ÉAMON KELLY

THE STORYTELLER

MERCIER PRESS

MERCIER PRESS
Douglas Village, Cork, Ireland
www.mercierpress.ie

Trade enquiries to COLUMBA MERCIER DISTRIBUTION,
55a Spruce Avenue, Stillorgan Industrial Park, Blackrock, Dublin

First published in two volumes:
The Apprentice (1995), *The Journeyman* (1998)

© Éamon Kelly 1995, 1998; Estate of Éamon Kelly 2004

ISBN 185635 439 3

10 9 8 7 6 5 4 3 2 1

Mercier Press receives financial assistance from
the Arts Council/An Chomhairle Ealaíon

Printed in Ireland by Colour Books Ltd

CONTENTS

A Turn of the Wheel

I was just six months old when I was brought to the house in Carrigeen where I spent my life until I was twenty-three. I often heard about the journey and often too have I tried to imagine what it was like that morning as we drove in Danny Maurice O'Connor's sidecar from Shinnagh Cross to Carrigeen. I was born in March 1914 so it was a September day. I always see my father and mother on one wing of the jaunting car and me sitting on my mother's lap, Danny Maurice on the other wing and conversing with my father in a loud voice over the noise of the horse's hooves and the grinding of the iron-shod wheels on the road. All our belongings were on that car. My mother's personal possessions were stored in the well, as the deep receptacle at the back of the sidecar was called. There was a bundle on the box seat in front, and under the seat the tools of my father's trade. He was a carpenter. Some more things, probably bedclothes, on the seat beside the driver, and on the flat surface over the well a box my dad had made with tableware and maybe a kettle and a few pots.

If I took any notice of the countryside as we drove along I would have seen the behind-the-times farmers still making hay which had become a little discoloured because of bad weather. At this time the stalks would be beginning to fade in the potato gardens and men would be busy drawing out turf from the inner bog and stacking it by the roadside to be carted home later. I like to think of it as a sunny day; a pet day coming to brighten up the countryside after a lot of rain.

Then I would have seen the mountains that ring, or half-ring, that great saucer of land from Castleisland to the county bounds. Their names are the first five beads on my rosary – the MacGillicuddy Reeks, Mangerton, Stoompa, Crohane, and to the east and looking down on our sidecar, the Paps. The old people called this twin mountain *An Dá Chích Dannan*, the two breasts of the goddess Dana. Maybe I wasn't looking, my mouth on another breast that sustained me. A Rathmore man told me once that when people climbed the Paps each man took a stone and placed it on one of the two cairns at the top of twin peaks. In time these two cairns grew to be the nipples on the breasts of Dana. Further upland towards Boharbue you can see the mountain range in its entirety and you can make out what looks like the torso of Dana stretched out in the sun. One breast, they say, is something higher than the other, as if she were lying a little on her side. Up there Fionn MacCumhaill stood and, bending down, he washed his face in the waters of Doocorrig Lake.

In the shade of the Paps were born the poets Eoghan Ruadh Ó Súilleabháin and Aodhagán Ó Rathaille. Each day as the sun shone they saw those perfect shapes against the sky, and maybe the old gods who lived up there inspired them. At the foot of the Paps is 'the city', *Cathair Chroibh Dhearg*, a ruined fort. When it was in its glory it was walled and circular like Dún Aengus or Staigue fort. I see *Crobh Dearg* as a high priest of the pagans and his hand was red from slaughtering animals – and for all we know maybe humans – as a sacrifice on the high altar when Our Lord was a boy or even before Homer nodded.

Since Christian times 'the city' has been associated with Gobnait, the Ballyvourney saint. The first of May was the Pattern Day, a day of pilgrimage. From early morning the way was black with people going up the rising, twisting road to the ruined circle. The lame, the blind and the halt sat or lay by the roadside. They carried placards on their breasts or exposed a mortified limb, crying aloud their ailments and calling on our charity. Often I did the rounds at 'the city', walking inside and outside the circle, praying and pausing at a station marked by a rock fallen from the once high wall. The prayers, as far as I remember, were the Creed, the Our Father, three Hail Marys and a Glory be to the Father. At one station I waited my turn to take the pointed stone and draw the sign of the cross, three, five or seven times on the rock. From the rubbing of one stone on the other over the centuries the cross is worn deep into the rock. In my young days the bush beside the holy well was festooned with giobals, pieces torn from the pilgrims' clothing. At the base of the shrub, buttons, old combs, hairpins and safety pins were placed by pilgrims making the old pagan gesture of leaving their troubles behind. People prayed to be cured of their afflictions and once I saw a pair of crutches by the holy well.

To complete the round, the last thing a pilgrim did was to drink from the well and give a penny to the poor woman who filled the mug for him. The well was said to have curative properties and bottles of water from it were brought home to treat humans and animals. Traders' stalls, often in tents, were set up around the circle where sweet cakes, buns, apples and lemonade were sold. As evening fell, young boys and girls drifted away from their elders and danced to the music of the fiddle in Duggans' field.

The Paps looked down on our sidecar as we journeyed west. These twin mountains would colour my youth. When they donned their cloudy nightcap the weather was about to change. When they looked distant the coming week would be fine and when they were clapped up to you it would rain tomorrow. When a man was making something clear in conversation and that something wasn't readily grasped he would protest that the point that he was making was as plain as the Paps. A priest, new to the parish, had a jumble sale and a young lady bought a crocheted cardigan. It was very open crocheting, a string of holes tied together. The priest asked the girl's mother how her daughter liked the cardigan, and the mother said, 'It is like a screen, Father. You could see the Paps through it!'

'Ah,' the priest answered, 'can't she wear a blouse underneath?'

Crossing the railway bridge this side of the Bower, we came to a crossroads where a ghost was said to appear. The ghost was known as the spirit of Béalnadeega. She waylaid and attacked men late at night. She was able to pull a rider from his horse and blind him by squirting her breastmilk into his eyes. Some held she was the evil sister of the goddess Dana or a female demon of that far-off age. The parish priest was helpless in his efforts to get rid of her. A very holy man, a friar, read over the spot where she used to appear and the spirit was never seen again. He banished her from Ireland, people said, and her penance was to drain the Dead Sea with a silver spoon for all eternity.

After climbing the steep hill above Barraduv Bridge we came to the village itself and my father asked the driver in for a drink. My mother thought we should keep on going but the men said it wouldn't take a minute. The horse stood outside the pub, well accustomed to such an exercise. The bar was dark, with a low ceiling and only a small window to allow in the light. We were well known in that house. My grandfather, on his way from town, was a regular customer there. The pony that pulled his tub trap stopped at John Dan's of her own accord.

When Kate Connie, the publican's wife, had filled the two pints for the men she took my mother into the kitchen. It was only then that Kate spotted me, wrapped in my mother's black shoulder shawl. I was held up to the light. The back door was opened to let in the sun and I was admired. 'What age is he? Who's he like? He's a Cash, I'd say!' She put a silver piece into my little fist and poked my middle playfully, saying, 'Kutsie, kutsie, kutsie!' She boiled the kettle to make a cup of tea. My mother would rather that than any alcoholic beverage. 'Drink!' she used to say. 'If you were spilling it at my feet I wouldn't touch it.'

When the men had finished – and I'd venture to say that they had two pints a man, reminding each other that a bird never flew on one wing – we set out, leaving our goodbyes with Kate Connie. We boarded the sidecar and began the last leg of our journey. We passed by the church that later in life I would attend every Sunday, down on one knee beside my father at the men's side and listening to the word of God. Once every five years I would hear the missionaries thunder in that small church.

We were passing now through countryside that would become familiar to me as the years went on. Not only would I come to know the name of each townland but in time I would learn the names of fields or some prominent feature of the landscape and the story behind each name. When we drew up outside our new home we were in the middle of the half-circle of mountains to the south. Mangerton, Ceapach and Stoompa I would see every day and watch their changing faces. The house was almost new and had become vacant because the tenant had died of consumption. In the three rooms there was a circular black mark, the size of a saucer, on the boards, where the disinfecting candle had burned itself into the floor. The Murphys, our new neighbours, who knew we were coming, had a fire down and had brought a jug of milk and some vegetables to go with our first meal. The few sticks of furniture were old but in time my father made a new bed, a better table, a few chairs and a dresser. The bed I remember best because I slept in it with my parents. It had a high board all round, the inside was filled with straw and on top of this was an enormous feather tick. My mother, when dressing the bed, would flounce this up and down and when the sheet was spread she would place me on the bed and I would sink gradually into the feather tick, laughing up at her as she tickled me.

My father was busy every day. He used the new kitchen table as a bench, and before he turned his hand to building a workshop at the gable of the house he made a cradle for me. My mother had had the use of Mrs Cronin's old cradle when we were living at Shinnagh Cross. The cradle my father made was a much swankier affair, with a hood and two rockers. On a fine day he'd lift the cradle out to the corner of the house along with a chair for my mother. She sat under the shining sun doing her knitting, rocking the cradle with her foot and singing to me as she kept her eye on our new cow in case she strayed out on to the road. A cow uneasy in her new surround-ings would try to get back to where she came from. But when she had her calf she settled down. Then my mother had two youngsters to look after. The calf didn't drink all the cow's milk. There was plenty for the house and my mother skimmed the pan where it was set and made butter by shaking the cream in the big teapot.

The girls from Murphys' next door came to mind me if my mother had to do some shopping, doing the messages as it was called. When I was older they often told me what I looked like as an infant. They said I had a fine head of flaxen curls.

In time my mother got hens and a cock. When I could sit up in the cradle I loved watching this proud bird as he strutted through the yard with measured pace, his red comb like a crown on his head. I clapped my pudgy hands as he flapped his wings and crowed. There were two out offices going with the house. One of these was now turned into a fowl house, the other was later to become a piggery. My father had built a cowshed with space for a stable when we got the pony.

We were now well established, with a workshop at the gable end of the house and customers were coming. As well as being a carpenter my father was a wheelwright. When I was well able to stand up my mother would put me in a tea-chest in the workshop. My father as he worked could keep an eye on me and she was free to do whatever she wanted. The hens made nests in the workshop and a hen when she laid an egg proclaimed to all creation her great achievement. As she clucked her way to the door a ring of shavings would become entangled in her leg. She would drag it with her to the yard, trying to shake it off as she went. I chuckled at this and my father, seeing me laugh, laughed to himself and went on running the plane on the straight edge of the board.

Neighbours who came with an order sat for a while and watched my father working. 'A trade is as good as an estate,' they'd sometimes say. 'And a man who knows his trade well can hold his head high in any community!' The skill of making a wheel was the admiration of many. The materials for it were bought in Lord Kenmare's sawmills, all the wood grown locally: elm for the stock or hub, elm too for the felloes or rim and oak for the spokes. The stock was turned on the mill lathe, the felloes were sawn and the spokes split with the grain for strength, like a hurley stick. There was a special wheel-stool made by the carpenter for wheelmaking. It held the stock firm between four stool pins while it was being mortised to receive the twelve spokes. Each mortise was bored with an auger and finished with a chisel.

A sharp tool is the craftsman's friend and my father prided himself on being able to put up a good edge. Tools had to be ground down to cut away the proud steel behind the cutting edge, and for this purpose there was a grindstone. It was a wheel of sandstone which my mother turned. She twisted the handle with her right hand and poured the water on the wheel with her left, while my father held the chisel firmly on the sandstone. She complained that it was tiresome doing two things at the same time so my father, always inventive, made a wooden trough underneath to hold water. The wheel, when spun, went through the water and it was better than the old way, for an even amount of water was always on the wheel. When the chisel was ground, the sharpening was completed on an oilstone. Fast back and forward movements and then the front of the chisel laid flat on the stone to remove the burr. My father would clean the edge between his thumb and first finger and look at it closely in the light. If he was satisfied, he took up the wooden mallet and sent the chisel singing through the wood.

The stock mortised, my father turned his hand to the spokes. Each spoke was given a face. This was a straight flat surface made with the plane while the spoke was held firmly in the vice. Then with a drawing knife he shaped the spoke, an oval in cross-section, and finished it with the spoke shave. The chips and shavings from the wood, in this case oak and elm, gave rise to a compound of smells. My small nose twitched and I thought the speckled hen coming from her nest twitched her beak a little too. The stock was fixed firmly in the wheel stool and each of the twelve spokes was driven home with a heavy hammer.

There was a mark on the stock at each side where it had been held in the lathe. A hole was bored in the front mark and a long arm called a trammel was screwed into it. This arm could be spun around and used to mark the ends of the spokes, equidistant from the stock. Dowels were formed at the ends to go into the felloes. My father placed the appropriate template on a roughly sawn felloe and marked it off, sawed it to the length and with a hatchet cut off the surplus wood on the convex side and with a tool called an adze shaped the concave surface. Holes were bored in the felloes to receive the spoke dowels and each felloe had a smaller dowel to connect them together. When the wheel was rimmed my father rolled it around my tea chest and said, 'Wheel'. I was too young to get my tongue around the word. All I could say was 'Dada'. I said that and it pleased him.

My mother brought me in her arms and put me sitting on the grass by the river the day of the wheel shoeing. The diameter of the iron band was a little less than that of the wheel. This iron hoop would expand when heated and go down easily over the rim of the wheel, then when it was quickly cooled it contracted, tightening the wheel together. To measure the new band for the blacksmith, who made it, the carpenter had an instrument like a large disc which he ran around the rim. It was called a traveller.

To heat or 'redden' the iron band a great fire was put down. While this was lighting the band was placed on stones to lift it about six inches from the ground. When the fire was red, the hot coals were heaped around the band in a circle of fire. More turf was added and in time you could see the red ring inside the fire. Many neighbours came to see the operation. A fire is always an attraction. The wheel was flat on the ground, an indentation made to receive the jutting stock. When the band was red-hot, men with hay forks helped my father lift it from the fire. As the white-red band hit the air you could see thousands of little white stars winking all round the circumference. The band was held directly over the wheel and gradually lowered into position. As the hot iron touched the rim, white-blue smoke shot up, the hay forks were thrown away and with hammers the band was put in place. No delays now as the iron would burn too much into the wood. Buckets of water were dashed on the rim and the hot iron bubbled and sizzled. White steam came up in a burst to mingle with the white-blue smoke of the wood. As the band cooled it tightened its grip on the wheel. You could hear the crackle of the felloes as they came together and of the spokes as they sank a little deeper into the stock. The fire was put out and my father bowled the newly shod wheel up the road to the workshop. The water spilling on the oak acid of the spokes stained them black.

The wheel wasn't finished yet. The centre of the stock had to be chiselled out to take the metal box which encased the axle. The box was a cleverly thought-out affair, narrower on the outside so that the pressure of the axle tightened it in the stock. There were two ridges left proud on the outer surface, which ensured that it could not twist in the stock. It was wrapped in jute and driven home with a sledge. Now a chase was chiselled out in the front of the stock where the axle protruded to take the lynchpin. A band of iron was put inside and outside on the stock and when the wheel was painted with red lead these bands and the edge of the big band were touched in black paint. More black in the chase and the wheel was complete. When my father made a cart the finished article was painted the same colour as the wheels, and all the ironwork, boltheads and so on in black, with a pair of guards in a shade of Reckett's Blue. If you made it yourself you would stay up all night looking at it!

THE HANDS OF WAR

My first faltering steps I heard about from my mother. I stood in the field, she often said, wavered a little and then stumbled three paces into her outstretched arms. She was sitting on the grass playing 'gobs'. She hadn't yet forgotten the games of her schooldays. To play you used five pebbles the size of a robin's egg. You put four pebbles down, marking the four corners of a square with the fifth in the middle. You threw up the middle one and tried to pick up as many of the others before you caught the first one falling. The person who could pick up the four on the ground before the first one fell into her hand was very expert. My mother added a complication to the game by catching the falling pebbles on the back of her open hand.

I didn't wear trousers at first. I walked around in petticoats, as did all the male children until they were three or four. The petticoat was a sensible enough form of attire as with little train-ing I could perform the minor call of nature without wetting myself. I was able to carry out the natural functions in a manly fashion before I stuck my legs into a trousers. I remember the occasion: the little pants came to just above my knees. But the longest memory in my head is of sitting in my father's lap – I can still smell the tobacco from his waistcoat – and fitting on a pair of shoes my aunt sent me from America. When my father put me standing I stamped and stamped my feet on the floor, fascinated by the noise I made.

When my brother was born about two and a half years after me I wasn't the centre of attention any more, and I moved out of the kitchen and spent more time in the workshop. My father had his work cut out for him to keep me away from the sharp tools. He made a small wooden hammer for me and gave me pieces of wood to play with. I sat in the shavings and listened to the men who came with jobs for my father. They all spoke to me and those who knew my grandfather were surprised that I wasn't called after him. The custom then was to call the first son after his father's father and the second son after his mother's father. The same rule applied to the first two girls. They were called after their grandmothers. If you walked into a house at that time and there were two boys and two girls in the family and you knew their grandparents, you could name the children. Both my male grandparents, who were inseparable friends, objected to my father's and mother's marriage. They claimed there was a blood relationship, though fairly far out, and the slightest trace of consanguinity had to be avoided. My mother was very upset by this attitude and called me after my father to annoy the old man. My father's Christian name was Edmund, Ned to everybody, and so was I.

Years after, as a young carpenter's apprentice, I worked with my father on the building of Clifford's Hotel in town. Old John Clifford became confused because when he called me my father used to answer, and when he called my father I often replied, 'Yes, John!' He decided to call me Éamon but the name never stuck; at home and to my neighbours I was always Ned.

The house I came to as a child was a rural cottage with a slate roof. Slate roofs were rare then; all our neighbours' houses were thatched with straw and had but two rooms and an enormous kitchen. By comparison our kitchen was small but we had three rooms. The kitchen had an open fireplace not as big as the fireplaces in the farmers' houses but big enough to seat a large company around it when in winter our house became a visiting place, what was known in our district as a rambling house. The stairs went up from the kitchen to the two rooms overhead, and now that I had got over the crawling stage and was able to walk, climbing the stairs became my greatest ambition. My mother, dreading that I would fall, often rescued me from the third or fourth step. A chair was placed at the bottom to impede my passage but this created the danger that I could pull it down on top of me. This problem was solved by my father making a small door bolted on the inside to the newel post, and that door remained in position until the family, all eight of us, grew up.

The kitchen floor had 12"x12" fireclay tiles. Concrete

hadn't yet become a popular floor-making material. A big turf fire burned in the hearth, making the men who came at night push back their chairs. All the men smoked pipes and pipe smoking induced spitting, hence the spittoons and sawdust on public house floors. One of our visitors who had two lower front teeth missing could manipulate a spit, triggering it with his tongue and sending it soaring through the air in a flat parabolic curve to land on a burning coal on the hearth. His accuracy was amazing. The spit sizzled on the red coal for an instant, then the spot went black but in no time was red again until another spit landed on the same place.

When I was very small my mother put me to bed before the company came in at night. As I lay in my parents' bed I could hear the men talking below me in the kitchen. The rise and fall of the voices had a soporific effect on me and gradually I fell asleep. When I got a little older I stayed up longer and as my bedtime came I went up the stairs, my mother walking behind me in case I fell, to a chorus of 'goodnights' and 'codladh sámh' (sound sleep) from a crowded kitchen. My mother stayed with me, telling me about 'Jackie Dorey in his red cap who went to the wood' until I fell asleep. Then she tiptoed down the stairs with a 'ssh' to the men; and all brought their voices down. Little by little the voices rose again but by this time I was far away in dreamland.

The men who rambled to our house were the married men of the locality. Some of them were old, there were a few bachelors who hadn't yet embarked on the choppy sea of matrimony, and a teenager or two. The programme for the night was varied. It started with news, worldwide and local. Those who attended fairs or markets that day had their newsy contributions to make. Men who were at a funeral or at a wake the night before started to talk about the deceased and about those who attended his obsequies. During Shrovetime there was talk of matchmaking and weddings. In times of high emigration those who had been to the railway station to see young men and women bid a fond farewell to their native place talked about our neighbours' children who had gone. They talked fondly of those who, for some time, had made their home on a foreign shore. They showed their pleasure at the news of local men

18

who had made good and were saddened by the fact that men and women went away and were never heard of again.

War in foreign lands claimed the men's attention and as I grew a little older the Great War raged in Europe. News came to us from New York that my mother's brother, Eugene, had been drafted into the Fighting 69th contingent. Letters came from him while he was in the training camp in Albany, and one letter when he went overseas to France. It was Eugene's last letter and it was kept in a small box with a sliding top which my father had made for my mother. The rent book was kept there and other small precious belongings of her own. When my brothers and I were a little older she would take Eugene's letter out of the box and read to us as we sat on the floor around her. He described what it was like in the trenches: the sound of the big guns noising overhead, the mud and water and rats in search of little morsels of food. 'Not far away from where I sit in this dug-out,' he wrote, 'a young German soldier is taking his long last sleep, reminding me, Hannah, that unless God is very fond of me ...' My mother, who had been holding back the tears, would cry openly and we would cry too, as much for the young German soldier as for our uncle Eugene. He never came back. He died of the great flu on 22 November 1918, eleven days after the Armistice. The American government offered to send his body home, and my grandfather spoke to his neighbours who had come to share his sorrow. One neighbour said, 'How do you know, Tim, that it is your son will be in that box?' He sowed the seeds of doubt in the old man's mind and he declined the offer. My uncle lies in an American cemetery at Meuse, Argonne, north-west of Verdun. There are neat rows of graves with white crosses and his name and his rank are on his. 'Cpl Eugene C. Cashman, 307 Infantry, 77 Division, State of New York.'

As well as the war many is the subject the men would discuss. Politics were ever high on the agenda, the work of the Board of Guardians and the goings-on in the British Parliament where our local MP sat. 'Will I get in this time?' the sitting MP said once to one of our neighbours, coming up to polling day. 'Of course you will,' the neighbour told him. 'Didn't you say yourself that it was the poor put you in the last time and aren't there twice as many poor there now!' Sullivan and Murphy were the two contenders for the Westminster seat and their followers, the Sullivanites and the Murphyites, fought with ashplants on fair days or at sports meetings. The cries of 'Up Sullivan!' or 'Up Murphy!' echoed long into the night.

The 1918 election, with victory for Sinn Féin, put an end to that era. And on the heels of the 1918 election came the first rumblings of the War of Independence. There were echoes of the Somme and the Dardanelles nearer home now. Young Flor Donoghue, who worked at Dineens, and Mick Lynch came into our house and my mother gave them tea. Their rifles leaned against the newel post of the stairs and sitting on the floor I rubbed my hands along the polished stocks. At night when we heard the noise of the Crossley tenders coming up Mac's Height we ducked under the table as my mother's hand reached up to turn down the wick of the oil lamp. We crouched in the darkness as the Tan lorries came near the house and we held our breath until they had passed. Then as the sound died away by the Gap of the Two Sticks we gradually emerged and my mother turned up the wick of the oil lamp.

The men didn't come rambling to our house during the Tan War. A list of the occupants of the household was nailed up inside the front door. I can still see it. Parents: Edmund Kelly, Hannah Kelly. Children: Edmund Kelly, Timothy Kelly, Laurence Kelly. If anybody else was found in the house when the Tans called we would have some explaining to do. My father was one day working in the open beside the workshop. He was sawing a board and I was blowing the sawdust off the pencil line. Two English soldiers came in asking questions about who was living in the neighbouring houses. The Daniels, the same day, were picking stones in the high field and when the horse butt was full they heeled it into a gripe. The loud noise of the falling stones made the soldiers spring to attention.

'What was that?' they said, as they backed my father against the wall. He explained what had happened and he showed them the young boys working in the field. They went and inspected it for themselves. If my father wasn't telling the truth God only knows what would have happened to him. People said that the British Tommy was a civilised enough individual, but the Black and Tans were a murderous crew. Many were the stories told about the burnings throughout the country. A man well known to my father and mother – he came from where they were born – was tied to a Tan lorry and dragged live behind it until he died; and the day after Headford Ambush, in which twenty-three English soldiers and two IRA men died, the Black and Tans went through the countryside shooting anything that moved, even the animals in the fields.

But they weren't alone in the cruelty of their ways. Two young English soldiers deserted from the ranks. They went into hiding and lived away from the towns until they came to a secluded place where they worked for farmers and lived a happy enough existence in that small community. Nothing would convince certain elements in the IRA but that they were spies. They were tried in their absence and sentence was passed on them. One night the two young soldiers were playing cards in a neighbour's house when there was a knock at the door. Two armed men came in and despite the pleadings of the people that the soldiers were innocent their hands were tied behind their backs. They were blindfolded and taken to a cowshed. The armed men wanted someone to hold a candle in the cowhouse. The men listening made no move. 'So much for spunk!' a woman said. 'I'll hold it myself.' Maybe the terrible story of that night expanded in the telling. By the time it reached us we were told that one young soldier asked for a priest. There was a delay in the pretence that one was being sent for, and when he arrived the blindfold was eased. The 'priest' was one of his executioners who had donned a black coat and placed a folded white handkerchief around his neck. Kneeling in the half-dark the frightened soldier confessed his mild transgressions that wouldn't bring a blush to the cheeks of a saint. What an obscenity! When I heard that part of the story I thought of my uncle Eugene dying far from home. What did republics or empires mean to him or to these two young men cut off from life and the love and the opportunities the future could bring? 'I must give you my address,' the young man said to the 'priest'. 'You will write to my mother?' he asked quietly. The other soldier kept his silence. He never groaned or cried out but went to his death without a word. They were buried, half-alive some claimed, in the bog.

I thought of the animals in that cowshed and I wondered did the cows jump with fright when the shots rang out, or did one cow give a low moan of agony as a cow often does when she is bringing her calf into the world.

The truce came. I was seven years old and helping the Daniels with the hay in the leaca field. It was a July day and the lorries of British soldiers drove up and down Boher Vass. They sang and cheered and waved to us and we small people waved back to them. The men came again and sat in our kitchen, and when the subject of the two young soldiers came down, one man said of the armed men who perpetrated that awful atrocity, 'They will melt,' he said, 'like the froth in the river!' Bloodstains remained on the walls of the cowshed. No water could wash them off.

FIGHTING AMONG OURSELVES

❧

I was over seven years of age when I went to school in the autumn of 1921. I was always a delicate child and my mother thought she'd never rear me. She swore by beef tea and chicken broth as body builders, but the sustenance failed to fill out my spare shanks. Molly and Nell Murphy called for me that first morning. They were a few years older than me. My mother held back the tears as I went out the front door in a navy suit, Eton collar and no shoes. All the scholars went barefoot until the winter months.

'How old are you, Edmund?' Mrs O'Leary, the schoolmistress, asked me. Jerry Mac, Jer Daniels and Con Dineen nearly burst out laughing when they heard her calling me Edmund. To them and everyone at home I was Ned, young Ned. 'How old are you, Edmund?' she said again.

'I am seven years since last March,' I replied.

'And why did it take so long for you to come to school, Edmund?'

'Well the way it was, Ma'am,' I said, settling myself and talking like one of the men in my father's rambling house. 'The way it was, we were every day waiting for the Tan war to be over!'

'Now that you are here, Edmund,' she told me, 'you'll have to learn very fast to make up for lost time.' And she gave me a new penny. My mother had taught me how to count up to twenty, and I knew most of the letters of the alphabet. Indeed I recognised words like 'cat' and three-lettered words in a sentence like, 'Ned put his leg in the tub.' I had a little head start and I made good progress.

As the autumn died and the winter came, a fire was lit in the school. The pupils supplied the fuel. Well-to-do farmers brought a creel of turf, heeled it out at the gate and boys in the big classes brought it in the armfuls and put it in the turf box in the hall. Those of us who couldn't afford to bring fuel by the creel brought a sod of turf to school each morning. My mother went through the turf shed to find a small sod for me.

With my mother looking after me at home, the two Murphy girls taking me to school and Mrs O'Leary's daughter teaching me, I began to feel that I was too much under petticoat rule. Having so many women around me was bad for my image. I made friends fast with boys of my own age and even though of a shy nature I managed to get into a few fights. In the playground one day I got a puck of a fist into the throat, sinking the big stud of the Eton collar into my Adam's apple. I cried from pain but soon dried my tears. That belt of a fist hardened me. I left the house on my own every morning and sought the company of the boys going and coming from school. I never again sat down with the girls as they played the game of gobs on the grassy patch by Mac's Well.

Older brothers of the boys going to school were out in the IRA. Not yet carrying arms, they acted as scouts, and one morning we saw Jimmy Williams with a spyglass scanning the countryside. He wasn't on the lookout for English troops. It was 1922 and the Civil War was on. That war divided neighbours. In one case it divided a household as two brothers fought on opposite sides. And it divided us schoolchildren. In the playground and on the way home from school we fought the Republican and the Free State cause. I was on the Republican side. I didn't know what it meant. All I knew was that my Uncle Larry, who worked in Dublin, was a prisoner of the Free State Government and was on hunger strike.

We fought with our fists. We squared out in front of an opponent and called, 'Come on! Put up the dukes!' and the boy who couldn't keep his guard ended up with a bloodied nose. Boys whose fathers accepted the Treaty called us Republicans murderers and looters. And looting did go on. The men talked about it around my father's fire. They told of a prominent citizen who took a cartload of furniture out of the Great Southern Hotel before it was taken over by the regular army. He unloaded his booty in a laneway off College Street and went back to the hotel for a second load. When he returned to College Street the first load was gone. Lifting his eyes to heaven he shouted to the clouds, 'This town is nothing but the seed and breed of robbers! A man couldn't leave anything out of his hand!'

Running battles took place along the road when we were freed from school. Opposing armies lined up and threw stones and clods of earth at each other. The Dineens and I soon found that our Republican allies deserted us, not through cowardice, but because of the fact that they had reached their homes. Now that we were greatly outnumbered by Free State forces, we had to leg it out of the firing line, and take the short-cut home through Mick Sullivan's fields.

But our schoolboy war came to an end when we were brought face to face with the real thing. One day when we were out to play, two Republican soldiers, young Mick Sullivan and Dinny Connor, passed by the school. I can still see their gaitered legs, the rifles slung from their shoulders and the bandoliers about their breasts. One wore a hat and the other a cap. They didn't slope along. They walked as if they were marching to music. The big boys out of fifth and sixth classes walked along with them, chatting all the while. 'We heard shots,' the big boys said. 'The military are somewhere near.' 'That firing,' one of the men replied, 'is as far away as Millstreet.' We watched them as they passed by Jer Leary's house until they were out of sight around the bend towards Fordes' cottage.

Playtime over, the bell rang for us to go back to the classroom. Some time afterwards we heard gunfire, then the sound of lorries. Standing on a desk and looking out, one of the boys said there were soldiers everywhere. It seems when the two Republicans had got around the bend out of our view they looked down into the village of Knockanes and saw that the place was full of military. They decided to engage them and fired into the village. If the soldiers advanced they could easily retreat. They were local men and knew the countryside. Advance the soldiers did, and some say that, hiding behind fences, they put their caps on the tops of their rifles to draw the Irregulars' fire, while others fanned out to encircle the two men. Realising that they could soon be trapped, Connor and Sul-

25

livan split up and made a dash for it. In the getaway Mick Sullivan was wounded in the arm. Dinny Connor made his escape and Sullivan barely made it to Jer Leary's house. The Free State advance party was there as soon. Because of his wounded arm Mick Sullivan couldn't use his gun. The soldiers burst into the kitchen. Sullivan surrendered but despite the protests of Jer Leary and his wife they dragged Mick Sullivan outside the front door and shot him dead.

When news came to the school that he was shot, the school missus and her daughter, later Mrs Spillane, were overcome with grief. We, seeing the anguish in their faces, tried to hold back the tears, and the big girls in the upper classes cried openly. It was then I saw my first Free State soldier. He came into the classroom and stood under the clock. He was a doctor. He wore a white coat which was open at the front and we could see his uniform and his Sam Browne belt. He spoke to Mrs O'Leary very quietly. As far as we could make out he said there was no need to be afraid, that the fighting was over. When he went out we heard the lorries going away. We knelt down and prayed for the soul of the young man lying dead two doors away. In a while's time, as no one could settle down to work again, the school was closed and we went home.

There was no stone-throwing on the road that afternoon. We went quietly and told our parents of the dreadful happening. 'You are too young,' my mother said, 'to be a witness to such terrible things.' I was put to bed early that night and when I came down in the morning there on the window-sill I saw a clay pipe and I knew that my father had spent the night at young Mick Sullivan's wake. The men sitting at our fireside talked the next night and for many a night about the shooting and the refusal of the parish priest to come and give the last rites to the man who died.

Other nights brought other stories. Young Republicans in Kenmare climbed a lean-to roof in the night time, entered a bedroom and shot dead two Free State soldiers as they slept. They were brothers, killed in their father's house when they were home on furlough. Stories of horror vied with each other for our attention: the blowing up of Republican prisoners at Ballyseedy, and forever etched in our minds remains the image of Dave Nelligan, a military officer, taking off his cap and combing his hair as he walked down Fair Hill in Killarney at the head of his troops after they had blown to pieces young Republicans on a mined barricade at the Countess Bridge. The Civil War was a black time. It blackened the people's minds. Neighbours disagreed as they followed their different loyalties. Old feuds, long dead, were reopened and hatred was the prevailing emotion. Men in Tralee who were being given back the dead body of a Republican by the regular army refused to accept the remains in a Free State coffin. They went down the town and brought a new one, and with hatchets smashed to pieces the coffin in which he had lain.

Our parish priest, who had refused the last rites to Mick Sullivan, preached continually against the Irregular soldiers. One Sunday he lit the church with language. So fiery was his condemnation of what he called looters and murderers that men of the same way of thinking as Mick Sullivan and Dinny Connor rose from their seats in the body of the church and walked out. A loose heeltip went clanging at every second step on the tiles of the aisle, as if in protest against the reviling of the Republican cause.

Going Away and Staying at Home

When I was very small I walked down Bohar Vass with my father, out under the railway bridge and along the road leading to the Iron Mills. We were hand in hand, my chubby fist holding on to his little finger. He was in his good clothes. It was Sunday and it was the first time I remember being alone with him outside the workshop. The signal pole gleaming white on the railway line attracted my attention. He explained how it worked. The red arm up to stop the train, and down when the way was free of danger. At night when the arm was up there was a red light and when it was down the light was green. Every night Jackie Ryan put a lighting lantern inside the glass.

A train came. Quite suddenly it appeared and the loud whistle frightened me. Smoke puffed from its chimney and steam hissed from all over the engine like the kettle boiling over the fire. In the blinking of an eye it flew past with a loud rattle and disappeared under an arch over the railway.

My father, with a piece of stick, drew in the sandy roadside the map of Ireland. There was no England or Europe, just Ireland with the sea all round it. With the point of the stick he indicated the towns and cities he could remember and he drew lines between the towns where the train ran. I watched the train many times before I was old enough to board it. I watched the train with Jer Daniels when his brother Dan, and other young men were going to America. We stood in the same place where my father drew the map and watched the train as it went slowly up hill on its way to Cork and Queenstown. Dan lowered the window and waved to us and we waved to him. We said goodbye and he shouted to us but we couldn't make out what he said because of the noise of the train. Jer Daniels cried after his brother. He had his big dog Shep with him and the dog, excited by Jer's crying, jumped up and put his paws on Jer's shoulders. With Jer's arms around him they both fell to the ground, Jer roaring crying and the dog licking the tears from his face.

The night before had been the American wake. Those going away and their friends came to one house where there was music, dancing and songs, sad and merry. I had learned a song from a gramophone that had come to Murphys' from America; a victrola the Yanks called the gramophone. That night, young as I was, I sang the song which opened with the line 'From this valley they say you are going'. When the music struck up the young emigrants danced with spirit, pounding the flags as if to vent the sorrow of parting on the kitchen floor, while the light from the oil lamp cast their dancing shadows around the whitewashed walls. By the fire the older people sat, fathers and mothers of those going away. The red glow from the fire lit their features as they kept time to the music with their feet. A mother, watching her fine son stepping it out, suddenly turned her face to the fire and watched the dancing flames as his young life up to that moment unfolded before her eyes.

Some emigrants danced throughout the night until it was time to go to the railway station in the morning. A line of horse-drawn cars, traps and sidecars then set out in time for people to have a drink in town and so that the mothers could buy a present for a departing son or daughter. It was usual to give a crown piece as a keepsake or a half-sovereign, and happy would be the one who got a golden guinea. As well as that, a present of wearables, gloves or the like, would be given to the girls, and the men got a silk handkerchief. It was sometimes thrown at the wall and if it clung to the mortar it was the genuine article. Those handkerchiefs waved from the train as it disappeared under the Countess Bridge.

Emigrants were lonesome leaving their own house and Paddy Murphy went back and opened the door and had one last look inside. I was old enough to be allowed go to the railway station that day. The train from Tralee ran out the Cork line and then reversed into the platform, where the young people going away were surrounded by their friends. It took eight to ten days to get to America in rickety old ships. You could feel the motion of the waves under your feet. A young man landing in New York had to work hard to put the passage money together to bring out his brother. That's how it was done. John brought out Tim and Tim brought out Mary. Maybe then the young man would get married and have responsibilities so when again would he have the money to come back over the great hump of the ocean? Now he stood for the last time among his relations. He started saying goodbye at the outside of the circle to his neighbours, his uncles, aunts and cousins, full of gab for everyone. But as he came to the centre the flow of words deserted him and it was only with a whispering of names that he said farewell to his brothers and sisters. His father held his hand, not wanting to let it go, and his mother, whom he had left until last, threw her arms around him, a thing she hadn't done since he was a small boy going to school, and gave vent to a cry that was taken up by the other women along the platform.

Oh, it was a terrifying thing for one as young as me to hear, and that cry used to have an effect even on older people. Nora Kissane told me she once saw a man race down the platform after the departing train so demented that he shook his fist at the engine and shouted, 'Bad luck to you oul' smoky hole taking away my fine daughter from me!' When those who were leaving boarded the train and put down the windows, their dear ones still held on to them, and when the train pulled out they were dragged along the platform until they had to let go. Some mothers collapsed on their knees under the great weight of loneliness and had to be helped to their feet, but the train gathered speed and the silk handkerchiefs waving from the windows was the last sight of them we saw.

> They travelled on for fifteen miles
> By the banks of the River Lee.
> Spike Island soon came into view,
> And the convicts they did see.
> They all put up in Mackey's Hotel
> Nine dozen of them and more,
> And they sang and danced the whole night long,
> As they did the night before.

In the morning they went out in the tender to the waiting

ship and sailed away. The first letters to come from them came from mid-Atlantic. It seems that east- and west-bound liners drew alongside and mail was exchanged. The letters told of their night's stay in Queenstown and of their first days at sea. They were poor sailors and try as they might they couldn't keep the food down. Their time was spent at the ship's rail retching emptily into the sea. The half-circle of white foam at the base of Sceilig Mhichíl was their last glimpse of Ireland. They promised to write when they had settled in America and when they got work they would send some money.

At home many families were reduced by half. But life went on. The tasks had to be done. Cows had to be milked, calves fed and the eggs brought in from the rogue hen's nest. The seasons brought different work to the community that lived around us and the first activity of the year was the setting of the potato garden. A large field went with our house. My father ran a wire fence through it, north to south. One part was known as East the Wire and the other as West the Wire. East the Wire was the smaller of the divisions, and here in the spring, if it had been under grass the year before, ridges were formed. These ridges my father, and maybe a helper, made with a spade. The spade was the implement of the strolling labourers of old. Eoghan Ruadh the poet worked with one and ridged a garden as he composed his songs, as far away from home as Cork and Limerick. The spade, made originally by the smith and later at Scott's foundry in Cork, had a sharp edge and a long handle and a treader. The operator cut the sod and turned it over, grassy side down, leaving a furrow as he worked along.

The ridges when completed with the spade looked a neat piece of handiwork and a furrow between each two ridges ran the entire length of the allotment. My father 'threw his eye' along the furrow and said with some satisfaction, 'As straight as a dye!' Each eye in a potato will sprout a shoot and as all that was needed was one stalk, the potato was cut into pieces, each piece holding at least one eye. The work of cutting the potatoes was done by women. They came to each other's houses and worked together, sitting on chairs in the kitchen. They talked, ribbed each other about their men, told stories and were high good company. My job as a child was keeping them

31

supplied with whole potatoes and taking away the eyeless waste pieces which were boiled and given to the pigs. The precious small piece holding an eye and maybe a young shoot was called a *sciollán*. There were many things in our district for which there was no English word and that was one. Fresh lime was shaken on the *sciolláns* to keep them from bleeding.

The planting on the ridges was done with the spade. His foot on the treader, the sower drove the spade deep into the ridge. Then, thrusting it forward and releasing it, he left a gaping hole. Into this the *sciollán* was flung from a home-made jute satchel which the sower wore around his shoulders. Each ridge carried three rows. I had the choice of two jobs when I was strong enough to be of help. One was to hold the satchel and shoot a *sciollán* into the hole as my father made it. The other was to strike down the sod on the gaping holes. I often ended up doing both.

There was a manure heap in the yard outside the cowshed on which the droppings of the animals were piled. To this, refuse from the kitchen was added. The manure was drawn out in the pony cart or in a creel basket and spread on the ridges. There was bag manure shaken on top called guano. This was the excrement of sea birds which came from the islands off Peru. I laughed to think that the droppings of colourful birds from South America mingling with the droppings of our hens and those of the cow and the pony helped grow our potatoes. With the spade we dug the earth in the furrows and with a shovel this earth was used to cover the manure on the ridges. Later on, when the stalks appeared and grew a few inches, the furrows were dug again and the soil, called second earthing, was distributed between the stalks.

It was an anxious time when the stalks were at this tender stage. A late frost could burn them up and all our work was gone for nothing. If the frost came my father was up before the dawn and with a piece of broom or a bunch of ferns or heather he would brush the frost crystals from the stalk leaves before the sun shone on them. The potato was an important item of food – king of the menu as one poet said – and the progress of the gardens was a topic of conversation in our rambling house at night. The men talked about the varieties of potato and the preference of different varieties for different soils. The Champion, all agreed, liked boggy ground. Potatoes from this type of soil were so clean when dug that they could be put in the pot without washing them.

Another anxiety for the people was the potato blight, which left the potatoes rotten in the fields in Black '47. When the stalks were high and closing in over the furrows, humid weather brought this dreaded disease. To guard against it the crop was sprayed. That day was a big day for me. I was kept in from school to help my father. We tackled the pony, a recent acquisition called Fanny, to the car and brought water from the river in an old wine barrel of which there was a few in every house. A second barrel was on the headland and the water in the barrel in the pony car was transferred to it. Bluestone and washing soda in certain proportions were put steeping the night before and when melted down were added to the barrel of water on the headland to make a bluish-green liquid. The back-board of the butt was placed on the barrel, not covering it fully, and the knapsack spraying machine rested on it.

This machine, to my young eyes, was an absolute marvel. It belonged to the shopkeeper who sold the bluestone and washing soda and was given free to his customers. It was about twenty inches square and about eight inches deep. The cover at the top had a rubber seal and with a little lever it clamped down tight when the tank was full. There was a handle at the right hand side and at the left a length of hose attached to a pipe, at the end of which was a rose head like that on a watering can. The sprayer was hollowed on one side to fit on the operator's back. When the tank had its quota of green-blue liquid and the cover was secured tightly, my father put his back to it and adjusted the straps that came over his shoulders. First he worked the handle at the right hand side up and down with a vigorous motion, pumping air into the liquid, and when he felt he had a good head up he released the tap on the pipe in his left hand and out shot a spray, making a sizzling sound. It was so concentrated that, as it came from the rose head, it turned into a cloud of vapour. He walked through a furrow, spraying a ridge at each side of him and as the spray dried on the stalks the dark green garden turned a bluish-green under the heat of the sun. When he returned with an empty tank I filled it with an old saucepan. Indeed my father could have done this himself but he liked company when he was working out of doors. We didn't talk very much but we enjoyed being together. Before he finished, with the tank just a quarter full, he let me put it on my back. Even at a quarter full the weight nearly knocked me down, but I struggled on, and working the handle I pumped in the air and released the spray. I got a great kick out of the feeling of power I had over the thing as I walked the furrow, my head barely above the stalks.

New potatoes were a special delicacy. The first meal was always on a Sunday in late summer. I loved the very small ones so clean and white they didn't need to be peeled. I put a knob of butter on top which melted and ran down the sides like lava down the sides of Vesuvius as the potato made its way from the plate to my mouth. It was a special day and as we made the sign of the cross we prayed that we all might be alive this time the next year. We thanked God for the crop and for the fact that there was no repeat of Black '47.

My Aunt Bridgie often talked about the famine and what happened to the people at that time. She told a story of little children weak with hunger tugging at their mothers' skirts and asking her to put down the potatoes. To keep them from crying, when they weren't watching she put small stones in a pot with water and hung the pot over the fire. The children sat on the floor, their eyes glued to the pot, and when they thought the potatoes should be cooked they kept imploring their mother to take them up. In the end, distracted from their pleadings and weak with hunger herself, she prayed to the Blessed Virgin to intercede with the Almighty to come to her aid. She took the cover off the pot and there to gladden the hearts of herself and the children were cooked potatoes. To a child's imagination everything is possible, but I caught my father winking at my mother and I hoped my Aunt Bridgie didn't see him.

Though my Aunt Bridgie was old she didn't remember the great famine but as a child she had heard older people talk about it. She described a house to us where distant relations of our own lived in Glounacoppal. The family lay on the kitchen floor too far gone from hunger to stand up. The father and mother had watched the younger children die one by one. He decided he would try again to find some sustenance for his wife and only surviving son. A raw turnip, maybe half-hidden and forgotten in the garden, or dandelion roots which he could dig up with his fingers. He crawled out of the house and was later found dead in a field clutching a bunch of dandelion roots in his hand.

Because of these memories there was always a deep respect for food in our house. Nothing was wasted. Not a single morsel was ever thrown out. What was left over was carefully gathered and added to the mess for the hens or the pigs. A beggar never went empty-handed from a door in our neighbourhood while there was food in the house, and my mother's most fervent request of God when we knelt at our prayers was, 'Feed the hungry!'

When the potato garden faded from dark green to brown and the ageing process had continued until the stalks were white and withered, the spuds were fit to dig. The same spade which was used for the sowing helped to reap the harvest. With his foot on the treader, my father drove the spade deep under the stalk and upturned the earth, revealing eight to a dozen potatoes. I marvelled at the bounty of nature that from one small shoot so many tubers could come. With the tip of the spade my father pitched them into a row as he went and we small people and my mother picked them and put them into buckets. For the winter the potatoes were stored in a pit in the garden. A trench about a foot deep was dug and into this the tubers were put and made into a small rick coming to a point. The neat heap was covered with withered stalks collected for the purpose and finally earthed over until the pit looked like the hipped roof of a long house. There the pit remained, the contents safe from winter frost. One end was opened when a supply was wanted for the table or to feed the animals. Farmers' sons, who were unpaid, raided their fathers' pits and sold a sack of potatoes so they could get pocket money coming up to Christmas.

In the potato garden there was room for an allotment for growing cabbages and a bed or two of onions. Cabbage plants were bought in bundles of a hundred in the town market and planted in neat rows with a generous helping of manure. The plants lay in the ground withered and forlorn-looking for a while. Then they perked up and grew with a fairish rapidity until in the middle of each plant the leaves hugged together to form the beginnings of a white head. While the plant was still growing the outside leaves were plucked and broken between the bands into a tub, topped with a mess of Indian meal and fed to the cow while she was being milked.

A cabbage leaf was used as a wrapper. When our cow was dry often we found a pound of butter in a cabbage leaf on the window-sill. It was left there by a generous neighbour before we got up in the morning. Boiled cabbage was the vegetable which accompanied cured bacon on our plates.

There was an iron frame, the rack, which hung like a gate over the fire. It had hooks that could be moved along the bar. When a pot was cooked it could be shifted to the side and another pot hung on. Red coals were also put at the side of the hearth on which rested the frying pan with 'a bit of fresh thing', as my mother called meat from the butchers. The fresh thing cooked with onions we got once in a blue moon. The staple diet for the principal meal was bacon and cabbage or bacon and turnips. When you sat down to such a meal there was a mountain of laughing Murphies in the middle of the table and as that mountain went down a small mountain of potato skins rose at each elbow. There was a bowl of semi-solidified milk to wash it down and every bite that went into your mouth was produced on your own holding.

FOOD ON THE TABLE

The fowl had a house in the yard with a hole in the door to give them air at night. My father made a ladder-like roost for them with a stick across fairly high up for the cock to perch on so that he could preside over his harem. When the last person was going to bed at night the word was, 'Did you kindle [rake] the fire?' and 'Did you close the door on the fowl?' Our front door was never locked, not even during the Tan war, but many is the man regretted not closing his fowl house door at night. The fox was always on the prowl.

When the men at our fireside talked about animals, pride of place for cleverness was given to the fox. Many is the time I heard them tell about the farmer who had a large hole in his fowl house door. The fox squeezed himself through it and having deprecated, as the men said, his stomach swelled and he was unable to come out through the hole in the door. The fox waited until the farmer opened the door in the morning, and was that farmer surprised to see a dead fox on the floor. He took the animal by the tail and swung the lifeless body over his shoulder on his way to dump him in a gripe. When the fox got into the open air, and out of view of the dog, he nipped the farmer in the back of the leg. With a cry of pain the man let go of the tail.

It was listening to the men talking in my father's house that gave me a life-long interest in animals. I heard them describe how the fox stole honey from the wild bees' nest in a summer's meadow. Reynard sat on the nest, his thick coat of fur protecting him. The disturbed bees crawled out and the fox, putting his snout down between his hind legs, sucked the honey from the comb. One of the breed became infested with fleas, according to one of our visitors, and to get rid of them he gathered a ball of wool in his mouth from bushes near where sheep grazed. When the fox came to a lake he dipped his tail, just the tip, and with infinite patience lowered himself slowly into the water, giving the fleas plenty of time to retreat before the advancing deluge. Finally his ears were going under and then his nose and the unwanted tenants, with nowhere else to go, took refuge in the ball of wool. Suddenly, letting go the wool, the fox submerged himself, saying in his own mind, 'If that ship sinks it won't be for the want of a crew!'

Badgers and otters were often the subject of conversation. A badger, separated from his mate, will defecate while on the move. The stool, falling in a certain way, indicates to his mate which way he has gone.

But domestic animals took pride of place in the men's conversation. They were very fond of their horses and their dogs, and the women sang when milking the cows and feeding the calves. People talked to the animals as city folk talk to their pets. There was a cat in every house, not so much a pet but a working member of the family. If the dog had to mind the sheep and bring home the cattle, the cat had his work cut out for him to keep the grain loft free of rats and mice. Men boasted about the intelligence of their dogs and told exaggerated stories about their cleverness. Stories about cats were exaggerated too. A carpenter who worked late at night trained his cat to hold a candle. The carpenter was proud of his achievement and wagered that training beats nature. A travelling man, hearing of this, laid a bet and let go a mouse in the workshop. Needless to say the cat dropped the candle and left them in the dark. Nature will out!

From the money my father earned in the workshop we were well set up in Carrigeen. By the time I went to school we had a cow and her calf, a pony, a flock of hens and a royal rooster and in the out office next to the fowl house two pigs fattening. My father bought them at the pig market when they were two small pinky-skinned *bonamhs*. He made a trough in which to feed them and we got straw for their bed. Pigs keep their bed and around where they sleep very clean and use the far end of the house for their calls of nature. My father put a half-door on the piggery so that we could look in on them. Neighbouring women passing by, having inquired about the health of the family, inquired about the animals. My mother usually brought them around to the back to see the pigs. It wasn't enough for the women to look at the two porkers; they opened the door, gave the animals a smart smack on the rump to admire them walking around, and then pronounced on how much they had improved since they last saw them. The owner of an animal likes to hear it praised and my mother was no different from anyone else.

On a summer's day my two small brothers and I loved to bring food out in the field. We would also provide some eatables for the pony, the cow and the calf and coax them to come near us while we all ate together. In our innocence we pretended that they were people. They were all tame and came quite close. The pony would eat bread and so would the cow, and when the pony grazed in Murphy's mountain we caught her by offering her bread or a handful of sugar. The cow, when her time came, was mated with Mac's bull, for which service we paid five shillings. Neighbouring farmers, who didn't have a bull of their own, availed of the services of Mac's 'gentleman'. They paid for this by giving a day's work to the owner, and when they came together to cut Mac's turf they were known as bull men.

I was still of tender years when I took our cow to the bull. There was no one else to do it if my father was away from home except my mother, and it was considered indelicate for a woman to go on an errand like that in our community. The cow was very giddy taking her there, darting in gaps and gates, jumping on other cows and lifting her head and bellowing. I drove her into the farmyard, the owner opened the gate and then opened the stall door. When the yard gate was shut the bull came out with a ring on his nose. His belligerent appearance terrified me as he pawed the ground with his front hoof. He lifted his head high, sniffed the air and let a bloodcurdling roar out of him.

Mrs Mac, a sensitive woman, called me into the kitchen, cut a slice from a home-made cake, buttered it and shook sugar on the top and gave it to me. I was troubled because I had heard the men say at our fireside when such matters came down that to be on the safe side a bull should jump the cow three times.

'Anything bothering you?' Mrs Mac asked.

'The men always said to make sure the cow got three jumps,' I told her.

'That will be all right,' she said, 'John will see to that.'

I finished the cut of bread and put the five shillings on the table. When the cow was left out of the yard I drove her home a much quieter and more contented animal than she was coming.

When the Civil War was over and some sort of order restored in the country, my father went off with Singleton, the contractor, rebuilding the bridges which had been blown up by the IRA during the two troubles. Singleton had a big red face and wore a broad-brimmed hat and wire-rimmed spectacles. He was always in a hurry and my father made sure he was ready when he called on Monday mornings. Singleton had an old Ford car with a canvas roof. He drove like hell and my father said that when they went over a humpbacked bridge the passengers were lifted out of their seats and their heads bounced off the canvas roof. When they were working in the Gaeltacht Singleton learned two words of Irish, *Brostaigh ort!* (Hurry on, you!), and used them to great effect on the labouring men.

My father, often I heard him describe it, made the platform which rested on the river bed, and shaped the huge mould to support the new arch. The original archstones and keystones were retrieved from the river and placed in position on the mould, and concrete was grouted down between them. The parapets were rebuilt and coped, and when the cement was set, they struck the fox wedges, the mould slipped down from the arch and in a day or two the road was opened for traffic. Local people who had to go through the river were now able to drive over the restored bridge. On Saturday nights Singleton brought my father home from places as far away as Duagh and Annascaul.

It was when my father was away that our cow – Buckley, called after the man we bought her from – decided to calf. We had watched her barrel grow bigger and bigger during the preceding months and her udder go dry. When the time came and she was in labour, I went and told my mother. She was too unwell to come downstairs as she was expecting another baby but she asked me and my younger brother, Tim, to sit by her bedside and she explained to us what we could do to help the cow have her calf.

Feeling very important we lit a candle and went out to the cowshed to sit and wait. The cow was lying down and the sign we were to watch out for was two hollows that would come on her back just above her tail. When this happened it meant that the pin bones were down and the new arrival would soon be on its way. The first thing that happened was that the water bag appeared. This was the 'blister' my mother told us to expect. That broke and the cow's behind opened very wide as the 'crubs' worked their way out. These crubs – my mother's word – were the calf's front feet. They hadn't come very far when the calf's nose came into view, resting on the feet. The nose was covered with mucus which we wiped away to give the little animal a chance to breathe. The cow looked back at us from where she was tied, giving a low moan with every stitch and with a wild look in her eyes. If the birth movement stopped, my mother told us to catch the front feet and give a gentle tug to coincide with the cow's natural ejection process. This we did and the calf came gradually into the light, his eyes shut. We heaved, holding a leg each, until all of a sudden the calf shot out, knocking the two of us back on the floor. He lay there, a slimy mess. His body was very small and when after a while he staggered to his feet he seemed all legs. His mother was pleading for him as she shivered with excitement. We coaxed him up, reeling drunkenly on his long legs, until he was under her head. She licked his face lovingly and licked his body.

We had plenty of hot water ready, to which we added bran in a tub. We placed it under the cow's head and she drank it greedily. We had to coax the calf away. He wasn't left to suckle the cow. He had to be taught to drink milk from a bucket. My father had placed the rail of the cart in the cowshed. We walked the little calf into this pen and put on the back gate. We went then and told my mother the whole story. She felt well enough to get up and milk the cow. Putting the milk in a bucket she showed us how to teach the calf to drink. She put her finger, dripping with milk, into the calf's mouth. No fear of being bitten, he had no teeth yet. He sucked the milk from her fingers as if he were sucking his mother's teat. It took him a few days to get the hang of it, but when he did he put his head in the bucket, drank what was there, and bellowed for more.

After feeding the calf there was plenty of milk left over for the use of the house, milk to colour our tea and to drink. We even managed to save some to put in a large shallow pan. In time the cream came to the top and was skimmed off with a saucer. When there was a fair quantity of cream collected it was put in a small table churn. When you twisted the handle, a ladder-like frame on the inside went through the cream. After much hard work – and everyone had to take a turn – the cream was made into butter. If you were passing a farmer's dairy on churning day it would be considered unlucky if you didn't give a hand. It was said if you purposely passed by without helping, you would take the size of your head of butter from the dairy. If you gave a hand I suppose the reverse was true. Anyway, many is the time when passing Murphys' dairy on churning day I was greeted with: 'Come here and put the size of your head in the churn!'

There were two products from the churning, butter and buttermilk. The fresh butter with just a little salt added was beautiful to taste and the buttermilk had a sweet-sour tang to it. We drank it and it was used for baking.

My mother baked all the bread for the family. It was only on a very rare occasion that shop bread made its way on to our table. My mother's soda cake was made from white flour but now and then she added Indian meal to make mixed bread. Locally this was called 'yalla buck' and steaming hot and with a plentiful spreading of fresh butter it tasted delicious. As a special treat my mother added cream when baking a white cake, and a little sugar. We loved the soft spongy bread. We cheered when we saw her reaching for the cream jug or taking two paper bags from the press, one with currants, the other with raisins, and adding the dried fruit to the small mountain of flour in the bread tray. As she tossed the flour the dark fruit turned white. When she had the flour thoroughly mixed and had added a pinch of soda, she made a hole in the middle of the heap and poured in the buttermilk, soaked the flour and kneaded the dough.

When my small sister, Eliza, Elizabeth, Betty and Bess my mother called her, was big enough to climb on a chair she loved to mess with the flour and the dough. If my mother was in a good humour she let her make a small cake. My mother's cake was round and almost a foot across. When she flattened it out in the bread tray (a *lasad* in Irish, sometimes pronounced losset) she cut the sign of the cross on the cake and put a small indentation between the four arms of the cross. Then, lifting it between both hands, she lowered the cake into the pot oven, which had been dusted with flour beforehand to keep the cake from sticking to it. She hung the oven over the fire and, placing the cover on it, she heaped red coals on the cover so that the heat to bake the cake was coming from above and below. Now and again she would lift the cover slightly to see if the cake was rising. When it was baked she took the cover off and a cloud of steam went up, filling the kitchen with the aroma of freshly baked bread. The cat sat up and twitched her nostrils sideways she found the smell so good. The new cake, covered in a piece of cloth, was put on the window-sill to cool. When my mother was in high good humour she would let my little sister put her small cake in an old metal saucepan with the cover on. The coals were piled on top and it baked at the side of the fire.

Many is the hour we gave on our knees in the field gathering *caisearbhán*. This was the dandelion plant. With strong knives we levered it up from the roots. My mother put her collection in her apron, and we small people had a bucket. This heap of greenery with orange roots was put on the kitchen table, chopped up very small and added to the hens' feed and the pigs' mess. With the care they got, the pigs fattened quickly. Sometimes they were let out for exercise. They grunted and made loud throaty noises as they enjoyed their freedom. If there was a muddy pool they rolled themselves in it and then started to root up the field in search of roots or whatever it is pigs find under the sod. It was amazing the amount of ground they turned up in a short time, but they were halted in their work of turning a green field black by having their noses ringed. A neighbour would do this for us. He had an implement like a pliers into which he put an open ring with two sharp ends. With a quick movement he clamped the ring shut through the soft flesh of the pig's snout. There was a loud squeal and a little blood came as the pigs ran off, but they rooted no more.

As the pigs got very fat and lay on their straw bed, I sometimes went in and sat between them. They seemed to like having their backs scratched and when a pig's hind foot was unable, because of his fatness, to reach a certain part of his body, I scratched the itchy place with my toe. This seemed to bring him immense pleasure. But the day would come when we would have to part company, for one pig would have to go to the market and the other would find his way into the pickling tub. When I was big enough I went with my father to sell one of the pigs in town. We were up at an unearthly hour that morning. Fanny the mare was tackled and the turf rail put on the car with the back gate taken out. A pig's big floppy ears made for a great hold. I grasped his left ear in my left hand and my father his right ear with his right hand. Then we reached under the pig's barrel and grasped our hands firmly and with a one, two, three, lifted the pig and walked him into the body of the car and put on the back gate.

We climbed in ourselves and my mother brought the holy water, as she always did when we were about to set out on a journey. She shook the water on us and the mare crinkled the skin on her back as the drops fell unexpectedly on her. The pig took no notice and as my father blessed himself we began our journey. Other cars on the same errand came out gates and out the mouths of boreens and on to the main road to join us. As we neared the town the road was black with traffic and the air filled with the squealing of pigs. When we reached the fair field on Martyr's Hill, the animals had to be taken out of the cars and walked around for the jobbers to see. I had my work cut out for me to keep our pig from getting mixed up with our neighbours' livestock or straying among the town pigs which were being walked to market. Each town animal had a rope tied to one of his hind legs and his owner had a light switch with which to tap the pig on the shoulder to steer him left or right. Many people in the town's laneways kept pigs at the backs of their small houses and collected swill at the hotels and lodging houses to feed them.

When the jobbers arrived there was a murmur of anticipation among the men. What would prices be like? The jobbers wore peaked caps and brown leather gaiters over strong boots and trenchcoats not unlike the uniform of the anti-treaty IRA. One of them walked around our pig, gave him a slap of the palm of his hand and said, 'What weight is he?'

'I suppose,' my father replied, 'he'd be shoving up to a hundred and three quarters.'

'What are you asking for him?'

'Nine pounds ten,' my father said with some conviction.

The jobber walked away as if he had been insulted. Other owners nearby had a similar experience and the feeling was that prices were down. My father brought his opening gambit down to eight pounds seventeen and sixpence when the next jobber came and after a bit of banter he too walked away.

'Don't come down any more, Ned,' a neighbour advised my father. 'You have a nice animal there. Don't let him go for nothing. Hold out!'

When the next jobber came around he asked my father, 'Are you selling the pig?'

'No,' my father said, 'I am taking him to Ballybunion on his holidays!'

The jobber and the men standing there laughed at that and the jobber and my father got talking.

'Aren't you the man,' the jobber said, 'that built the Tower Bridge on the road to Moll's Gap?'

My father admitted that he was. More conversation until the jobber said, 'Come on, the day is going,' and he offered a price for the pig. My father named his. The jobber went up a few shillings and my father came down as many more. The jobber walked away, came back and went up a few bob. My father came down a few. The jobber made his last offer and put out his hand, which my father refused. After some more talk, a neighbour intervened. 'What's between ye?'

'Ten shillings,' the jobber told him.

'Look,' says the neighbour. 'In the name of all that's high and holy split the difference.'

That was the final word. My father spit on his palm and the jobber spit on his and they shook hands on the deal. The pig went for eight pounds and five shillings. My father was satisfied. He had got what he considered was enough drama out of the scene. The pig jobber wrote a docket from the book he had in the pocket of his trenchcoat. That would be honoured in a public house later. Then with his penknife he cut his mark on the pig's rump. The pig squealed. I watched the spot where the knife had cut and after a while drops of blood oozed out, making the mark indelible. The pig had to be lifted up and put back in the car. We drove to the railway station, where he was loaded on to a wagon with the jobber's name on it. With a grunt he ran up the ramp and in no time he was lost among the other pigs. We tied the pony to the courthouse railings, gave her some hay, and I went with my father to Carthy Dennehy's public house where the jobber was paying out. He remembered my father.

'Oh ho,' he said, 'London Bridge is falling down, but not the one on the road to Moll's Gap!'

My father gave me a half-crown and called for lemonade for me. While the men talked over their drinks I walked out in the street and with a two-shilling piece my mother had given me in the morning I had a lot of money in my pocket. I went to Maggie Courtney's to buy sweets to bring home to those younger than me, and a currant cake I knew my mother would like. I didn't want to wander too far in case I got lost. I stopped to watch the sale of young pigs, pinky little *bonamhs*. They were in railed carts by the side of the street and in front of Dinny Sir John's. In some carts they were lying down and snuggled into each other, very tired after their long journey to town. Men who had sold grown pigs that morning were now buying young ones to fatten and so the cycle began again. When a little *bonamh* was bought, and the same bargaining had gone on as I had seen in the pig market, it was lifted out by the ears and transferred to the purchaser's cart. Sometimes a farmer cradled the small pig in his arms like a baby. There was much lamenting as the little fellow was parted from his comrades.

When I got back to Carthy Dennehy's public house my

father and the men, having downed a few drinks, were in good order. Men drank a whiskey first and then a pint of stout. Some drank the pint first and the whiskey followed as a chaser. On a very cold morning I heard it said older men called for two whiskeys, drank one and poured the other into their boots to warm their feet. In a while's time my father tore himself away from the company and we went to get the messages for my mother. When we got back to the courthouse railing the pony was glad to see us. She gave a neigh of welcome. We stood into the rail and she hurried home.

When we sat down to our meal, all the talk was about the market. My mother was pleased enough with the price my father got for the pig. He fished it out of his pocket and gave it to her and I knew it would find its way into the box with the sliding top. She wanted to hear any news we brought. Did we see anyone she knew? She was particularly interested to hear if we had spoken to any of her relations. I had news for her about the prices young *bonamhs* were making as I knew by next market day we would have space in our pigs' house for two new occupants. Then the big question was decided: the day was named for killing the pig we had kept.

When that day came, water was being boiled from an early hour. A wine barrel, not the one we used for spraying the potatoes, was cleaned out, and when the time came this was more than half-filled with scalding water. The pig butcher came, and two neighbours to help my father hold down the pig. The kitchen table was brought out in the yard and placed so that it was on a slight incline. A small noose was put at the end of a rope and the men opening the pig house door slipped the noose into the pig's mouth and tightened it over his upper jaw. He was led out to the yard, protesting loudly, and with a quick movement the men knocked him on the flat of his back on the table, his head where the table was lowest, and with a tight grip on his four legs they held him down. Pat Murrell, our next door neighbour, a pig butcher with a reputation of being quick to dispatch, had his coat off and his sleeves folded above his elbows. He took the gleaming butcher's knife so sharp it would nearly split a hair, and shaved the bristles along the pig's throat. He made a long lengthwise cut in the throat and when the flesh parted for a second it remained as clean as if he had cut a piece of cheese. Then the blood oozed out in little bubbles. My mother and small sister ran East the Wire to be out of earshot of the bloodcurdling squeals of the pig. With a swift movement Pat plunged the knife through the gash and his arm followed it to the pig's heart. The blood rushed out, the pig's voice gurgling through it, and into a large pan which I held. I was terrified to have to do it, but I wasn't prepared to appear cowardly before the neighbouring men. The pig's body was eased down the inclined table until his head hung over the edge. The butcher, his arm red like *Crobh Dearg* the pagan priest at 'the city', shouted instructions to the men to sway the body backwards and forwards and to keep moving the legs to get out all the blood. In the end the big pan was nearly full of red blood, with the last trickle of a slightly darker colour.

The barrel of scalding water was near the table and the pig was eased head first into it and worked up and down by the hind legs. Then he was pulled out and the other end was let slide into the barrel. When the boiling water had done its job of softening the bristly hair the carcass was hauled on to the table and the butcher began to shave the hairs from the skin. The men got what sharp knives were in the kitchen to help and I lent a hand myself.

When the carcass was clean the butcher removed the cloven hoof coverings from the feet, and inserted a piece of rope under the tendons of the pig's hind legs to hang him from a short ladder. There was a tub under the head, which had a spud in its mouth. Now with the knife the butcher cut the pig open from his tail to his throat and all his insides slid down into the tub. The liver and heart were removed and given to my mother and I got the bladder. It was like a small balloon with little nodules of fat stuck to the outside. I squeezed it and a squirt of urine shot out. I filled it with water and washed it well and put it in the shoulder of the flue over the fire. When it was dry I would blow it up, tie a cord at the neck and invite the neighbouring lads for a game of football.

At nightfall the ladder was brought into the kitchen. The carcass was too valuable to be left outside for wild dogs to feast on. When the lamp was lit the light fell on the hanging animal. As I sat at the fire I couldn't take my eyes off him. He was sad and comical with his front held open by three sally rods and his mouth held open with a spud. If you looked at him through half-closed eyes he could be laughing or crying. Holy God! I thought what he had suffered to bring us food for the entire winter. My mother, knowing the softie I was, suspected that I would be crying myself next. She gave me a cup of hot milk and walked me up the stairs to bed. 'That's the way the world is,' she said, 'and animals were put into it for our use and benefit.' The excitement of the day kept me awake for a long time and when I went to sleep I dreamt that it was I who was killed instead of the pig. I saw my naked body hanging from the ladder with a spud in my mouth. I saw the spud falling out of my mouth and my soul coming after it and floating up through the clouds. Heaven was full of pigs. Some had wings and a very fat pig looked like Singleton, the bridge builder. He was driving a car with a canvas roof. I couldn't mistake him. The same fat face under a broad-rimmed hat. He wore spectacles and had a gold ring in his nose.

Next morning the pig's intestines were taken in a tin bath to the river. I helped my mother to wash them; sometimes a neighbour's wife or daughter would also lend a hand. The running water was let flow through what seemed like miles of pig's gut and the gut was turned inside out so that it was thoroughly cleaned. The intestines were cut into lengths of from sixteen to eighteen inches, placed in the bath and brought home. where a busy day lay ahead for my mother and her helpers. Oatenmeal, milk, onions with seasoning of pepper, salt and spice were added to the pig's blood in the dish which I had held the day before. There was a big pot of boiling water over the fire. My mother took an eighteen-inch-long piece of intestine and tied one end with bageen thread. This was the thread which was saved when empty flour bags were opened out to make bed sheets and even articles of women's wear. Holding the other end of the gut open she spooned the mixture into it, and putting the spoon aside she squeezed the contents down along the intestine. When the length of gut was over three-quarters full – room was left for the pudding to expand – she tied the two ends together so that she had in her hand what looked like a small, pumped-up bicycle tube. Two or maybe three sticks were stretched over the mouth of the pot, and as my mother completed the filling of a pudding she put it in over the stick so that it hung down into the boiling water where it began to cook. She kept turning the wheels of pudding on the sticks to let the boiling water get to all of them and each one got the stab of a fork to let the air out.

When the job was ended the kitchen was full of puddings. We didn't eat them all ourselves. When God smiled on you you shared with your neighbour. It was my job to go to each neighbouring house with a dinner plate on which was a half circle of pudding and a pork steak. People were delighted to receive the gift and they would give the same to us and maybe more when God smiled on them.

When night time came there were two lamps lighting in our kitchen for the salting of the pig. The neighbouring farmer, Pat Murrell, who had killed the pig, and Daniel Moynihan came. The carcass was cut into flitches and the kitchen table was placed in the middle of the floor. My father nailed a board around three sides of it to keep the salt from falling on the floor. Two and a half stone of salt was bought that day and a little saltpetre was added to it. Each man took a flitch of meat and rubbed the salt well into it, into the skin as well as the flesh. Pockets were made in the flesh and salt stuffed in them as well as deep into the piece of meat that held a bone. The big wine barrel was placed at the bottom of the kitchen and the flitches of salted meat and the head now cut in half were firmly packed into it. When the last piece went in more salt was shaken on the meat and a large flat stone placed on top. A cloth was put over the mouth of the barrel and nine days later my father would look to see if the pickle was rising. If this liquid kept coming up until all the meat was covered the curing was a success.

In three weeks the flitches would be taken out and put hanging from the joists. They would drip for a day or two and we children avoided walking under them. It was said that if a drop fell on our heads we would go bald. But the curing process continued, with the smoke from the fire helping to mature the bacon. When our principal meal was being prepared all my mother had to do was reach for a hanging flitch and cut off what bacon she wanted for the pot, and while there were potatoes in the pit and York cabbage or turnips in the garden no one in our house went hungry.

RECEIVING

When the men came at night they picked a place for their chairs so as not to be sitting under a flitch of dripping bacon. Not that a drop of brine on their heads would make any difference for they all wore hats and caps. The men never removed their headgear except when going to bed or at Mass. Indeed it was on seeing the men bareheaded in the chapel that I discovered to my surprise that many of them had not a rib of hair between them and the Almighty. White-skinned domes topped weatherbeaten faces, faces that looked very different when I saw them again with their hats on that night. Two other places I saw the men bareheaded were in the wake room, when they knelt beside the bed to pray, and at the graveside, but as soon as ever the priest had said the final prayer, a decade of the rosary, the hats and caps were on again.

The men wore their working clothes when they came rambling to our house at night. This attire was once their Sunday best. The shirt was of flannel, something like an army greyback. There was a brass stud in front and a buttonhole at the back of the collar band to take another stud. Over the shirt on Sundays they wore a starched front with a butterfly collar attached. It was secured at the back and front of the shirt band with studs and was just large enough to cover the upper chest inside the waistcoat. With a necktie attached and the body coat on, it looked like a full shirt. It was as stiff as a board with starch and almost shone in its gleaming whiteness. With a navy suit, a velour hat and polished boots the wearer looked the picture of respectability going to the chapel on Sunday. But it was more the attire of the older men, and some of them as well sported a cutaway or swallow-tailed coat with two large buttons at the back. On St Patrick's Day a large spray of shamrock hung from the coat lapel and on Palm Sunday there was a sprig of palm in the hat.

My father wore a collar and tie on Sunday. The collar was starched and there often was a struggle trying to get the front and back studs through the starched clogged buttonholes. Standing on a chair I had to come to his assistance and with my tiny fingers try and force a reluctant stud through a starch-sealed hole. Somehow I succeeded and handed him the large handkerchief my mother gave me. He unfurled it, blew his nose with it and put it in his pocket. Younger men wore soft collars and many wore no collar or tie, just a plain collarless shirt with a brass stud at the front.

On Sunday my mother and the women of the parish had no opportunity to display their finery. They all wore shawls which, as the saying goes, covered a multitude. Only one lady, the schoolteacher, referred to as Mrs O, wore a hat and coat going into Barraduv Mass. The women's shawls, like the Kinsale cloak, lasted a lifetime. Pride of place went to the paisley shawl of two shades of fawn with a variegated pattern around the base and an abundance of tassels. There was a plain brown shawl, a green and black shawl and a black shawl which widows wore. From a distance a group of women in paisley shawls, their skirts sweeping the ground and with their heads together talking after Mass, looked like a cock of hay. The women always covered their heads with the shawl in the chapel, and a woman in the street who threw the shawl back on her shoulders, twirling the ends of it around her hands and with her arms akimbo while she talked and laughed, was a very outgoing person, something seldom seen.

My mother bought her shawl maybe when she was getting married and the only time she visited the shops was to buy a pair of high buttoned boots and clothes-making materials. Her skirt and blouse, a jacket she called it, she made herself. She made all my clothes as well. She bought the Eton collar, bow tie and of course my boots, but the jacket and trousers she made often from an old suit of my father's turned inside out. She knitted my stockings and my father's and when we put our toes or heels through them they were darned. Cardigans and jumpers she knitted for the household. My jacket, shirt and trousers were sewn by hand. Very few had sewing machines. The traveller, Mr Roycroft, called to the house in his gig trap but we never had enough money to buy one.

I wore a real suit made by Con the tailor for my first holy communion. He fitted me out with a nice body coat and a short pants in which I looked well with a collar and tie like the men and a navy skullcap with yellow stripes.

I dreaded the day before holy communion when I had to go to confession for the first time. The teacher acted it all out for us in school. The examination of our conscience, the going in the door of the confessional when our turn came, making sure to close it after us, waiting for the slide to come across and then saying, 'Bless me father, for I have sinned!' I could hardly go to sleep at night worrying about the sins I would have to tell the priest. I was afraid of what he would say if I had sins to tell and I was afraid of what he would say if I hadn't. I would have to get it right and I knew it was a sin to make a bad confession. 'I didn't do what I was told, father.' This was an example of a sin which the teacher told us. Her version of it was, 'I was disobedient, father'. Maybe it was a sin to make up a sin for the sake of having something to tell. 'I stole sugar, father,' and 'I cursed and swore,' were the other sins I could confess. I made up my mind before I went to sleep the night before that my last sin to tell him would be, 'I told lies, father.' The lies I told were harmless but it gave me something to say.

When the time came the biggest fright I got was the darkness in the penitent's side of the confessional when I closed the door. I wanted to dash out again, but when the slide came across a little light came in, and by rising off my knees I could see the priest inside. He never looked at me and didn't seem a bit surprised when I told him it was my first confession. He asked me to tell him my sins and I rattled off about being disobedient, stealing sugar, telling lies and cursing and swearing. It didn't knock a shake out of him. He gave me my penance, which was three Hail Marys and three Glories. Then for the first time he lifted his head and looked at me and whispered very earnestly, 'Pray for me, my child!' I came out of the box with a weight off my mind and thinking that the priest must be in some sort of trouble seeing that he was asking me to pray for him.

The following day was my first holy communion, the most

joyous day in all our lives, the priest said, when he visited the school. The day when we would for the first time receive the body of our Blessed Lord into our souls. The teacher had gone over it all with us. The going up to the altar, kneeling, and joining our hands. Opening our mouths and sticking out our tongues, not too far the teacher warned, to receive the sacred host. Then as we walked in line with our hands joined back to our places, we were to give thanks to God for coming into our souls as we swallowed the host. But what would happen if I couldn't swallow it, I thought, as I lay in bed the night before. Would the host melt in my mouth and then the body of our Blessed Lord would evaporate and not go down my throat and into my soul! Supposing I got a fit of coughing. I turned over on the tick and covered my head. Supposing I coughed the host out on the ground. What would happen then? I couldn't pick it up. The host was sacred and we were told that no hand could touch it but the priest's because his hand had been anointed. Everyone would notice me. The priest would be mad vexed at having to come down off the altar and pick the sacred host off the floor. My mother would be mortified and my father would be dying with the shame.

I went to sleep and dreamt that a frog came into the bed and was trying to get into my mouth. His huge protruding eyes frightened me, and he puffed and he puffed and his belly went in and out like a bellows. Then he began to swell into a monster and I woke up shouting, my body in a lather of sweat. I was in bed with my two younger brothers and my mother, hearing me shout, got up and lit a candle. She put me sitting at the side of the bed and noticing that my body was wet with sweat she dried me and put on a clean shirt.

'You'll be all right now, a stór. I'll give you a cup of hot milk.' My mother's cure for everything.

'You can't do that!' my father reminded her. 'The child is fasting.'

From twelve o'clock the night before no bite or sup went inside the lips of a person going to holy communion. A neighbour used to eat at half past twelve, claiming that from where we lived there was a difference of half an hour between Greenwich and God's time, which was the time he went by. I went

55

to sleep again and was up early next morning. There was a lot of fussing over me. My boots were polished and polished again. I had trouble putting a knot in my necktie. My father had to do it for me and my mother said that he made the knot too clumsy and she re-knotted it. Had I a handkerchief? On Sunday mornings there was a clean handkerchief for everyone from the pile of ironed laundry my mother had done the night before.

We had a tub trap for the pony by this time and very well she looked under it in a shiny set of harness. A shake of holy water before we set out to keep us safe on our journey. We all sat in. A rope rein guided Fanny the mare when she was tackled to the common car, but in the trap my father held a leather reins. He sat at the back with my mother and we youngsters at the front. I loved the motion of the trap when we were on level ground and Fanny could trot. Slow-moving asses and carts we passed and fast-moving horses and sidecars passed us. Neighbours waved to me, seeing me in my new rig-out, acknowledging that it was a big day for me.

We didn't have a family pew in the church. They were for the well-to-do farmers, shopkeepers and teachers, who could afford to buy a new pew and pay the yearly rent for it. Some of those seats were never full, yet outsiders never sat in them and I don't think they would be welcome. The family pew was private property in a public place. One year the parish priest put up the rental and a family, thinking the charge was dear enough, refused to pay. The parish priest ordered them out of the seat. They refused and the priest had the pew taken out and put behind the church, where in the end it rotted. The family never went to Mass in that church again during that parish priest's reign, but drove all the way to the friary in town. They never spoke to the parish priest after. Even when he came to the stations in their house they didn't speak, because they felt he had humiliated them before their neighbours and friends. There was a large space behind the seats and those of little property or none stood or knelt there, the men at the gospel side and the women at the side of the epistle. It was strange that among the poor there was segregation, while in the pews husbands sat with their wives.

I knelt with my father. He knelt on one knee, under which he had his cap. My mother, who was across the aisle, frowned when she saw me kneeling on my new skullcap. There was an understanding that the children for first holy communion would go to the altar first and when the time came I got the beck from my mother and I joined the other children as we moved towards the altar. Heads bowed, our hands joined, tips of fingers under the chin, and I with my skullcap under my left oxter. As I moved along I kept repeating the prayer before communion and reminding myself that when I had said the prayer after communion I should pray for my father and mother and all the family. I knelt at the rail, putting my hands under the long white cloth and holding it under my chin and I could hear the priest pray as he came from the far end. An altar boy accompanying him held a little silver tray under the ciborium as the priest laid the host on the communicant's tongue. O Dia linn! God be with us! The priest was at the next child to me and the altar boy was placing the silver tray under my chin. 'Corpus Christi,' the priest said and I opened my mouth and put my tongue out. I hoped my tongue would look clean. I washed it in the morning, making sure not to swallow a drop of the water. The priest placed the white circular host on my tongue and I felt the backs of his fingers touch my lips. I closed my mouth and forgot to get up so the boy beside me had to give me a nudge. As I walked back to my place, full of strange feelings of having God in my mouth, I swallowed and nothing happened. Sweet and Blessed Lord, what was wrong? I felt with the tip of my tongue and found that the sacred host had clung to the roof of my mouth. I tried to dislodge it and I couldn't. Terror seized me as I knelt by my father's side. I thought that God was refusing to go into my soul. Did I make a bad confession? Had I done something that offended Him?

'Are you all right, a leanbh (my child)?' my father said.

I nodded. I was afraid to open my mouth in case the host fell out. A corner of the host seemed to lift from my palate. I manoeuvred it on to my tongue and with a quick swallow it was gone. I could breath freely now. I looked up. My mother had been watching me. She smiled.

I was starving after the long fast as I came out of the chapel with my father. All the men put on their hats and caps and felt in their coat pockets for their pipes. These were lit and smoke began to rise as we came through the chapel gate. The men didn't make much wonder of me. One man said to my father, 'Is this Brian?' thinking that I was called after my grandfather. My mother came out with her friends. They all admired me in my new clothes. Relations gave me money, small coins, but I got a half-crown from my godmother, Bridgie Lar. I went then to Danny O's shop where my mother bought the messages. Danny O's sister Nora gave me a cup of tea and a currant bun. I took a bite of the bun and a slug of the tea and I was in heaven. We trotted home. Fanny the mare seemed in a hurry. She was hungry and I was too, despite the bun and the tea. A neighbour had killed a pig two days before and last night the gift plate had come to our house. 'Bring in a few kippens (sticks),' my mother said. We did and the fire lit up and in no time the kettle was boiling and a circle of black pudding was sizzling in the pan.

FORBIDDEN FRUIT

୶

Not long after receiving my first holy communion I came home from school one evening to be told by my mother that she had met her distant cousin in town that day. Her cousin was Miss O, a teacher at Lissivigeen School, about the same distance in the other direction from our house as the school we attended. Miss O was teaching infants, first and second class and she asked my mother to let her two boys come to her school. My father was opposed to the change but my mother got her way and one Tuesday morning my brother Tim and I set out for our new school at Lissivigeen. We didn't start on Monday because there was a superstition about beginning anything on Monday. My neighbours began no enterprise on Monday. If a burial was on that day the first sod of the grave was dug on Sunday. Our hair was never cut on Monday and the clippings were not put in the fire, but carefully placed in a hole in the ditch until we came back for them on the day of the resurrection.

Through some misunderstanding, my brother and I were put in the same class. He was better than me at many subjects, which proved an embarrassment to me for the rest of my schooldays. Miss O was exceptionally nice to us at first, although we could see how strict she was with the others. One of her punishments for mistakes was holding a pencil between the first and second fingers of her closed fist with a little of the pencil protruding and hitting you hard on the top of the head. This was extremely painful, as I found out when I failed to answer a question which was easily answered by my brother. For grave offences like being late for school, offending pupils were sent up to the master to be slapped.

The master was at the other side of the glass partition and had charge of third, fourth, fifth and sixth classes. He had an ashplant fairly thin so that it almost swung around your hand when he hit you. The sting of the pain went to the heart and there was always a slap on each hand. It was a very hard case who didn't cry, and as they cried the pupils blew into their hands in an effort to ease the pain or pressed their palms under their armpits.

I was fortunate in escaping most of this punishment and my brother was so good that he was never reprimanded. If we were late in the morning I was blamed because I was older and always took the rap. We left home early enough but when we met up with the other scholars on the way we dallied, talked, argued, even sat by the roadside and watched the farmers working in the fields. A horse-drawn mowing machine because of the noise it made we found fascinating. Losing all sense of time, we spun castle tops, and then, of a sudden, realising the lateness of the hour, we plucked a yellow birdsfoot trefoil flower which grew by the roadside. We called it 'no blame' and put it in our books, hoping it would save us from the rod. But it never did.

Only once do I remember being severely slapped and that was when I went with some other boys to rob Owen Keeffe's orchard at play hour. Between getting there and stealing the apples and eating them the time flew and we were very late getting back to school after the bell went. Our hearts sank when we saw that there were no pupils in the playground. We heard the voices in the classrooms reading aloud or doing their tables. For a moment we thought of running away but we had to go in – our satchels were inside. Very timidly and in hangdog fashion we sloped into Miss O's classroom. We were late, we told her, because we had gone to Healy's shop for tobacco for our fathers. Where was the tobacco? We had nothing to show but the telltale apples left over after the feast.

We shook at the knees as she ushered us into the master and told him what we had done. He talked about the seventh commandment and he got the pupils who were preparing for confirmation to recite for us what was forbidden by that commandment, 'unjustly taking what belongs to another ...' He took the ashplant, looped it almost double and let it go with a swish. He told us to empty our pockets of the few apples we had left, and they were placed on his rostrum. He motioned us then to stand by the wall. Anticipating the pain of punishment as we stood under the map of the world was very near unbearable. When the time for class change came, we were called out one by one. It was better to be first because you didn't know what was coming. What did come was four slaps, two on each hand. The second slap on an aching palm was the hardest to bear and we went back to Miss O's classroom contrite and tearful. When she wasn't looking, my brother, who didn't go on the raid, asked me if I had any apples left. The punishment changed my attitude to robbing orchards for a long time to come. Later when the boys went on another raid, after school this time, I refused to go, remembering the sting of pain from the ashplant which went through my system like an electric shock.

Ashman was what the pupils nicknamed the master, because of his dexterity with the rod. But to be fair to him he didn't slap all that often. After I moved from Miss O's section into third class I don't think I was ever slapped again. When things went well and everybody did his best and attended to his homework, life in class was great. The master was kindly and had all our interests at heart. There was a lesson once a week to which we all looked forward. This was the hour we spent in the garden attached to the school residence. The big boys dug with spades in the spring and made drills for potatoes and ridges for onions. We were shown how to grow carrots, parsnips, lettuce, and one year we grew a giant vegetable marrow. Currant and gooseberry trees were added to the garden and there was much celebration among the boys the spring we planted four apple trees, winks and nudges, as much as to say we won't have far to go when these bear fruit. In the autumn we harvested the fruits of our labour. Peas and beans were spread out to dry on the wide sills of the school windows, the ripe onions filling the classroom with their pungent smell.

It took the apple trees in the school garden ages to bear fruit, and then one spring there were blossoms on a tree. Not a great number but we watched with the master as a honey bee perched on a flower and, poking for the honey, brought away on its hairy legs the yellow dust which pollinated the next flower. We watched too as the blossoms faded and in time a nut-like little apple appeared. In September there were four apples on the tree. We raced ahead of the master on each weekly visit to see how they were progressing. Coming to the end of the month the apples got larger and the master was very proud of his crop but there was many a young stalwart whose teeth swam in his mouth for a bite of one of the apples. There being only four one would easily be missed if stolen. But a greedy descendant of Adam tasted the forbidden fruit without plucking the apple. He took a large bite from the side away from the public gaze so that it was some days before the master noticed. There was an inquiry, the rod lying waiting on the rostrum, and even though we suspected who the culprit was he was never brought to book. The incident was forgotten and we continued to enjoy the hour we spent each week away from lessons in the garden, out in the open air, preparing the soil, planting the tiny seeds and waiting for them to show above the ground and grow to maturity. It brought us more satisfaction than we got from reading, writing and arithmetic.

When it came to geography, in our first year with the master, he got us to draw a map of the place where we lived showing the house and the fields around it. My map was small, one field, but that was divided into the potato garden, onion and cabbage patch and pasture for the cow and the pony. We were to add in as an extension of our own map the main road, byroads, streams, rivers and any landmarks. There was a *gallán* stone standing on a hillock like a mighty grave not far from our house. We suspected that under the great mound of earth and with the *gallán* stone to mark his resting place, a king or giant of old was taking his long last sleep. The road to school and beyond it to the town we drew, and showed the course of the river Flesk as it wound its way to the lakes of Killarney. We put in the range of mountains which stood on guard over our territory and named them from the Paps to the MacGillicuddy Reeks. If we craned our necks in the schoolyard we could see Carrauntoohil, the highest peak. From our home-made map the master took us to the map on the wall where we learned about Kerry, then about Ireland and a little about the globe. Having started at home and learned about our own surroundings gave us a better understanding of the wider world.

Mangerton Mountain we could see by standing up in the classroom. Mangerton was volcanic maybe a million years ago, the master told us. The crater can still be seen up at the top. It is now a bottomless lake known as the Devil's Punch Bowl. The master laughed as he told us the tall story, often related by the jarveys and boatmen to the tourists, about the man who fell into the Punch Bowl and came out in Australia. Later in a higher class when we came to study *Mo Scéal Féin* (My Story) by an tAthair Peadar Ó Laoghaire, we read of a description of a visit to the top of Mangerton which the priest had undertaken as a young student. From up there he could see north to the Shannon, east to Tipperary, south to Bantry Bay and west to the mighty Atlantic pounding on the coast of Kerry. The master was full of admiration for the young student who set out on that trip and we marvelled at the wonders he saw.

Going home that evening we sat on a mossy bank and looking up at the great mountain we said to ourselves why shouldn't we climb it. The idea took root and there and then we made up our minds that we would climb it tomorrow. We would meet at Mac's arch and go over Gortacoosh and up by the shores of Lough Guitane to the foot of Mangerton. We were not sure if we should tell our parents. Maybe we should say that we were going playing football. I went to bed early that night and spent a long time awake, thinking of what I would see from the top of Mangerton. What would our house look like from away up there? Maybe I would not be able to see it with all the trees and bushes that were growing up around the place. I went to sleep at last and dreamt that I was walking like a mighty man and stepping from Mangerton to Ceapach, then to Crohane and Stoompa and finally standing with a foot on each of the twin Paps Mountains. From that position I bent down and washed my face in Doocorrig Lake. It was the sound of the water trickling through my giant fingers and falling into the lake that woke me up. I listened in the darkness and heard the rainwater gurgling from the eaves into the downpipe and the raindrops falling on the roof.

It rained all the next day and the day after. In time, other things happened to claim our attention.

Two Christian Brothers came to the school one day and

talked about their order, their work in foreign lands and the importance of devoting one's life to God. They made the life of holiness, teaching, caring for the sick and travelling abroad very appealing and asked us to join the order. So as not to disappoint the master, who was a very religious man, I was tempted to join up. When they asked us again and with more fervour this time, I was carried away and put up my hand. The master with a smile on his face and a whisper of 'good man' wrote my name and address and gave it to one of the brothers. He took me out into the hallway and asked me all about myself. My age. Was I a good scholar at school? Did I like games? Did I go to the sacraments regularly and what did my father do? He put his hand on my head and said, 'Give yourself to God!'

Then I thought of what my father would say. I had been helping him in the workshop and he often said he was waiting for the time when I would be confirmed and leave school to become his apprentice. He deserved my help as much as God and the black people of Rhodesia. I kept to myself on the way home from school. I didn't know whether the boys thought me very brave or a right ould cod for doing what I did. One boy took out his handkerchief and folded it into a narrow band and put it around his neck to look like a Roman collar. 'Forgive me, Father, for I have sinned!' he mocked. I was encouraged when his comrades said, 'Stop that, Johneen!'

When I reached home I didn't go into the workshop, which was the first thing I always did. Instead I went into the kitchen and told my mother that I was joining the Brothers. In a way she was sort of pleased about it and was full of questions about where I was going, what the Brothers were like and what the Brother said who questioned me in the hall. 'I must pray,' she said, 'and we must all pray and ask if your decision is the right one and if God wants you.'

We went out together to the workshop and she told my father. He was furious. I'll never forget the look he gave me. He threw a tantrum. He kicked things around in his anger. My mother was consoling him and saying what good I'd be doing in the world. 'He'll be praying for you, Ned!' she told my father. 'He'll be praying for you and praying for all of us.' 'Praying won't bore holes in oak, ma'am,' he thundered, as he sank the axe in the chopping block and rived it in two. At the rosary that night I never mentioned a word to God about being a Christian Brother and my mother never asked Him to enlighten me in my decision. She knew if she brought up the subject even at prayers my father would get up off his knees and go out and commune with the stars, something which he did to avoid fighting with my mother in front of us. Some time later a letter came from the monastery saying that I was accepted as a postulant in the order. My mother showed it to me, but by now my mind had changed. 'I think I'll be a carpenter,' I told her. She wrote back to say that I had no vocation.

The Gaelic League in Killarney proposed holding a feis in the old cricket field. Now that the English had gone, men in whites no longer played there. The feis, or festival, celebrating the Irish language, was held in the month of June. We went in the pony and trap. The master had made up a conversation piece in Irish, a *comhrá beirte*, for my brother and myself. We were to act the parts of two old farmers selling a pretend cow at a fair. As well as the *comhrá beirte* section there were short plays and sketches, school choirs, storytelling for adults and schoolchildren, stepdancing and solo traditional singing for young and old. Platforms were erected here and there throughout the field so that the audience moved about from competition to competition. Lorries were driven in and with one side butt left down they took the place of platforms.

I was interested in seeing boys and girls of my own age in school plays. One of these was being acted out on the back of a lorry. Pieces of cardboard had fireplaces, doors and windows drawn on them with coloured chalk and placed on the lorry to give the effect of a kitchen scene with the barest essentials in furniture. The first child to enter the stage set stood inside the door and talked back to the one coming in after him. They stood there arguing their case. As each extra actor entered they moved a little bit to make room and the entire play went ahead as they stood in a bunch inside the door. Fireplace, window, chairs and table were all ignored. The man of the roads character wore a white wig and a red beard. His back was bent; he was a martyr to rheumatism. A girl played the grandfather and a boy his wife. They were dressed suitably for the parts but this did not conceal their gender. Their teacher sat on the hood of the lorry prompting them and was overcome with paroxysms of laughter at every funny thing they said. The pupils must have come from an Irish-speaking district for their language was clear and beautifully spoken and because of that the judges had no hesitation in giving them full marks.

My brother and I did fairly well with our *comhrá beirte* but spent too much time trying to control an imaginary, recalcitrant cow and lost marks. There was a section for music and this and the school choirs drew the biggest audience. There was an interest too in the child storytellers and a greater interest in the adult exponents of the art. One old man told the story of *Bithiúnach Mór Gleann Fleisce* (The Great Rogue of Glenflesk) and those who could follow what he was saying knocked a tremendous kick out of it because Glenflesk was our parish. The Glenflesk rogue had a school for training young rogues and the storyteller said that many of these students emigrated afterwards and wound up as the biggest gangsters in America.

The official opening was not at the outset of the feis but well into the proceedings, when a full crowd had assembled. It wouldn't do to have a prominent person giving the *óráid na feise* (feis oration) to the few people who would arrive on time. The man who opened our feis was a *duine mór le rá*, a very important person, one of the foremost politicians of the day. There was a great surge forward when he appeared on the platform, such was the esteem in which he was held by most of the people. He spoke only in Irish in a dreary, matter-of-fact tone. The day was very hot and as he went on and on the older women, who had rushed to the fore because of their admiration for him, were now melting with the heat in the tightly packed crowd. They were easing their heavy shawls back on their shoulders to get some air. At first among themselves they had been full of praise for the speaker and mentioned in tones of adulation that it wasn't Irish alone he could speak but French and German. The great man droned on and as the women were being overcome with the heat and unable to get out and not understanding one word of what he said their interest waned. One old lady, shifting from foot to foot, the sweat running down her face and glistening in the little hollow below her throat, remarked in a voice of pure desperation, 'Oh God, will he ever stop the *cadaráling*!' She knew at least one word in Irish, which meant meaningless meandering. Suddenly the oration was at an end; the people parted, letting the air circulate, and the women, feeling cooler, went off to get themselves some refreshment. The same as at 'the city' or a sports meeting, there was lemonade for sale. This on a hot day was in great demand, as were the fat biscuits which went with it.

In one part of the field there was a tug-of-war between schools to give those not too proficient in the language a chance to show their talents. There was high jumping too and a bag race and spoon race. I was on the tug-of-war team from our school and so was Paddy Furnane. Paddy had his head down and with his heel he was making an impression in the ground that he could dig into while straining on the rope. Two priests, one with an umbrella – some priests carried umbrellas at all times – were walking along deeply engaged in conversation and not watching where they were going. One of them thrust his patent leathered foot under Paddy's heel as it was coming down and got the full force of the steel tip on his toe cap. The priest growled with pain and lifted the injured foot, hopping on the other one. He was red-haired, a sign of temper, and seeing Paddy and associating him with his agony he upped with the umbrella and landed Paddy the father and mother of an ecclesiastical clout on top of the head and floored him. Paddy got up, staggered around holding his head and then made a beeline for the gate of the cricket field, leaving us to pull the tug-of-war without him. We were beaten badly. The proceedings were closed by a pipers' band playing for a while and then marching out the gate. We all followed them.

A STRONG AND PERFECT CHRISTIAN

The one time while I was at the master's side of the partition when he became very angry was when we were studying for confirmation. The religious doctrine we had to learn was much harder than that for holy communion. Reams of the catechism had to be got off by heart. Our not too supple tongues had to get around words like consanguinity. 'Big rocks of words,' our elders used to say, 'that you wouldn't break in a county council stone crusher!'

> Q   *What else is forbidden by the sixth commandment?*
> A   *All lascivious looks and touches, idleness and bad company; all excesses of eating and drinking and whatever may tend to inflame the passions.*

God help us! All we ever saw in flames was a furze bush! My mother held the book for me and listened to my answers, and was as liable to lose her temper as the master if I got them wrong. I didn't mind her getting mad with me and anyway she didn't slap as the master did. There was no explanation from the master or my mother as to what the words we didn't understand meant. I had only to guess what was implied by, 'Thou shalt not covet thy neighbour's wife.'

The men had a story in our rambling house when they heard me mention that commandment. It seems a young lad who had been away for a long time with his uncle in county Limerick missed out on the sacrament of confirmation. When the lack was discovered he was almost twenty and even though of a wild and obstreperous nature he was sent back to school where he sat with boys nearly half his age learning his catechism. On the appointed day the bishop came to the church to confirm the children. He walked down the aisle not yet in

68

his full canonicals and questioned a class as they sat, school by school, in the body of the church. The bishop couldn't help noticing a grown man sitting in the middle of the children and he consulted with the parish priest who was at his side. In whispered tones he was told of the circumstances. The bishop commenced to question the young man and he gave a good enough account of himself until he was asked what was forbidden by the ninth commandment. 'Thou shalt not converse with thy neighbour's wife,' he said. The bishop smiled and gave the correct answer. And then in an effort to make the meaning plain he said, 'Would it be correct for you to fall in love with your neighbour's wife?' 'Why should I do a thing like that, my lord,' the young man said, 'and the country full of young lovely girls!'

Well, our day came to go under the bishop's hand. The priest came to the school, examined us and gave each one of us a ticket. We were seated school by school in the lofty cathedral, the teacher responsible for the tuition standing or kneeling with each group. Surpliced priests walked among us asking questions here and there. Then the bishop came out of the sacristy followed by two young priests. They remained behind the altar rails, one of them holding the bishop's mitre and the other his crozier. The bishop had a surplice over a red soutane and a big cross on a gold chain hung from his neck. When he came nearer we saw the huge ring with a red diamond bulging from it on his right hand; the sign, we were told, of his authority. The bishop paused and asked a few questions of a school and if the answering was good he passed on to the next class. But when he came to a school where the answering was indifferent he stayed and questioned them thoroughly and then spoke to the parish priest, as if voicing his disappointment at the quality of the religious instruction. Small as we were, we had pity for that school's master standing there as red as a turkeycock.

I thought the bishop was going to pass by our school but no, he paused and looked straight at me. I began to shake, I was so nervous. He asked a question but it was the boy beside me who answered it. He moved on. The question was about perjury. Perjury was a reserved sin in our diocese. Maybe that

69

was why I got tongue-tied. A while earlier I had been before the court as a witness in a lawsuit between two neighbours over a right of way. One party had erected a gate in the passageway to which the other party objected. I used to help drive the objector's cattle and said in court that the gate was always closed against us, which wasn't exactly true. There were a few, very few times when it was open, but I didn't tell the court that because it would weaken my party's case. I would have been as well off telling the truth because we lost the lawsuit and the gate is still there.

How well now the bishop wanted to ask me about perjury. My heart missed a beat. I hadn't confessed that transgression and I was going to receive the sacrament of confirmation with my soul in a state of sin. A small consolation came to comfort me. I remembered the judge had said that day in court that I was too young to be sworn in. 'Where will you go, my boy,' the judge asked me, 'if you tell a lie?' 'To hell, my lord,' I told him. I was becoming easier in my mind now because I couldn't have committed perjury if I wasn't sworn in. It was just a lie. Bad enough, God knows, but I would make an act of contrition with a firm purpose to sum up enough courage to tell the priest about it the next time I went to confession. I said an act of contrition then and I put my whole heart into it.

The candles were lit on the altar, the choir sang and the priests helped the bishop to finish his vesting. The mitre was given to him, he took it in both hands, looked into it and put it on his head. Then he put his hand round to make sure that the two broad ribbons that fell from the mitre hadn't gone down inside his chasuble. He took the crozier in his left hand, drew himself up rooster-like to his full height and stood as still as eternity for a moment in all his finery; it was an impressive sight. If I ever became a priest I'd want to end up as a bishop.

We went to the altar rails school by school and knelt down. Almost everyone had new clothes. My suit was navy blue and made by Con the tailor. The bishop approached along the line, preceded by a priest holding a vessel with holy oils or chrism into which the bishop dipped the thumb of his right hand. He made the Sign of the Cross on my forehead. Holding his hand over me he pronounced the words of the sacrament and gave me a light slap with his open palm on the cheek. I looked up at him and he eyed me back. I didn't flinch. My mother always told me to look the world in the eye. 'Make no excuses for yourself,' she said. 'You are as good as anyone else.' Words which echoed what the master made us learn by heart from Ó Cadhlaigh's *'Slighe an Eolais'* (The way of knowledge):

Is gael mise agus mise im Ghael,
Ni thuigim gur náir dom é
Ni chasfainn mo chúl le fearaibh an tsaoil;
Is ní fearr d'fhear cach ná mé.

(I am Irish and Irish I am,
Of that I am not ashamed.
I would not turn my back
To the men of the world,
And there is no man
Better than I am!)

Walking back to my place I thought to myself not alone was I as good as the next but after confirmation I was a strong and perfect Christian, provided of course that God accepted the act of contrition in place of my bad confession. God is good, I always heard, and he has a good mother. I prayed to her now as my own mother had told me do and asked her to intercede for me with her divine son, and for all the family.

Now that I was confirmed I knew that my days at school were numbered. I'd leave when I was fourteen and follow the trade of my father and grandfather. Already during the school holidays I was helping my father in the workshop, keeping a car shaft steady while he was mortising it for the cross laths or turning the handle of the grindstone. I tried my hand at planing and sawing or drilling deep holes in wood with the auger or bit and brace. At night on the kitchen table I'd rewrite, so that we'd have a copy, the long list of materials down to the last nail, when my father was engaged to do the carpentry work of a new house. Masons built the house in stonework and my father made the doors and windows, staircase and partitions. He put on the roof and slated it and put down the timber floors. Away from school in the summertime I loved getting on the roof and helping to nail the slate laths to the rafters. Nothing

71

gave me more pleasure than clouting two-inch wire nails into timber. When the last lath was on, I'd walk on the inch-and-a-quarter ridge board, with my hands out like an acrobat on a tightrope from chimney stack to chimney stack. My father would nearly have a heart attack watching me but he wouldn't shout in case I'd fall.

In a short time my father was allowing me to cut the 'bird's mouth' on the heel of a rafter where it fits over the wall plate, or letting me chisel out the chase in the string boards of the staircase to receive the step and the riser. The rough preliminary work I would do like Michelangelo's apprentice and my father would finish it himself. He had the name of being a great man at his trade and it was a joy to watch him working and a pleasure to see him when a job was finished, the staircase for instance, complete with balusters, handrail, newel post and bull-nosed step, and the way he would stand back from it, his head a little to one side, admiring his handiwork. I looked forward to the time when school would be over and I could be with him every day.

The master's father, a stately old man with a King Edward beard, lived in the school residence. Now and again he came to the school and looked us over with a practised eye, picking out the boys with the brains. He had a tub trap highly polished, and with yellow stripes on the shafts and on the spokes of the wheels. This classy contraption was drawn not by a high stepping horse or pony but by a jennet, a stubborn and cantankerous animal who'd kick the stars and often left the marks of his hind hooves on the under carriage of the trap. One morning on our way to school we met the master's father in the trap. As he passed us he lifted the whip crop and said, 'Good morning, boys!' To which we all answered, 'Good morning, Master!' The jennet must have taken exception to this greeting and as the gate of Mick Horgan's field was open the jennet suddenly wheeled across the road, almost knocking us down and dashed into the field. The old man stood up in the trap and, tugging at the reins, tried to bring him to a halt but it was no good. The jennet galloped three rounds of the field, making a strange neighing sound, with his tail stuck above the front board of the trap. Then he ran out the gate again and continued on his journey. We would have cheered that morning at what looked like a one-jennet chariot race but we knew the story would go back to our own master and we'd never hear the end of it.

Sometimes when the master's father came to the school he would say to his son. 'I want two boys to come to the house and clean out the jennet's droppings.' We were afraid of the jennet but still if picked out we would go gladly because it could kill maybe an hour away from lessons. One day I was selected with a boy from Ballaugh. We plodded after the old man over to the house. He showed us the shed where the jennet was stabled and gave us a fork and coarse brush to clean out from him. We thought it strange that he didn't take the jennet out of the shed while we were cleaning it. Maybe he forgot. We opened the door of the shed and went in. The jennet was tied with a rope running from a halter to a ring in the wall beside his manger. When he saw us he bared his teeth and put both his ears lying along his neck, a sure sign that he had evil on his mind. He threw a few kicks in our direction and collected himself up near the manger. We availed of this opportunity to clean and brush the droppings on to the dunghill outside. We put in fresh straw, going as close to him as we dared. As we made for the door he let fly with the hind hooves. Mercy of God that he didn't brain us. We told the old man that the job was done. He came and looked and was satisfied and gave us sixpence each. When we came back to class the master asked us how we had got on and the boy from Ballaugh, hoping that the master might be talkative, as he sometimes was, asked him why jennets were so cross. The master thought it had to do with their not being a definite species. He took off his glasses and began to polish the lens with his handkerchief, a sure sign that he might spend some time on the subject.

The jennet was a crossbreed, he said, and so was the mule. In the case of the jennet the mother was a horse and the father was a donkey, and it was the other way around for the mule. He paused for a moment as if he wasn't too sure of that statement. These hybrids, he explained, did not breed again, which was just as well as there were enough strange looking animals in the world. They were very rough, stubborn, bad tempered creatures, but were great workers and lived longer than either of their parents. The jennet and mule were in great demand during the Boer War for pulling small cannons over rough ground and when they became scarce large donkeys were used for the same purpose. Then with a half-smile as he warmed to his subject he told us that it was announced in the British House of Commons that an army representative was coming to Ireland to buy as many large donkeys as he could find. Our local MP, seeing an opportunity for farmers to make money, asked that the representative come to Kerry. Spanish donkeys were rounded up in readiness for the sale but the army man never turned up. Very disappointed, the MP asked in the Commons why he hadn't come, to be told that he got his full needs of large donkeys in the midlands and Connemara. 'He made a mistake,' the MP said, 'he should have come south for the biggest asses in Ireland are in Kerry!' We all laughed, ending in a hee-haw. The master looked at us for a while and then, getting serious, said, 'Maybe that MP was right!'

THE REAPER COMES

⚜

'Go for the priest!' was the shout we heard from Daniel's high field, the same field where we were saving hay when the British soldiers drove up and down Bohar Vass singing and cheering on the day of the Truce in 1921. Daniel had been working at the hay when he had a seizure. Immediately his son was on his bicycle to the presbytery and someone else went to town for Dr O'Donoghue. Neighbours arrived quickly and one man recited an act of contrition into Daniel's ear as he lay on his back on the ground. His family, the blood drained from their cheeks, were a pitiful sight to see. His wife, her arms around him, cried, 'Don't go! Don't go from us!' As we waited for the priest – and it seemed ages before he came – everything was done to make the sick man comfortable. The neckband of his shirt was loosened and someone brought a bolster from the house to put it under his head. The priest came in long strides across the field. We all moved back as he knelt beside Daniel, feeling for the pulse in his left wrist. With a grim face he took the penitential stole from his pocket, put it about his neck and pronounced the words of absolution. Then he anointed his eyes, lips, ears and we had to take off Daniel's boots and socks so that the last oil could be put on his feet. The young doctor came in over the fence, running from his car. He knew immediately what everyone suspected: that Daniel was dead. The family wept bitterly. His wife, cradling his head on her lap, raised her eyes to heaven and asked God why he had done this to them.

The kitchen door was taken off the hinges and the body placed on it and taken by able-bodied men and placed on his bed. Older women who had done this job before came and washed the corpse. With his own razor he was shaved and, dressed only in his long shirt, he was put lying on the white sheet of the bed. White sheets were draped over the head and foot of the bed. Two blessed candles were lit, one at each side of a crucifix. The clock was stopped and a cloth hung over the only mirror in the room. Later, when supplies for catering at the wake were brought from town, there was a brown friar-like habit which was put on the corpse. Two pennies were put on his eyelids and a prayerbook under his chin. These would be taken away when rigor mortis had set in and the face with the eyes and the mouth shut would look serene. The hands were joined and a rosary beads entwined around the fingers. The white cord was tied around his waist and his grey socks that his wife had knitted for him were put on his feet.

The wake was about to begin. People were already coming in. Women of settled years, near neighbours and relatives of the family by blood or marriage, sat in the wake room with the widow. Men took off their caps coming into the room, knelt by the bedside and said a prayer. Then they sympathised with the widow or any of the family in the room and spoke a few words in praise of the man who was gone. The wife was dry-eyed and composed after hours of weeping, but when a near relative of her own or her husband's came into the room she took them by the hand and cried openly.

Her husband was a great loss, his family not yet reared. The older members had emigrated and were now in America. They wouldn't hear about their father's death until a letter came and then news would spread to his nephews, nieces, cousins and one-time neighbours. They would all come together and there would be another wake three thousand miles away in New York. With the candlelight flickering on the pallid face of the corpse and paler on the faces of the women there was an eerie atmosphere in the wake room. Voices were subdued except when a near relative arrived and cried out on seeing the corpse on the bed. It was heart-warming to see the feeling of love, sympathy and the sense of loss displayed by all who came and the deep respect they showed for the dead.

The kitchen was brighter. There were two oil lamps lighting. Preparations were going ahead for catering for the crowds who would come to the wake, not only tonight but tomorrow night. Neighbouring wives and daughters would see that tea, white shop bread and red jam were provided for all those who came. The provisions brought in the horse cart from town were still being taken into the house. Some families beggared themselves with the amount of money spent on food and drink. Men were tapping a half-tierce of porter and setting it up on a small table in the bottom of the kitchen with a white enamel bucket under the tap. When the last sympathiser had come and everyone was seated, snuff went around in a saucer as the people settled down to wake the corpse. Each person took a pinch of snuff, praying for the soul of the departed. There was much sneezing, which brought choruses of 'God bless us!' or 'God bless you!' In a while's time a man went around with the white enamel bucket full of porter and each man of the older generation got a bowl of the liquid. When they raised the bowl it was not to say, 'Good health!' but 'The light of heaven to his soul!' The women, girls and younger men sat into the table and drank tea and ate bread and jam.

In a corner of the kitchen there were men cutting and crushing tobacco and putting it in clay pipes. Men, again of the older generation and close friends of the man who was gone, were given a pipe, and as they lit the pipes and the smoke curled up, prayers ascended to heaven for their dear friend. The talk among the men and women was about the late owner of this fine house. They spoke about the age he had reached, about his farm and the great warrant he was to work. The men talked about the times they met him at fairs and markets, at wakes and weddings and in the work they did when neighbours came together for threshing oats or cutting turf. They remembered him as a young man at house dances before he married and how when the music struck up he knocked sparks out of the flagged floor. Those feet were now stilled. They looked at the concertina on top of the dresser which his wife played for set dances in this kitchen. That would now be silent. For twelve months his wife and daughters would go to town or church in black mourning, and his sons would wear a black diamond on the left sleeve.

By degrees the talk took on a general tone and as the white bucket went around again the volume of the conversation increased but never so loud that people forgot the sadness which death had brought to their midst that day. In groups men put their heads together the better to hear old men tell stories until before midnight, when it was time to say the rosary. This was started in the wake room and the person who called the mysteries stood in the short passage between the room and the kitchen. After five decades were recited, the Hail, Holy Queen was said and then the litany for the dead began. When God's name was mentioned the response was, 'Have mercy on us!' and when the name of the Virgin or the saints was called the people responded with 'Pray for us!' After the rosary many people went home, but near neighbours and relatives sat and watched and talked and prayed until the grey light came in the window. The next day, relatives who lived far away would come, and that night Daniel would be waked again. On the third morning the funeral would set out for Muckross Abbey.

As the mourners were assembling for the funeral, a tall, stately woman arrived. She was a distant cousin and the first and last person I heard to cry the lament for the dead. At the wicket gate leading to the house she dipped the corner of her apron in her mouth and wet under her eyes to give the appearance of tearstained cheeks. She threw her shawl back on her shoulders and gave a loud cry which sounded like, 'Oh, oh, oh, ochone, oh.' She brought her voice up to a fierce wail, which subsided into a singsong as she walked in the pathway. When she saw the family coming to the door her grief knew no bounds and they all added their voices to hers. Other women joined in as they went through the kitchen to the wake room where the family cried their hearts out. Just as suddenly as it began, there was silence and, as if having shaken off a weight of sorrow, those nearest to the dead man smiled and were contented. I had seen for the last time what had once been the dirge for a dead chieftain, when his genealogy was recited in the old days. It was now only a pale imitation of the ritual it had been then.

The coffin came through the door and was borne on the shoulders of four men of the same surname. Each man wore, as did every male relation, a black crêpe piece on his left coat sleeve. The older men put the length of crêpe around their hats. The crêpe was tied with a black ribbon. A white ribbon was used if the deceased was a young person. The coffin was placed in the horsedrawn hearse. There was a pause then while people got into their transport, and when everyone was ready the hearse moved off, followed by sidecars, then traps and common cars and last in the procession were men on horseback. As we were going through the town, shop doors were shut and in some cases a single shutter put up as a mark of respect. The grave was open when we arrived at Muckross Abbey. Neighbours' sons did the work. Every act connected with the wake and funeral, the catering for the numbers who came to the house, the washing and laying out of the corpse, its placing in the coffin and now the burial, was performed by relatives and friends. All these services were given as a mark of respect for an esteemed neighbour. Death the reaper brought the people together.

The priest read the prayers and sprinkled holy water on the coffin. In the sunlight, drops fell on the breastplate which read, 'Daniel Moynihan, 49 years.' When the coffin was lowered into the grave two men went down and, unscrewing the wing nuts on the lid, placed them in the sign of the cross by the breastplate. This meant something, a nod maybe in the direction of rising on the last day. During the prayers the relatives remained calm. The great cry at the lament that morning seemed to have drained them of their sorrow, but now as the first shovelful of clay fell with a loud noise on the coffin lid they cried out again. Red-eyed and pale-faced, the wife and daughters wept in their black mourning clothes. The lid covered with earth, the noise was reduced to a dull thud and then no noise as the grave was filled and the green sods beaten down with the backs of shovels on the new mound.

The priest led a decade of the rosary and that over, people waited for a while and then drifted away to pray at a family grave before making their way in twos and threes to the graveyard gate. The men and women would go for a drink when they reached the town. Many of the women who didn't like sitting in a pub would crowd into the snug. The man who was gone was the talk of the last three days, and he was talked of again when the men came that night to my father's rambling house, a place where he himself had sat three nights before.

They mentioned all the people who came to the dead man's wake and funeral and they all agreed a king couldn't have got a better send-off.

THE STATIONS

My mother always wanted to have the stations in our house but it was not to be. The station Mass was said in the farmers' houses. The powers-that-be decided that the occupant of an artisan's dwelling would be unable to meet the expense of catering for a big crowd the morning of the stations. The men around my father's fire did not know the origin of the stations unless they were necessary in the penal times when there were no churches in which to say Mass. They did say that the priests in those days travelled long distances and were put up in the station house the night before. There were at least seven obligations the owner had to meet in connection with the priest's stay: a room, a bed and a fire, food, polish for the priest's boots, oats for his horse and an offering. The men heard tell of the days when the priest was hunted and of the time when there was no presbytery in our parish and only a shack for a church. The parish priest and his curate lived in a one-roomed hovel. The curate was an exceedingly holy man. He'd give the shirt off his back to the poor. One day a beggar asked him for help. The curate told him he had no money, that he had given his last ha'penny to a poor man the evening before. The beggar persisted in his plea for help and asked the curate in the name of the Virgin to give him something. 'Look!' says the curate, turning out his trouser pockets. Half a crown fell on to the road. He gave the money to the beggar and nothing would convince the holy man but that the Blessed Virgin had put the money in his pocket.

At mealtime he told the parish priest about it. 'I am sure and certain,' he said, 'I had no money. It was a miracle!'

'Ah, miracle my hat,' the parish priest replied. 'You'd want to watch whose trousers you are putting on in the morning!'

Twice a year, in the springtime and in the autumn, the

station came to our area. There were three small townlands with not many more than a dozen houses in the station district. The station Mass went in rotation and when a man's turn came there was feverish activity in that house to have the place ready for the morning of the big event. The walls were whitewashed inside and out, the roof freshly thatched and the furniture varnished. Varnish put on too late and in a smoky kitchen didn't always dry, and many is the person stuck to the chair he sat on the morning of the stations. Two brothers put their backs to a sticky dresser and when they went to go on their knees before confession, they brought the dresser down on top of them. Such a clatter of broken delf! The parish priest in the room thought it was the end of the world. In the old days we are told, green rushes were cut and spread under the feet of a visiting king, and the muddy approaches to a farmer's door were covered in a similar way under the feet of a priest the morning of the stations.

When the stations came to a neighbour's house my mother would let me and my brother go on before her. I was always there in plenty of time to see the people arrive. The women went straight into the house. Their husbands lingered in the yard in their Sunday suits and polished boots, talking. No pipes – they wouldn't smoke until they had received holy communion. When the parish priest arrived, driven by the parish clerk in a horse and sidecar, the men took off their hats and caps and greeted him. He exchanged a few pleasantries with them and went into the house.

The curate came a little later. He had his own horse and every year a collection was made for the support of the priests' horses. It was called the oats money. After a few words in the kitchen the parish priest went into the parlour where there was a blazing fire, and began to hear confessions. He sat sideways in the chair with his head turned away from the penitent as he heard his sins. The curate heard confessions in the other room, and the parish clerk made the kitchen table into an altar on which to say Mass. The table was raised almost to elbow height by putting two chairs under the cross rails.

The parish clerk had a very large and battered suitcase from which he took the consecrated altar stone and placed it centre-ways and a little to the back of the table. This stone is said to contain a relic. The altar cloth was put over it and let fall down over the sides of the table. The Mass book, two large candlesticks and a chalice were set in their proper places. There were three cards, each with a large ornamented capital letter, from which the priest read during Mass. One was placed at each end and one in the middle with the words of consecration. Over the chalice the clerk put a smaller card and on this was draped a square of cloth of the same material as the priest's vestments. The two sides of the cloth were pulled out at the bottom to give the draped piece the shape of a pyramid without a top, and the letters IHS were at the front.

The parish clerk put a ciborium on the altar and took out a handbell which he put on the floor near him to ring when the chalice and the sacred host were raised at the consecration. I wondered how he fitted everything into that old suitcase. There seemed to be no end to what it revealed, and the last things to come out were the priest's vestments. They were neatly folded and placed at the end of the altar in the order in which they would go on the priest. I followed the parish clerk's work with a keen eye and my hands itched to help him. Most of all the vestments caught my attention and for a moment I wished I were big enough to put them on. I tried to remember the different names of the pieces. When we were studying for confirmation the master had put pictures of the vestments on the board and told us their names several times.

The parish priest came from the parlour, leaving whoever was remaining for confession to go to the curate. In the crowded kitchen and in the small space in front of the altar he vested himself. First the amice, a square piece of white cloth which he wore like a cape; the two strings which hung from the corners he tied around his middle. He stooped and the parish clerk put the folded alb over his head, he put his hands through the sleeves and the long white garment fell to the floor. He was now handed the cincture, a long white rope-like cord which he doubled and tied it around his waist, leaving the tasselled ends fall down his right side. One tassel almost reached the floor and the other swung a bit above it. The priest pulled up the alb at the front and back inside the cincture so that now I could barely see his boots. Next he put the stole around his neck and crossed it over his breast, tucking the two ends inside his waistband to keep it in position. Then he took the maniple, a piece of vestment material like a short stole, doubled and sewn in such a way that it ran over his left sleeve and rested between his wrist and elbow. The last thing to go on was the chasuble, a sleeveless, open-at-the-sides garment. The parish clerk had rolled its two sides up and when the priest showed him his stooped head the clerk put the opening down over it and the chasuble rolled down his front and down his back like two maps rolling down a wall.

The parish priest, taking a card from the altar, went on his knees and recited the acts of faith, hope and charity. Now the Mass proper started, answered by the parish clerk, and the Latin sounded strange in the small space of the crowded kitchen. At the consecration the priest whispered fervently the words which we had never heard in the chapel as he rested his elbows on the table and thrust his body back towards us. Soon he would raise the host and as the bell rang every head bowed down as we beat our breasts. In my way of looking at things I thought we bowed down because human eyes could not stand the blinding splendour of God coming on the altar. When I glanced up the chalice was rising in the priest's hands towards the darkness of the interior of the thatched roof, and many women in a voice above a whisper said, 'My Lord and my God!'

The parish clerk had counted the number of people who were to receive holy communion and that number of breads or small hosts had been put in the ciborium to be consecrated.

After the communion the priest put his back to the altar and the kitchen table, so unstable on the chairs, nearly capsized. The priest quickly put his weight back on his feet and the clerk, reaching out, caught the table and saved us all from a calamity. The priest didn't raise his voice as he did in chapel. He gave the sermon in a conversational tone and it was about the truth. 'Thou shalt not bear false witness against thy neighbour.' He was very serious in his condemnation of the liar in everyday life and in the courtroom. Perjury was a reserved sin in our diocese. The priest in confession could not absolve the penitent; he had to go to the bishop. I thought of the day of my confirmation and about the doubts I had, but I had made a good confession since and I wasn't going to worry any more about it. After the sermon the priest turned his back to us and faced the altar and it wasn't long until he came to the last gospel. I followed it in my child's prayer book, 'In the beginning was the word and the word was with God ...' After the Mass proper there were three Hail Marys and the Hail, Holy Queen.

The priest, getting up from his knees, took off his vestments and gave them to the clerk, who folded them and put them back in the large suitcase. The priest spoke to the men about their work and about the weather. Men considered it an honour to be singled out and spoken to by the priest and a singular honour if he remembered their names. With the table back in its former position, the parish priest sat at the head and the clerk gave him a large account book from which the priest read the names of each householder in the station district. As each name was called out the man or the woman came forward and put the station offering on the table. Seven and six it was. It had gone up since last year. Each three half-crowns as they were put on the table sat there in a little stack, which made one woman remark to the priest, 'You're making hay, Father. Lots of meadowcocks in your field.'

When the dues were collected the parish priest and the curate, who had been talking to the young men in the yard, were invited into the parlour for breakfast. The owner of the house sat with the priests and one or two other men noted for being able to give a good account of themselves. Some parish priests preferred to eat alone, and it was said that one man used to bring his red setter which sat beside him and to which he talked and gave small morsels of food during the meal.

There was much excitement among the women to see that everything was right. These were the most important guests the woman of the house would ever have in her parlour. If the priest's preference was for boiled eggs the timing of the cooking was vital so that the eggs didn't end up too watery or in bullets. A priest who had been in the parish for a long time, his likes were known, but when a new priest took over the duties of the parish many enquiries were made as to what his preferences in food were. There was always toast: slices of shop bread browned on a long fork in front of the fire.

In the dim and distant past a new priest came and it was said that he liked tea for breakfast. That commodity was unknown in our community then. The woman of the house where the stations were coming was a know-all who had never seen tea in her life but sent to the city for a pound packet of it. She made no inquiries about its preparation but on the morning put the whole lot down in a large saucepan and stewed it well. Then she drained off the liquid, put the tea leaves in a dinner plate and said to the priest, 'Is it a shake of salt or pepper you'll have on it, Father?'

My mother and the other women sitting in the kitchen would give their eyes out for a mouthful of tea. It was a long fast since twelve o'clock the night before, and good enough, when the priests' needs were seen to each woman got a cup in her hand. There would be a full breakfast for everyone when the priests were gone. That was the flurry of excitement when the parish priest got up from the table – getting his horse and the curate's horse. After the goodbyes and when they were well out of sight the bottle of whiskey was produced. With a hint of ceremony the owner tilted the bottle upside down ever so slowly and back again so that the goodness was evenly distributed through the contents. There was more than a tint for all the men of the older generation. Some savoured the golden liquid, others gulped it down, and there was a drop too for the women if they fancied it. The breakfast was taken in relays. The women took over the priests' place in the parlour and the older men were given the first sitting in the kitchen. There was tea, bread and butter and boiled eggs and red jam for those with a sweet tooth.

If the owner of the house could rise to it there was a bottle of stout for the men and wine for the ladies. Indeed it was not unknown for a man to have a half-tierce of porter, and our ramblers had the story of a house where the barrel of stout was put too near a blazing fire. While the priests were hearing confessions in the rooms the bung flew out of the barrel and a spout of Murphy's stout shot up the chimney. Strong men were quick to the rescue and lifted the half-tierce out the door, one man holding his palm over the bung. They hid it in the cow-house and nearly wept at the loss of such precious liquid. The kitchen was clean again and everything in its own place when the priest came to say Mass. Even though there was the unmistakable smell of stout he didn't pretend to notice but the theme of his sermon was strong drink.

Friends of the family who couldn't make it to morning Mass called during the day. There was an air of festivity in the townland, a kind of local holiday, and in the house that night there was a station dance. Michael and Brian Kelly brought their concertinas and the room where the consecration bell had rung some hours before now echoed to dancing feet.

AT THE THRESHING

There was always a dance in the houses the night of a threshing. It was a celebration when something was achieved, a kind of thanksgiving like saying thank you to God for visiting the house the morning of the stations. The first threshing machine I saw was in Murphy's haggard, and it was worked by a pair of horses running in a circle and turning a shaft which turned another on which there was a wheel which operated the threshing machine. The next thresher I saw in the same place was worked by a steam engine. It had a funnel like a train engine and when coal was fed into it and it had water in the tank it belched smoke and steam hissed out of various parts of it. There was a huge wheel at the side, which carried a belt attached to the axle of the threshing drum. When in operation it made a loud throbbing noise that could be heard miles away.

The corn ripened around Puck Fair, 11 August, and men with scythes fell in to mow it, cutting the standing stems towards the growing corn. The swathes lay with the ears of grain falling in the same direction. The takers lifted the corn in bundles from the swathe and laid them in rows. Then the binders came and took some stems of corn and twisted them rope fashion and tied each bundle near the base to form a sheaf. My mother was a neat binder. Being a farmer's daughter, she had worked in the fields as a young girl. She would give a day binding to a neighbour and afterwards there would be a present of a sack of potatoes and fresh vegetables for the table. The farmer would let her glean the stray stalks of corn. She brought a huge bundle and shook out the straw for our hens. They enjoyed scratching their way through it and pecking up the grain. The cock was very much to the fore in this operation, and when he found a choice morsel he made a loud clucking noise and with a little side dance called his favourite hen to share it with him. When the hens had pecked the grain we had the straw to use as bedding for the cow and the pony.

A mower in full flight was a pleasure to watch. The rhythmic swing of the scythe and the swish of the blade as it cut through the corn was music to the ear. His feet were spaced about eighteen inches apart and as he never lifted them from the ground his boots left two marks in his wake like the track of a car. The mower worked without coat or waistcoat with his sleeves folded up and his braces hanging down his trouser legs. The good mower was a man who could keep the blade of his scythe sharp. There was a narrow board attached to the scythe which had a coating of carborundum at each side, and after mowing a few swathes the mower placed the tip of the blade on the ground and sharpened the back end of it. He rubbed the board to the two sides of the cutting edge with a quick semi-circular motion making a dit-dit dit-dah sound. Then, holding the blade over his shoulder he sharpened the tip and the sound went dit-dit dit-day.

Towards evening the sheaves of oats were put standing on end and leaning together in the fashion of rifles stacked in a barrack yard. The stooks were placed in neat rows and a few days later, in case of rain, the stooks were capped by putting sheaves around them. Building a load of corn on a horse car to bring it into the haggard was a skilful piece of work. The ends of the sheaves were to the outside and by leaving the wheel guards on the car the square load was built out over the wheels and sloped forward over the horse's back. Two ropes slung over it tied the load down to the car. In the haggard, circles of stones were put down to form the base of the stacks. The stones saved the corn from the damp. The base was covered with rushes or briars and the sheaves of corn built on that. When the circular stack was at a height of about ten feet it looked like a truncated inverted cone widening as it went up. At this stage an eave was formed from which the roof of the stack tapered to a point.

A farmer with a good crop of oats would have four or five stacks in his haggard. Sitting all together they looked like a village of strange houses in some distant land. One stack was thatched with green rushes and sat there for the winter. Sheaves were pulled from it evenly all round so that the stack sank down smaller as time passed. These sheaves were fed to the horses or hand-scutched if straight unbroken straw stems were needed for thatching the farmhouse.

It could be late September before the threshing mill got round to every farm. When the mill was set up in the haggard, neighbouring men came to help feed the sheaves into the drum, and neighbouring girls came to assist at the catering for such a big crowd or to draw the grain to the síogóg (straw granary). People of the district came together when a job needed many hands. The system was called comhairing and the labour was returned by the farmer or his servant boy.

The straw granary to hold the grain was what I loved to see being made. A circular stone base was prepared and covered with old sacking. Then an endless súgán, a straw rope about six inches thick, was twisted and laid in a circle on the base. This circling of the rope was continued, making a circular wall, four feet in diameter at the bottom and widening out like the haystack as it went up. The grain was poured into the middle and when it was packed down it kept the straw rope in place. It reached its required height when there was no more grain to go in. A wide eave, made with sheaves, was added, and a conical roof of straw which was thatched with rushes. The síogóg sitting there as the daylight faded looked like a fairy house with its dark green roof and golden base. It was flanked by a rick of straw and a rick of hay. The day's work over, they stood in the now silent haggard as the moon shone and the sound of music came faintly from the farmhouse, growing louder each time the kitchen door was opened.

It was the night of a threshing I went out in my first set dance. I was still a schoolboy in short pants, but I had been watching the dancers for a long time in the houses and at the Sunday evening dancing deck near Mac's Arch. People said I had dancing in my feet from the way I used to tap out the time to the music. I knew the figures of the polka set; the jig set, I thought, was a little more complicated. I'd never have had the courage to go out only that my father said he'd make up the three other men to stand in the middle of the floor. I stood opposite my father so that he would be my co-dancer in certain figures of the set. As we stood there we talked for a while, as was the custom. Then we asked our partners.

The girls, all eager to shake a leg, had their eyes on the men on the floor There was no formal request. The women responded to a nod or a wink. I thought this method a bit too grown up for me and I walked to the side and said to a young woman who was a good dancer, 'Will you dance, please?' When the music struck up the women came and stood by the men's right hand. My partner guided me and told me what was coming next in each figure of the set. I became so confident after a while that like my father and the other dancers I added a little embellishment to the step. A bit of heel and toe work. The first time I did this a cheer went up in the kitchen and shouts of "Tis kind father for you!'

I danced many a set after and pounded many a stone-flagged kitchen at station dance or on threshing night, but the first time I squared out with my father standing opposite me remains the clearest in my mind. Mick and Brian Kelly had a concertina which they played in turn. It was Mick who played for our set, polka tunes for the first three figures and then 'Pop goes the Weasel' for the slide. In this figure my father and his partner danced towards my partner and me. We met them halfway, did some fancy footwork and retreated. Then forward to meet them again, our right feet hitting the floor in perfect timing. The music gathered speed as we danced to form a square and this went into a swing. The swing, or wheel as it is called, is a tricky thing to get right. The dancer pivots on one foot and wheels his partner around him. Faster and faster we went to keep up with Mick Kelly's music until my head swam as the dancers' faces and the entire kitchen, floor, ceiling and fire went into a mad spin around me. People cheered, egging on the musician. I lost my footing and as the legs were taken from under me, I landed on my backside on the floor, my head still spinning. I must have fainted because I could hear the loud laughter fading as if the wireless were suddenly turned down. My father's face and the faces of the dancers bobbed up and down in my mind's eye, twirling and swirling and turning different colours until they melted into darkness.

Gradually I heard the voices coming back. When I came

to I was sitting on a chair and someone was holding a cup of water to my lips. I took a long drink, shook myself and stood up. 'I am all right,' I said to the many enquiries as to how I felt. My father wanted to take me home. No, I was feeling fine. And I was. When the dancers lined out for the final figure in the set I took my place. Mick Kelly didn't race the music and my partner took care that we didn't overdo the dancing. After the dance there was a cup of tea and I was right as rain. On the way home my father talked about what had happened. He was anxious about me, and we decided not to tell my mother. She would be very troubled if she heard that I fell in a faint in my first set dance. She always held I did not have the sturdiness of other young lads of my age and that anything over-strenuous would knock the wind out of me.

They were all in bed when we went home. 'A nice hour to have him out!' my mother complained to my father. I got into bed beside my brother, worn out from the dancing and helping at the threshing. As I fell asleep the events of the day ran through my mind. Stacks of corn going down and the síogóg and the straw rick going up. The movement from hand to hand as the sheaves of corn found their way to the thresher, the black smoke belching from the engine and boo-ooo-ooo of the machine mingling with the racing music of Mick Kelly's concertina. I don't remember going to sleep and it seemed as if only minutes had elapsed when my mother called me and my brother for school. When I came downstairs I dashed the cold water on my face and dried myself. I put my lunch in my coat pocket and brought my strap of books to the table. As I sat down opposite my father my mother looked at me anxiously.

'He was talking in his sleep,' she said to my father, 'Did anything happen to him?'

My father was taking the top off a boiled egg and putting a dust of salt in it. He said, 'These eggs are hardly done, Hannah.'

By Train to the Seaside

❦

In my last year at school and coming up to the summer holidays the master put forward the idea of a school outing. 'Hands up,' he said, 'all of you who have been to the seaside?' Not a single hand went up. None of us had ever seen the sea. In fact very few of the older generation had seen it, though my mother, before she married, was on an excursion to Youghal. The sea was a mystery as far as we were concerned and we were delighted when the master announced that he would take the upper classes to Rossbeigh the week before we closed for the summer. He thought that the infants and first and second classes were too small to take them on such a long journey. We agreed with him. And as Sullivan from Ballaugh said to me, 'What do they want there for!' We were very excited at the news. 'Calm down,' he told us. 'This outing will cost money.' There would be the train fare and expenses for the day. Not too much. We could bring our lunch the same as if we were coming to school and get a cup of tea there. He told us what the train fare was and he told us to collect this and bring it to school.

I was up early on the appointed morning. I got into my best clothes, my confirmation suit. Boots, stockings and a skullcap completed the outfit. We had seven and sixpence between my brother and myself, and my father slipped us a two-shilling piece which I think my mother didn't know about. She warned us to be wary of the sea and if we went paddling not to go out too far. My father drove us to Killarney railway station in the pony and trap and we picked up a few boys on the road who didn't have a drive. We were away too early for the train and the time was spent running up and down the platform and counting the boys every now and then to see who was missing. As sure as anything, we said, someone would be late. But they were all there when the train came puffing in from Cork. We were lined up and the master shepherded us into whatever vacant carriages he could find when the Killarney passengers got out. There were no corridors. Each compartment had two seats running the entire width of the carriage. Once you were in and the train moved off you had to stay there, but you could change to another compartment when the train stopped at a station.

It was everyone's first time on a train. We soon got the hang of how to work the leather strap to lever the windows up and down, so that as many of us as could fit were looking out both windows when the train got to Ballyhar. The master got out there and ran along the platform to see that we were all right. He warned us to keep the windows up in case we'd fall out. At Farranfore we all got off and changed to another train. Such excitement! We were like sheep set free from a pen. When everyone had settled down I took my place at the window and watched the guard wave his green flag. He blew on his whistle and with a chug, chug, chug, the train was off. He ran a few steps with the train and then hopped on to the end carriage.

We halted at Killorglin and we promised ourselves that when we were bigger and owned bicycles we would cycle here to the famous Puck Fair held each year on 11 August. At the next station the guard alighted and shouted, 'Mollahive!' but no one got out or got in. It was full steam ahead to Glenbeigh. All out and into line but a few of us ran forward to have a look at the engine. The furnace door was open and the stoker shovelled coal into the glowing fire, darkening the glow momentarily. When the stoker shut the door the driver put his hand on a lever and a huge jet of steam shot up. There followed a whistle. We got back into line and watched the train gather speed on its way out of the station to Kells and Cahirciveen.

The master, as pious a man as you could meet, marched us out of the platform and into the chapel to say a prayer. Going up the aisle, Sullivan from Ballaugh suddenly genuflected prior to entering a seat and I, not expecting the genuflection and walking close behind, was thrown out over him. This brought more than a titter from the rest of the class. The master's face clouded at such a display of mirth in a holy place and when we came out we were spoken to very severely. Cafflers, a great word of his, he called us. As we walked down towards the fork in the road where we would turn right for Rossbeigh our hearts sank. A mist started to come down. As we walked along, the fog got thicker and when we arrived on Rossbeigh Strand the master was panic-stricken as our vision was now only a couple of yards. The master was afraid that some of us might stray away and get lost. He collected us in a bunch and warned us to watch him and not to move anywhere unless he was in eye view. We were down in the dumps with depression at having come all the way for a glimpse of the sea and now that we were standing on the strand it was nowhere to be seen.

There was movement in the mist. It seemed to be blown in from the ocean. Sometimes it thinned out and then got so thick you could hardly see the boy next to you. We kept our eyes peeled for the master's black hat, and he kept talking loudly so that if we couldn't see him we knew where he was. Even though a vision of the sea was denied us we were conscious of its presence from the sound of the waves and the smell of the seaside. The master had an idea. We all moved back from where we perceived the sea was and sat on the dry sand and on a heap of stones. He called the roll – everyone was present – and he suggested that we should wait in the hope that the mist would clear, and while we were waiting as it was a long time since breakfast we would eat our lunches. Afterwards he would arrange that we got a cup of tea. As we sat and ate, maybe it was a prayer the master said or maybe it was our visit to the chapel, but the mist got lighter. We took off our shoes and stockings and placed them on the stones and ever so gradually the sea came into view. Only the white surf on top of the waves at first as they chased each other to the shore. When it was clear enough and the master gave the signal, we raced barefoot towards the water's edge. We stopped and watched the waves rush in towards us only to peter out on the sand and flow back into the sea again. The game now was to run after the receding wave and turn quickly so that it didn't catch us as we ran back. We weren't always successful.

The water felt cold at first but after a time we didn't feel it. By pulling up our short pants we paddled in as far as we could and when we got tired of that we raced up the strand and the dry sand stuck to our feet and shins. We found if we sat for a while on the bank of stones the sand dried, little particles of it glistening in the sun, which was now coming out. By rubbing our feet with our hands we got the sand off.

The master said what about a cup of tea. No one found any fault with that. We put on our shoes and stockings and went to an eating house perched over the strand. The lady of the house had a huge teapot as big as a kettle and she filled out a mug of tea for each one of us. There were tables with milk and sugar and chairs where we could sit. The master paid her for the tea and said we could have a second mug if we felt like it. There was a shop at the end of the dining-room. This was a chance for us to spend our money. We bought buns, cakes and fat biscuits, and even though it was only a little over an hour since we had our lunch we sat down to a royal feast. Afterwards we bought *tómhaisíns* (conical paper measures) of sweets, bullseyes and NKM toffees.

When we got back to the strand the master talked to us about the sea. He explained the coming and going of the tide and how the waters were influenced by the pull of the moon. He showed us the nets laid out upon the rocks and how a fish working its way through a hole was caught by the fins and held a prisoner. He told us the names of the fish that were netted along the coast, and as the sky cleared the day got warmer and we saw black shapes rolling in the sea. These were porpoises. We wondered would there be any chance we'd see a whale or a shark, but wherever these animals were that day they kept far away from Rossbeigh. Outside where the waves rolled on to the shore the sea was like a sheet of blue glass stretched away to where it met the sky. We were delighted with the variety of seashells and we collected some to bring home to show the smaller members of the family. I got one huge white shell something in the shape of the house the snail carries on his back but miles bigger. The master said if I put it in my ear I could hear the sound of the sea. I brought it home and showed it to the neighbours. They put it to their ears and swore they could hear the sea quite plainly.

The master suggested that we play games and enjoy the sun. Some of the boys had a football but a party of us opted to play ducks off. This was a favourite game which we played at home or by the roadside on our way from school. We selected a big stone with a flat top from the bank and positioned it on the sand. This was the granny. We marked the throwing point about twenty feet back from it. Each player picked a stone about a pound in weight and this was his duck. One boy, a volunteer, placed his duck on the granny. He was the granny man. The others in turn threw their ducks at it, the aim being to knock it off. When a good shot knocked it from the granny there was a mad scramble by the other players to retrieve their ducks from behind the granny. The granny man replaced his duck as quickly as he could, and having done this if he succeeded in touching a boy before he got back to the mark that boy's duck went on the granny. And so the game was played. Every boy as he threw the stone had to shout 'ducks off!' If he omitted to say it the penalty was that his duck went on the granny. It sounds a very dangerous game with all those stones flying, but it wasn't. All the players had to remain behind the mark while the ducks were being thrown.

In time there was an argument. A player claimed that he wasn't really caught before he got back to the mark. This led to a row and the master had to intervene. 'No more rounders!' he said. That was his name for ducks off. We turned our attention to the sea, and noticed that while we were in the eating house and playing ducks off the waves had receded. The water was away out now and we had to race down to it. There were round jelly-like platters on the sand. The master said if we stood on one of those jellyfish we might get a sting. The very big ones which he called Portuguese men o'war were especially dangerous. We were disappointed we didn't see any fish but we did take stock of the birds. They were very different from the crows, pigeons, blackbirds and thrushes which we saw at home. Most noticeable were the white herring gulls with grey backs. They swirled and screamed overhead and landed on the sea. In a way I envied a creature that could walk on land and fly and swim. To my mind that was a form of complete freedom. There were smaller gull-like birds called terns. We

97

had the master bothered asking him the names of the different species. There were very small birds keeping in flocks with a smart walk like a wagtail when they landed and only a short butt of a tail. These were sandpipers.

All in all it was a great day. The one regret we had was that nobody told us about bathing suits. The master never said a word. Maybe he didn't want our mothers going to the expense of buying togs and our using them only once. We would have dearly loved to strip off and dive into the sea and frolic around in the water like we saw some other children do. We really envied them and the bathers running against the high incoming waves and being covered over for an instant and then washed in towards the shore. We saw men swim out to sea and I was as jealous of them as I was of the seagulls who had the best of three worlds. I was firmly planted in one.

It was time to head back for the village of Glenbeigh. On our way past the eating house we saw a woman in a white apron selling sea grass. We decided to invest in a pennyworth. It was of a purple shade and tasted very bitter and salty but after a time we got used to chewing it. We weren't too keen on swallowing the sea grass so when it was all chewed up we spat it out. The master thought our conduct was disgusting. We went back and bought another few pennyworths of it to bring home. When we reached the village I counted my money and with what we had left my brother and I bought sweets for those at home and a barmbrack type cake for my mother. The train came into the station. When the engine stopped, steam seemed to escape through every bit of it. We climbed in and when the porter banged the door shut and the guard waved his green flag and blew his whistle the train chuffed out and we all began to sing. Sullivan from Ballaugh had two lines of a song which went:

We came to see sights that would dazzle the eye,
But all that we saw was the mountain and sky!

And we chimed in with,

We saw the sea, ah ha, ah ha, we saw the sea!

98

When we changed trains at Farranfore my brother and I broke company and joined with the boys in another compartment to see what the fun was like. Not so good. They were mostly a crowd from Minish and one of them got sick after chewing too much sea grass. We had to pull the leather strap very quick so that he could put his head out the window. With every heave we all went 'Aaaah!' to give him encouragement. His brother took umbrage at this and a row developed. They shouted at us, 'Bealach an chabáiste!' (Ballaugh of the cabbage; market gardening was a sideline by the small farmers there) and we shouted at them, 'Minish hold the bag!' In no time the dukes were up and fists flew. Even the sick man turned from the window and joined in the melée. There would have been skin and hair flying only that the train stopped at Ballyhar. My brother and I got out and joined the Ballaugh crowd in another carriage for what turned out to be an uneventful final run into Killarney.

My father met us with the pony and trap, and when we reached home there was a great welcome for the two heroes. My mother had kept the dinner for us with some roasters (potatoes) sitting on the red embers. We weren't too hungry after all we ate at the seaside, but we didn't refuse a slice of the cake we brought home to my mother. She gave a piece of that to everyone.

When the ramblers came in later the table was cleared and we put out the assortment of seashells we had brought home and two roundy stones of a bluish tinge and shaped like duckeggs. My mother thought it was a pity we didn't hide them until morning and put one of them in an egg cup for my father's breakfast! All the small people got shells and sweets and we showed the men the big shell I brought and just to please us they listened to the sound of the sea. We had enough sea grass to give everyone a piece. The men chewed and twisted their faces at the bitter taste. The man with the famous spit when he had the grass well chewed sent it flying towards the fire where it landed on a red coal. The coal went black and it was a while before it burned red again. We answered all the questions the men asked us about the sea. They remarked among themselves that sea water was very good for pains in the bones.

One old man said he had heard of houses where a person could have a hot sea water bath with plenty of oily seaweed in it. He said that a couple of dippings in a bath like that would loosen the stiffest joints. We told him we hadn't noticed such houses.

Young Jack was interested in the tide. The coming and going of the tide was one of the three things which the great Aristotle couldn't understand. The other two things were the work of the honey bees and a woman's mind. 'Na mná go deo,' my mother said (always the women). The storyteller continued, 'There was a man inside in this parish who had never heard of Aristotle or who had never seen the sea or the coming and going of the tide. The same man, Crowley was his name, suffered greatly from pains in his bones. One night at a wake he heard it said that a dip in the sea would bring great relief. Crowley wanted to know would he have to strip off in public and he was told that he would. A very modest man, he had no notion of doing this so he hit on a plan of going to the seaside and bringing home a quantity to bathe in at home in privacy. He set out for Rossbeigh with the horse and car to bring home a barrel of the brine. When he arrived at the seaside there was a fisherman mending his nets. "Are you in charge of the water?" Crowley said. The fisherman not knowing what to make of the question said that he was. "And how much are you charging for a barrel of it?" Crowley asked. "Seven and six," the fisherman told him, saying in his own mind, "They're biting on land today!" Crowley paid him and as the tide was full in he filled the barrel with saltwater and brought it home. He heated a quantity of it over the fire and when night time came he bathed in the barrel. This went on for a week, with Crowley bathing in the barrel every night. True enough it brought relief from the pains in his bones, but as time went on the jizz was going out of the water and he decided to go back to Rossbeigh for another supply. When he arrived at the pier the same fisherman was there. Crowley paid him the seven and six and then looking he saw that the tide was away out. "You'll have to pull out a lot farther to fill your barrel today," the fisherman pointed out. "So I see," says Crowley, "It must be in great demand; 'tis nearly all gone!"'

As we went upstairs to bed I thought of school tomorrow. No doubt the master would ask us to write a composition about our day at the seaside. If he did I would put into it the story Young Jack told. I lay then in the dark thinking about the day's excursion. When I fell asleep I was in the sea rising and falling with the mighty waves. I was swept away from the shore. Then blessed hour! a huge whale approached me and opened his mouth. I went down into his belly. My shouting as I woke up aroused the house. My mother gave me a drink, saying to my father, 'The excitement of the day was too much for him!'

THE LIGHT OF THE FIRE

The source of light in our house was the paraffin oil lamp. It hung on the wall and was made of tin, with a mirror at the back to reflect the light. The burner had a wick which went down into a container and soaked up the oil. With a twister the wick could be turned up or down. Some lamps had a double burner which gave a far better light. Our lamp had a glass chimney called a globe, though it didn't resemble one except where it bulged out around the burner. Each night my mother trimmed the wick and lit the lamp with a spill from the fire. When she put the flame to the wick it blazed up. Then she turned it down very low until you could hardly see the flame and put the chimney on. This done she turned the wick up very gradually and the flame that had been yellow turned white and filled the kitchen with light. She took a hairpin from her hair and straddled it over the glass at the top of the chimney. This was supposed to attract some of the heat and prevent the chimney from cracking. The only other light came from the fire or the candle in a sconce which lit us to bed.

We loved to sit around the fire before the lamp was lit and watch the glow from the burning turf throw our shadows on the wall. My father had shown us how to cast the silhouette of a rabbit's head and front paws with the fingers of both hands. We often populated the gable and side walls of the kitchen with rabbits and even set them to fight each other. The cat or the small dog, Charlie, loved to sit at the fireside. We used to hold Charlie up and watch his shadow catch a rabbit.

The turf for the fire we cut and saved in Young Jack's bog, but the oil for the lamp we bought in Eugene the Boer's shop. Often I brought it in a can when I was seven or eight. Paraffin has a very strong, unpleasant smell and a gallon of it is very heavy. I had to keep shifting it from hand to hand to relieve the pain in my shoulders. In our house we small people were expected to work from an early age – jobs like minding the cow, feeding the hens and pigs and bringing hay into the cow and pony when they were in their houses for the night. We had to draw all the water for use in the house in buckets and cans: the water for washing from the nearby river and the water for drinking and cooking from a well which was in Sullivans' bohereen a half mile away. The sparkling spring water came out of a spout and the buckets filled quickly. We found that plucking a fan of fern leaf and placing it on top of the bucket kept the water from splashing as we walked. The well was a meeting place for neighbouring women and they sat and talked for a while.

We were nearly always on the go and the seasons brought new work. In mid-summer we helped save the hay when my father bought a field of it at the auction in Danny Mullane's. When things were slack at home we helped in a neighbour's meadow and loved when a gallon of tea and piping hot mixed bread with plenty of fresh butter was brought out from the house in the evenings. Tea always tasted better in the open. When we were working in the bog, a fire was started with sticks and turf, and water from the well put boiling in a can. When it was bubbling the tea was added and then the milk and sugar as the can was taken off the fire. You filled your cup by dipping it in the can and as you sat in the heather drinking tea and eating buttered bread you wouldn't call the king your uncle.

When it came to the time for us to cut a year's firing my father engaged a group, a *meitheal*, of men. They brought their own *sleáns* and turf pikes. We'd set out for Young Jack's bog, where we had rented turbary, early on the appointed day. From the time when I was very young I would plead to be let go with the men that morning. I joined my father in the pony and car, which brought the food for the meals the men would get. The day before the turf-cutting my mother spent baking bread and boiling bacon. Plates of this bacon and rolls of butter with plenty of sharp knifes were put in a covered basket, and the wheels of mixed and white soda cakes in a white cloth bag.

The turf bank was cleared of its top sod the day before by a man with a hay knife, a spade and a length of line. The cleaning measured about two and a half feet. The turf-cutting implement was like a spade with a piece jutting out at right angles on the left hand side called a horn. This *sleán* was very sharp and cut through the soft peat to turn a sod of turf say four inches by four and a foot long. The *sleán*sman stood directly over his work and in one fluid movement he cut down straight through the peat, thrusting out and up as he landed the freshly cut sod on the bank. There a pikeman pitched the sod to another pikeman and he to another who laid the sods in a neat row at right angles to the bank. When it came to a second row the head of each sod lay on the tail of the one before. In time at least three *sleán*smen would be working on the bank, one behind the other, each succeeding one a foot or so lower as if they were on the steps of a stairs. When they got into full swing there was a lovely rhythm to the work, with the sods leaving the *sleán* in quick succession and being pitched by the pikemen to join their brothers on the heather on the bank. Some *sleán*smen sang as they worked or carried on a conversation with the nearest pikeman. The work was hard and on a hot day the sweat poured off the men. Now and again the whole rhythmic machine would come to a halt to draw breath and go on again. My job was to bring a bucket of water from the well and be ready to hand a tin mugful to the thirsty. I remember one *sleán*sman taking the bucket and putting it on his head and drinking from it. The first big break from work came for the midday meal.

On the day of the turf-cutting my mother came to Young Jack's house about twelve o'clock and boiled water. She thought it quicker than building a fire in the bog. Tea was made in a white enamel bucket on which there was a cover. When the men saw her appear in the field below Young Jack's house a cheer went up. A place was selected in the dry heather of the *cois* (a lower level from which the turf had been cut away), and a cloth spread to hold the plates of bacon and butter. The bread was cut and buttered and a slice of bacon put between every two pieces. Milk and sugar were added to the white bucket of tea and the men dipped their cups into it and ate away to their heart's content. There was a rest then as pipes were lit. There were stories and a discussion on whatever were the latest happenings of the world.

My father would not be the first to make a move to return to work. He would leave that to a neighbour who, putting his pipe in the top pocket of his waistcoat would say, 'This won't pay the rent. Back to the grindstone!' In no time the men were in position and the *meitheal* resumed its rhythmic motion. The black sods tumbled from the *sleáns* on to the bank and were pitched by the pikemen into place. The intake of food put the men in good humour and a song was heard drowning the sweeter sound of a disturbed lark which rose in little leaps higher and higher until it became a small speck and its song was lost and we were left with the strains of the ballad 'My Mary of Loughrea'. At four o'clock on the dot my mother would appear again in Young Jack's field with the white bucket. This time there were two large cakes of currant bread. These were sliced and buttered and washed down with cups of hot tea.

The men worked until the bank was cut and a carpet of black sods covered a good half-acre of bogland. The bank was seven sods high and the bottom sod, the blackest and the best, was spread in the *cois*. The carpet of turf remained that way for some weeks and when a thin crust formed on the sods they were lifted and made into foots. Footing turf is the hardest work I know. As youngsters our backs used to ache from the constant stooping. If we didn't keep our heads down and work hard we'd never be done. I used to pick a place ten or fifteen feet in front and vow I wouldn't lift my head until I had reached that spot. Four sods were put standing by leaning them together and two sods were placed on top. Standing so the drying wind went through the sods and the sun lent a hand in the saving process. From the constant handling of the hard-crusted sods the skin at the tops of my fingers wore thin and began to pierce so that I was driven to take the sod by its under or soft side. The butter-soft peat eased the pain in my fingers but as evening came the blood showed through the skin.

A couple of weeks later the turf was stooked. Three or four foots were put together and a number of sods placed on top. By the dint of drying, the fat sods were now growing thin and shrunk to no more than three quarters of their former size.

Towards the end of the summer the turf was drawn out from the inner bog by the donkey and cart to where there was a metal passageway, and made into a large heap. From here, when the chance came, it was carted home. The turf creel was put on the pony car and Fanny the mare, helped by a neighbouring horse or two, brought the winter's fuel supply to the house. There the turf sods were built into a neat rick, narrowing as it went up and about nine feet high. When the men rambled in as autumn came, they noticed the new turf burning in the hearth. They took up a sod and passed it around and commented on its quality. It was a good year when turf, hay and oats were got into the haggard. God be praised! The talk would turn from the light of the fire to the light of the lamp, and one night Young Jack spoke of God's two lamps in the sky. And he told the men about Copernicus, who was the first man to discover that we went around the sun instead of the sun going around us, which was the belief up to then. Always in top gear when having a go at the Church, Young Jack told us that Galileo, who promoted Copernicus' discovery, was put on trial by the Pope for going against the belief of Ptolemy, which was that the earth was stationary and flat. Galileo was sentenced but because of his age he was confined to his house for the rest of his life. And there are men who still believe the earth is flat, Young Jack maintained, and he told us of a man of the Humphreys who came back from New York. Humphrey, entertaining his neighbours at his father's fireside, filled them with stories of the wonders of America. He claimed he went so far west in the States that he came to the end of the world where there was a cliff, and looking over it he saw all the suns, moons, and stars that pass overhead thrown there in one great heap. 'Only that I had no room in my trunk,' he said, 'I would have brought some of them home to hang up for the Christmas decorations!'

CHRISTMAS

[⌒]

With the drawing home of the turf the days began to shorten as the sun sank lower in the heavens. The big round cock of hay with a green cap of rushes kept the rick of turf company in the haggard, and a small pile of sheaf oats was stored in the house where the pigs lived during the summer. The hay and oats meant that the cow and the pony were provided for during the winter months. There was turf to keep us warm and with potatoes in the pit, York cabbage in the patch, hanks of onions seasoning over the beam in the workshop and flitches of bacon hanging from the kitchen joists, we humans were sure of our share when the winds blew loud and the rain and the sleet slashed against the window pane. The lamp was lit a little earlier now and the men came earlier to the nightly parliament that was my father's house.

The news of the day over, the men debated the affairs of the nation. Having our own government and the recent Civil War made politics more immediate. In the old days matters of Irish concern had been lost in the largely British business of the House of Commons. In the springtime, great interest was taken in the budget and when there was a sharp rise in the price of tea, beer, spirits and tobacco, our native rulers came in for some castigation. One man, looking into the empty bowl of his pipe, complained, 'John Bull wouldn't have done it to us!' To which a joker added, 'He was a better bull than the bull we have now!'

When it came to the time for us small people to go to bed the men might claim our attention for a little while. It made us feel important when they spoke to us and knew us by our names. They asked us about school. Could we spell lynchpin and consanguinity? I don't know how many times William Murphy told us about the two schoolboys who killed a bull.

They lived near Mangerton and one evening on the way home from school they went up the side of the mountain. They continued climbing until they could see their own house, and the cattle in the fields seemed small below them. They came to a place where there was a sizeable round stone balanced on a flag. The stone must be nearly a hundredweight. They kept rocking it on its bed until it rolled off the flag and sped down the mountain. It gathered speed and went by leaps and bounds. Sometimes it jumped as high as a house until it crashed into a farmer's field and a prize bull looking up from his grazing got the full force of the careering stone between the eyes and he fell down as dead as a doornail.

They avoided the farmer's land on the way home. There they told their father what had happened. He was greatly troubled because the owner of the bull was the crossest man in the barony. The father advised the children, if the farmer was before them on the road to school in the morning, to deny all knowledge of the incident. 'Say you saw no bull,' their father told them. Sure enough the farmer was outside his house in the morning in a tearing temper. He asked them were they up the hill yesterday. The big boy said nothing and the farmer, thrusting his threatening face into that of the small boy who was only about six, said, 'Were ye up the hill yesterday?'

'We were,' the small boy said, 'but we killed no bull though!'

We were terrified of bulls and on the way to school we knew the farmers who kept one and we stayed far away from their land. The darkness frightened us too and my brother and I would go out together for company when we had to bring in turf from the rick in the dark moon. We were afraid of the boodyman (bogey man). We were threatened with him when we were smaller. If we weren't good the boodyman would come with his bag and take us away. The *púca* we also dreaded. He was supposed to be out at night and according to the men he was a mischievous creature. They described him as a cross between a pony and a hornless goat. He had a flowing beard and big blazing eyes, and with a jerk of his head he could hoist you on his back and gallop off with you through the night. When he came to a black lake he would stop suddenly and send you flying out over his head into the water.

The men used to say with a half-smile and in language we weren't supposed to understand that a man unfaithful to his wife could meet the *púca* coming home in the small hours after visiting the lady of his dreams. The *púca* would lever him up on his back and galloping through furze and briars would never draw rein till he landed in the man's yard. He would then stop short and the nocturnal Romeo would go sailing over his head into a dark pool of *múnlach*, a dirty pond of cattle urine and liquid manure. By the time he had dusted himself down all amorous notions would be banished from his mind! The mischievous creature gave a strange laugh when he had done his impish deed. It was a sound something between the neigh of a horse and the bleat of a goat.

I was often roused in the night in the month of November by a loud bellow. I thought it was the *púca*. No, my father told me, it was a wild stag from Muckross Estate deer park. He had been defeated in his fight for the supremacy of the herd, and would roam the countryside looking for another herd where he could fight again and maybe be king.

Jack o' the Lantern was another being that used to be seen at night. He was a wandering soul and when he was in this world it was said that he committed some heinous crime like killing his father. When he died St Peter wouldn't let him into heaven. He went down to hell and the devil wouldn't let him in there either. Jack pushed his face inside the door and the flames were so great and the heat so intense that his nose caught fire. The devil slammed the door shut and Jack o' the Lantern is going around at night ever since, his nose glowing in the dark. He is seen in marshy places dipping his face in the water to cool his burning nose.

We wouldn't put our heads outside the door on Hallowe'en. All kinds of spirits were said to be abroad that night. We passed the hours playing games we heard our elders talk about. With a length of string we suspended an apple from the joists. Then the participants had their hands tied behind their backs and tried to take a bite of the apple. A useless exercise until two of us came at each side and by pressing our mouths succeeded in getting bites out of the apple. A variation of this childish innocence was to try to take a bite of an apple floating in a dish of water. When the water spilled all over the kitchen a halt was put to this activity.

Especially for Hallowe'en night my mother bought a barm-brack. Three objects were hidden in the cake: a pea, a stick and a ring. Whoever got the pea would be forever poor. The finder of the stick would be master over all and the one who got the ring would be next to marry. If you put the ring under your pillow you would dream of what your wife would look like.

Now that November was on the wane Christmas was on its way. Throughout the year we dreamed of Christmas. It couldn't come soon enough, and when it came it couldn't stay long enough. We small people worked hard on Christmas Eve helping my father set the tall white candles in crocks of sand, one for every window in the house. Holly sprigs from the huge holly tree which grew at the corner of our house were spiked into the sand around each candle. These sprigs were decorated with flowers which my mother made from coloured crêpe paper. We decked out the kitchen with holly, laurel and ivy, placing it around the window, over the door and on top of the clevvy and the dresser. Two mottoes had been kept from the year before, and were put by the fireplace. One read 'Happy Christmas' and the other 'A Bright New Year'.

When darkness fell on Christmas Eve the youngest child in the house lit the first candle, my father's large hand making the sign of the cross on his small head and shoulders. The other candles were lit from this and we raced from room to room revelling in the new blaze of light, and out into the yard to see what the effect was like from the outside. We watched the bunches of lights come on in the houses of the townland. They were like clusters of stars as they appeared down the valley and up the rising ground to Rossacrue. Our principal meal was always in the middle of the day. One o'clock was dinnertime, but on Christmas Eve, big Christmas as we called it, the main meal was after the candles were lit. First we all knelt down to say the rosary. Kneeling at the head of the table my mother gave out the prayer in the voice of a high priestess. After the creed she said the first decade. Tonight it was the glorious mysteries. My father said the second decade, I the third and my brothers completed the five decades. Even though my mother's thoughts were soaring on a high plane of piety she didn't forget now and then to look towards the fire to see how the dinner was cooking. Most rosaries ended with, 'Hail, Holy Queen, mother of mercy, hail, our life, our sweetness and our hope,' but ours didn't. When we touched our breasts, calling on the Sacred Heart to have mercy on us, my mother launched into the trimmings:

> Come Holy Ghost send down those beams
> Which sweetly flow in silent streams.

She prayed for the lonely traveller, for the sailor tossed by the tempest, for our emigrants, for the poor souls, for the sinner who was at that very moment standing before the judgement seat of God and last of all for all of her family:

> God bless and save us all,
> St Patrick, Bridget and Colmcille guard each wall,
> May the Queen of Heaven and the angels bright
> Keep us and our home from all harm this night!

Our knees ached as we got up from the floor, and it took my father a long time to get the prayer arch out of his back. We all helped to lay the table. The good tablecloth for Christmas Eve. We were ravenous, but as the eve of a feast was a day of fast and abstinence we, like all our neighbours, had salted ling, a type of cured fish. We saw it opened out flat and nailed to shop doors when we were in town doing Christmas shopping. It was over an inch thick and hanging on the door with the tail at the top, it seemed to be three and a half feet long and two feet wide. The shopkeeper cut squares off it and weighed them. These were put steeping in boiling water the night before to get rid of the salt. When the ling was properly cooked it tasted fine, especially when my mother added to it her own special concoction of white onion sauce. We had whatever vegetables were in season, big laughing potatoes and home-made butter in which you got the barest taste of salt. It was a simple meal but we ate until we could eat no more. We leaned against the backs of our chairs and sighed, 'We're bursting!' 'A nice grace after meals!' my mother said as she started, 'We thank Thee, O Lord, for these Thy gifts …' As my father finished the signing of the cross after the prayer he remarked half to himself, 'This house is turning into a monastery!'

After the dinner we helped my mother prepare some food in the cow's feeding tub and my father gave an extra sheaf of oats to the pony. The cow dined alone as her calf had been sold at the November fair at Martyr's Hill. Then we all sat around the fire. The Christmas log, *bloc na Nollag*, as the old people called it, with sods of turf built around it, was catching fire. The green moss still attached to the bark was turning brown and little jets of steam shot out which made the cat sit up. In a while's time when the heat got to the log it aimed sparks at us, and the cat, rising and humping her back, spat in the direction of the log and moved under a chair. The dog ignored the fireworks.

It was time now for my mother to open the Christmas box she got in Reidy's shop where we dealt in town. There was a bottle of wine for herself. That was put away to share with the women who called on small Christmas night, the women's Christmas (6 January). There was lemonade for us and biscuits, and last to come out was a Christmas cake. We had slices of this and cups of lemonade. My father would never look at the Christmas cake. His eye was on the big brown jar full of porter and resting on top of the bin. He wouldn't drink unless he had company. Knowing this, my mother sent me for our next door neighbour to come and sit with us. Our candles lit my way for one half and the neighbour's lit my way for the second half of the journey. Pat Murrell came with a 'Happy Christmas everyone!' and after the exchange of small pleasantries my father took the cork off the brown earthenware jar and poured out two glasses of porter, black as night when it settled, with two creamy collars on top. He handed one to Pat, and he by the way taken by surprise said, 'What's this?' 'Go on take it,' my father urged. ''Tis Christmas night and more luck to us!' Pat's face brightened and, lifting his glass, he wished us health and happiness and prayed that we all might be alive again the same time next year.

It was bedtime for us and when my mother went down to

the kitchen I came out of the bed and sat on the return steps of the stairs to hear the conversation between Pat and my father. When he got his second glass Pat said, 'I hope we don't go too far with this, like the militiaman in the town of Tralee. He was a raw recruit,' he continued, 'and on pay night he got so drunk that on the way home he passed the barracks and walked out into the country. He sat on a mossy bank and thinking it was his bed he took off all his clothes. He folded his uniform and put it as he thought under the bed. Where did he put it but into a gullet that was there. He lay down and tried to sleep. The night began to freeze and after a while he woke up still tipsy but if the cat went a pound he couldn't find his clothes. He walked off and I can tell you he was feeling the cold now. He kept going until he saw a light in a house in a bit from the road. He threw a stone at the door and it was opened by a young woman. She invited him in.

'"I can't go in," he told her, "I am as naked as when I came into the world!"

'"Well," says she, "There's an old suit of clothes here that won't be wanted any more. My husband is after dying on me!"

'She prayed for the dead and the soldier did so too. Then she threw him out the suit of clothes and he got into it. When he went into the house he saw her husband's corpse laid out on the settle bed. The young woman gave him a glass in his hand. A nice drop it was too and it put the life back into him. As he sat by the warm fire he could hear the young woman talking and laughing with a man in the room.'

'Tch, tch, tch,' my mother said, and began to busy herself around the house.

'Sitting there by the fire,' Pat went on, 'and with the light from a candle, the militiaman was taking stock of his surroundings. Whatever look he gave at the corpse's face he thought he noticed the left eyelid fluttering a bit.'

'The Lord save us!' I could hear mother saying.

'On close examination,' the storyteller said, 'he saw the beads moving that were entwined around the corpse's fingers. All of a sudden the corpse turned his face and beckoned the soldier to come over to him.

'"Bend down your head," he whispered, "until I tell you. I

am an old man married to a young woman and letting on to be dead was the only way of finding out if she was unfaithful to me. I have proof now. Do you see that three-pronged pike at the butt of the kitchen? Bring me up that and put it here beside me in the bed!"

"'Go up now," the old man said, keeping his voice low, "and turn down Jack the Cuckoo and my wife out of the room."

'The soldier went to the door of the room and called them and when they came down the "corpse" was dead again.

"'What's wrong?" the young woman said.

"'You know well what's wrong!" says the old man, jumping out of the bed. Jack the Cuckoo gave a gasp and made for the door but the old man put the imprint of three prongs in his backside as he went out. The young woman was going to close the door when her husband said, "Take your shawl and go with him; it will keep the two of ye warm in a gripe!"

'She took the shawl from the peg and went out and as she closed the door after her the old man said to the soldier, "An unfaithful woman is only an encumbrance to a man. You can keep the clothes. I have a good Sunday suit I can wear."

'The soldier had a warm bed for the night and at dawn he set out for the barracks in Tralee. When he went in the militia were drilling in the square and when they saw the raw recruit in a suit miles too big for him they roared out laughing. He was hauled before the captain to explain himself, and he told the story the same as I have told it to you. A major on horseback went out the road to where the soldier described and found the Queen's uniform in a gullet. I forget now what punishment he got. Maybe a week confined to barracks. That's my story. If it didn't happen I can't help it. It wasn't me who thought it up in the first place.'

The story called for another glass and then my father went to the storyteller's house to sample what he had in for Christmas. My mother warned my father as he went out the door not to come back with the signs of drink on him. 'Everyone is for the altar in the morning,' she reminded him. I stole into bed, thinking of the naked soldier going along the road in the dark and the old man lying dead with one eye blinking. It was dark in the room now. All the candles had been quenched except the one in the kitchen window, which would be left lighting all night and the fire kept in. That was the custom as Sigerson Clifford remembered it:

> Don't blow the tall white candle out,
> But leave it burning bright,
> To show that they are welcome here
> This holy Christmas night.
> Leave the door upon the latch,
> And set the fire to keep,
> And pray that they will stay with us
> When all the world's asleep.

There was a picture of Mary and Joseph in the kitchen. In the clothes they were wearing I couldn't imagine them walking down Bohar Vass in the dark. My mother believed in their presence about us tonight and every night. My father didn't. I once heard him say, 'If that holy pair passed our house on Christmas night, they'd have strayed a tidy step from the road to Bethlehem!'

It was still dark when my mother called us in the morning to go to early Mass. My father was dressed and ready for the road when we came down to the kitchen. We had put our stockings hanging on the crane by the fire the night before. There was a small mouth-organ in mine. In other stockings we found a Jew's harp, a small doll, an orange and a new penny. Father Christmas didn't break his heart but we were satisfied with what we got. Our own father had the pony tackled and under the trap. He was fixing a short piece of candle in the lantern to light us on our way. We all piled in, my mother holding the smallest one in her lap. It was pitch dark and we noticed the single candle lighting in the kitchen window of the houses as we drove along. The road was dry with a slight touch of frost and the clippity-clop of the mare's hooves sounded loud and echoing in the morning air. As we neared the village there was a stream of traffic, the dismal gleam from the candle lamps throwing small pools of light on the road. Some people were in sidecars, some in common cars and a few on the lowly ass and cart. The pony was tied to a bush opposite small Bessie's house. We all climbed out and were warned to stick together and not get lost in the dark. And it was dark, people bumping into each other and then a chorus of greetings as men and women recognised each other. 'Happy Christmas, Con!' 'Happy Christmas, Julia!'

The only light in the chapel was the light from the altar candles and from the shrines of the Blessed Virgin and the Sacred Heart. We couldn't see the rafters of the church and could only barely make out the figures in the big picture of the Assumption into Heaven on the wall behind the altar. The priest and the altar boys looked like shadows when they came from the sacristy. It didn't matter that it was dark because very few read from prayer books; they told their beads. The sermon was very short. The priest wished us a very happy Christmas and said a few words about the nativity and the coming of Christ. Nearly everyone received when it came to holy communion. My father was unaccustomed to the trip from the bottom of the chapel to the altar, but he always went at Christmas and at Eastertime. He and the other men seemed awkward and ill at ease approaching the light at the rails and were happy when they were back in their old place again, kneeling on one knee and telling their beads.

The dawn was breaking as we emerged from Mass. The men stood outside the gate facing the chapel in lines of three or four deep and took out their pipes. The women moved towards their carts and sidecars or collected in bunches talking and exchanging Christmas greetings. The day brightened and the lone vigil candle was still lighting in Pakie Richie's window.

The hunger picked us as we drove home. Except for the few small children we were all receiving and had been fasting since the night before. The kitchen fire was still in and when we added a few sods of turf and sticks it was soon blazing again. Back rashers cut from a flitch of bacon hanging from the joist had been steeping to wash some of the salt away. They were put in the pan with eggs and a circle of black pudding. Slices of shop bread, it being Christmas time, were toasted at the fire and buttered. 'Eat enough now,' my mother advised. 'It will be late before I'll have the dinner ready.'

Darkness had come and all the candles were lighting again before it was on the table, and by that time the postman had called. He was always late on Christmas Day. Jer, the postman, was in high good humour from sampling a little of the season's cheer in the many houses along the way. In the front carrier of his bicycle he had a big parcel for us from our aunts in Dittmar's Boulevard, Astoria, New York. It had small items of wearing apparel, a tie for my father, a colourful apron for my mother, a cotton dress for my sister and knee breeches and jacket with a belt at the back for my brother and me. There was a doll and a small metal brightly painted carriage drawn by two horses with little wheels on their hooves so that we could run the carriage on the table or on the floor. There was a letter, too, with a robin redbreast Christmas card, and when the card was opened out popped three ten dollar bills, which was a small fortune to us. The letter made enquiries about our health and it was signed Mary, Margaret and Elizabeth.

On St Stephen's day we were never allowed out in the wren. Numbers of children, three or maybe four in each party, came to our house and standing inside the door sang:

The wran, the wran, the king of all birds,
St Stephen's day he was caught in the furze.
Up with the kettle and down with the pan,
And give us a penny to bury the wran!

They would get a penny or maybe more if we had it. As well as singing, two of them would lilt a tune and the third would dance a step. They always carried a holly sprig with a coloured paper flower or a dead wren in the middle. The candles were lit in all the windows on the night of St Stephen's day, also on any Sunday nights that fell within Christmas and on New Year's Eve and New Year's Day. New Year's night was the night of plenty. Everyone ate enough on that night. The men used to talk of a custom of hitting a cake of bread against the open door and chanting:

I banish all hunger to the land of the Turks
For a year and a day and every day
From here to eternity!

The feast of the Epiphany was the last night on which the candles were lit. It was believed that water was turned into wine on that night. My father always put a white enamel bucket of water standing outside the door, but the miracle never happened. Small Christmas, the Epiphany was called, and after the supper neighbouring women visited my mother. A portion of Christmas cake was kept for this occasion, and the wine which came in the Christmas box. After a while they would adjourn to another house and it would be late when my mother came home. Next morning the holly and ivy decorations were taken down, the mottoes were put away for another year and what was left of the long candles stored to light us to bed in the long nights ahead. Candle grease droppings clung to the candles and to the sides of the crocks which held them. We collected the grease and when we worked it between our palms it became soft and pliable. Sitting by the fire we made it into different shapes, little animals and small houses. When we got tired of this, by putting a piece of cord in the middle, we fashioned the lumps of grease into small candles. These we lit in the windows and the tiny light they made revived for us the delight we felt when the tall white candles were first lit twelve days before.

Christmas was gone!

The Apprentice

I left school at fourteen and began my apprenticeship as a carpenter to my father. I was no stranger to the bench. I had been helping him during school holidays for the past few years. Jack Brosnahan was getting out of his time as an apprentice when I started and I was given his place at the bench. At first my time was spent tending my father, holding the board he was sawing or keeping the car shaft in place as it was forced on the body laths, and painting the spoke tenons before they were driven into the wheel stock.

My instinct was to watch how the tradesman did the job and to store up the knowledge against the time when I would be experienced enough to do it myself. There was advice from my father when I came to use the handsaw and the jack plane. I soon learned that to rush the situation gave poor results. The implement had to be given its time to work. There was a rhythm in the movement and sound of the saw or plane when used properly. The correct actions of a craftsman sawing, planing or mortising with the chisel were as fluid as those of an expert hurler on the playing field. In my first year I did much of the easy preliminary work, like removing the proud wood from a wheel spoke with a drawing knife in the fashion of a sculptor's apprentice chiselling away the surplus stone and leaving it to the artist to finish the work.

Now that I was engaged in a man's job it was time for me to get into long trousers. My mother got the suit length in Hilliard's drapery, and I took it to Con the tailor and he measured me for the new suit. A week later I went for a fitting. He put on the sleeveless jacket and with a wedge of white chalk marked where it should be taken in or let out and the positions of the buttons and the pockets. I tried on the basted trousers and felt a little surge of pride as I saw them extended to my feet, covering my knees for the first time since I was born. A week later I went to collect the new suit with the money, as they say, in the heel of my fist to pay Con. The next day was Sunday and I wore the suit going to Mass, and the new cloth cap which I got to go with it. Everyone I knew took notice of me with words of greeting like, 'Well wear!' or 'You're a man now!' Well, I wasn't a man yet. My face was as smooth as the palm of my hand. Next I got a navy blue overalls the same as my father's. They didn't have my size in the shop but my mother cut one down that was many sizes too big for me. In the right trousers leg there was a long slender pocket into which I slid my two-foot rule. At the front there were three pockets for holding nails and the sturdy carpenter's pencil.

Sometimes our work took us away from the bench. This was when my father had the contract of doing the timber work for a new house. There were incentives now to improve rural housing in the form of grants and loans from the new government. If the work was nearby we crossed the fields in the early morning carrying our tools. I ran the leg of the auger through the handle of the handsaw and put it over my shoulder, and carried a bag in the other hand. My father slung a sack on his back with the jack plane, hammers, mallet, chisels and the sharpening stone.

At the farmer's house our first job was to make a temporary bench in the barn or hayshed. Door and window frames had to be ready for the masons to stand in position. Four stonemasons worked together, two outside the wall and two inside as they built against each other. The farmer and his sons tended the masons, mixing lime and mortar and drawing it and building stones to the workplace. The stones were normally found in the farmer's land. Fires were lit on big boulders – you'd see them burning in the night time. The intense heat split the rock right through in several places. By inserting a crowbar in the cracks the men prised the pieces away and broke them into portable sizes with a sledge. When you saw the irregular, jagged shapes thrown at the site you'd wonder how the stonemasons ever built a wall from such unpromising material. The tradesman, casting his eye over the heap, would pick a stone. He knew where the grain lay and by hitting a blow with the sledge on the right place he would split the stone open, revealing two fair faces. Then it was a matter of squaring a bed on the stone and levelling the top and he had two fine building stones. The stone sat on its bed on a layer of mortar with the face plumb at the front and touching the builder's line. The mason took great care when dressing the stone that the top horizontal side never sloped in. This would draw the rain. No tradesman worth his salt built a damp house and even before the joints were pointed with mortar, his work, as he might say to himself, was as dry as paper.

The cornerstone had two faces as near to right angles as didn't matter. They were faced, bedded, placed in position and tested with the plumb-board – as I heard one verbose mason remark, to ascertain their perpendicularity! A line marking the inside and the outside of the wall ran from one gable to the other. The masons built to the lines and from time to time put in a through bond, a stone extending right across the wall which bound the structure together.

About eleven o'clock the men fell out for a smoke. My father and I sat with them, pipes were cleaned out with penknives and the dottle put in the cover. If a pipe didn't pull, a blade of strong grass was run through the stem to free it. Wedges of tobacco were cut from the half-quarter of plug and broken with the thumb and first finger in the left palm. When it was ground to the satisfaction of the smoker he chased stray pieces from between his fingers into the middle of his palm. Then cupping the bowl of the pipe towards the little heap he coaxed the tobacco into the bowl with the first finger of his right hand and pressed it down, but not too hard. Last of all he put the dottle and the ashes in the cover on top, levelled it with his thumb and now he was ready to put a match to it. He drew in the white blue smoke and puffed it out and when he was sure the pipe was properly alight he put on the cover and sat back to enjoy the smoke.

Brian the men called me, thinking that I was called after my grandfather, who was well known to the older men. On the job a young apprentice is at the beck and call of the tradesmen. When they were thirsty I was sent to the farmer's old house for a canteen of spring water. There was a custom among the men of taking advantage of the apprentice on his first day by sending him on ridiculous errands such as to bring the round square and the glass hammer. My father had me primed in this regard and when I was asked to bring the glass hammer I enquired of the mason if the American screwdriver would do? The Americans were reputed to be so anxious to get the work done quickly that they drove screws home with a hammer. An apprentice who was asked to bring a round square went to the public house and got six bottles of stout on tick in the mason's name. Placing the drink in front of the mason he said, 'There's the round, you can square it yourself.'

The men rested for as long as it took to smoke a pipeful. They talked about the trade and about the men with whom they worked down the years. Some of them had been born into the trade and the signs of lime mortar had been on the boots of the menfolk in their families for generations. They talked of the masons being a thirsty tribe. 'Put a pint in a mason's hand,' one man said, 'and with the first swig he'll drive it below the tops of the church windows!' They blamed St Patrick for this state of affairs. It seems the saint came across a group of masons building a house on a Sunday morning and asked them why they weren't coming to Mass. They were Christians now and should observe the Sabbath. Their shoes were bad, they told him, and covered in mortar and not fit to be seen in church. St Patrick gave them money to buy new shoes, which they could do on Sunday morning for the shopkeepers were the last to be converted. 'I'll delay the bell,' he said, 'so that ye'll be in time for Mass.' When St Patrick turned on the altar to give the sermon he looked round the congregation but there was no trace of the masons. Later, coming up the street, the saint heard the sound of singing coming from a certain establishment. Going over, he looked into the public house, and there were the masons inside paralytic on the price of the shoes. 'I'll say nothing,' St Patrick said, lifting his eyes to heaven, 'I'll leave them to God!' 'And that's why,' one man said as he eyed his own footwear, 'you'll never see a good shoe on a mason. And another thing: there never was a man of them yet but wouldn't drink Lough Erne dry!' Two of the men working on that house would go on what was termed 'a tear' on Saturday night and wouldn't be seen again until Tuesday morning.

Back at the bench in the hayshed I helped my father. When we had the front and back door frames made, complete with fanlights, we turned our hands to making window frames. In that style of house, and it was the same style that was being built everywhere, there were five windows at the front and five at the back. Window sashes had to be made to fit the frames and a panel door for the front. The back had a plain boarded and ledged door. The old farmhouse was long and low and thatched and sat snugly in a hollow about half a field away. It had two rooms and a loft reached by a ladder from an enormous kitchen. When I got older and developed an eye for the fitness of things, I realised how much better the old house looked hugged by the hillside than the new one bleak and alone on the higher ground. I realised too that the farmer didn't want to go to the trouble of rethatching the old house every couple of years and good thatchers were getting scarcer as the years went by. The farmer and his wife wanted to get away from the yard where the cowhouse, piggery and stable were clapped up to their front door. The manure heap was under their noses. They wanted more space and a view from the front door. A parlour, too, was in the fashion and an upstairs, and all that glass of ten windows was a great attraction. I often thought that if the government grant and loan were given to add a new room to the existing house, to alter the entrances to the out offices so that the animals and the manure were kept away from the front door, and train new thatchers, how much better the countryside would look.

The turkeys, some say, put an end to the thatched house. As geese were falling out of favour for the Christmas dinner large flocks of turkeys were being kept by the farmer's wife. They were well fed to put up the poundage on the Christmas scales. When the turkeys got the full power of their wings to rise in the world was their sole ambition. The roof of the house was as high as they could go, where they scratched and scraped to their hearts' content, damaging the thatch and letting the drop down into the farmer. Men who couldn't afford new houses covered the thatch with corrugated iron. My father was an expert at this operation. Many is the time I

123

helped him place the rafters over the existing thatch, bind them with laths to the old roof, nail on the purlins and stretch the sheets of zinc on them. When finished, the house didn't look as well as when it had its amber coat of new thatch, but because of the situation and the way it blended with its surroundings it looked better than the new one. Leaving on the old thatch ensured that the house was warm and snug and the rain couldn't be heard pelting on the corrugated iron. In a few years' time when the zinc was painted tile-red, the house sat in harmony with the outbuildings and the hayshed.

In the hayshed where my father and I worked on our first day, the sun was now high in the heavens and our tummy clocks told us that it must be near dinnertime. The woman of the house came to the door and cohooed and beckoned in our direction. The dinner was ready. I ran to tell the masons and we all trooped into the huge kitchen of the house.

The deal table was in the centre of the floor, and the four masons, my father and I and the farmer and his son sat around it. Like the last supper it was an all male affair. There was a bageen cloth on the table. This was a couple of flour bags opened out, sewn together and washed and ironed, but the brand of the flour was still plain to be seen. 'Pride of Erin. 120 lbs.' The keeling over of a pot of potatoes soon covered the brand. The stray Champions which rolled off the table we caught in our laps and added them to the mound of laughing goodness from which steam ascended to the black roof. The farmer's wife and good looking daughter saw to our needs. Theirs was a friendly welcome and a friendly word for each one. Plates of home-cured bacon almost sweet to the taste were placed before us with lashings of white cabbage. Because there was only one fire the bacon and cabbage were cooked in the same pot. The bacon greased the cabbage so that it glistened when the light fell on it in the plate. The meal would be the same tomorrow and the day after except that now and again turnips replaced the cabbage as a vegetable.

There was a bowl of milk before each man, buttermilk which the men loved, or skimmed milk which had thickened almost to the consistency of jelly. As they drank this it left white moustaches on the men's faces. I often meant to count the number of potatoes a working man would eat. It wouldn't rest at a half dozen. A spud was selected from the heap, peeled with the knife and halved on the plate before it found its way to the mouth and thence to the digestive department. All the men blessed themselves before eating but some kept their hats on during the meal. First the men talked about the potatoes they were eating, and there were remarks like, 'They're good everywhere this year.' They knew that this particular variety had come off boggy ground because of the clean white skin. They knew by their shape that they were Champions. They spoke of other varieties, of Irish Queens, British Queens, Epicures, and a new kind making its appearance called Golden Wonders. They discussed the methods of cultivation, the difference between drills and ridges, first and second earthing and spraying against the blight. Then they turned their attention to the bacon. A tasty bit was the verdict. The man of the house told them he had added a dust of saltpetre to the common salt when curing, which gave it an extra flavour. The cabbage escaped comment except that one man wanted to know if it was York.

By the fire sat an old lady I took to be the farmer's mother. She wore a coloured shoulder shawl held with a brooch at the front. She had a white apron and on her head a lace affair with a starched linen front, a little like a nun's wimple, what my mother used to call a dandy cap. By her side she had a black walking stick with a crook. She reminded me of the bishop as he sat on the altar the day I was confirmed. She was very shy of the strange men the first day. She saluted each one courteously as he went to shake her hand. But as the days went by she blossomed out and in the end held her own in our mealtime conversation. She talked to the older men about the days when she was young, about the hardship when but a young girl she worked as a servant for a big farmer. Up at cock-crow and milking her share of eighteen cows. She helped the farmer's wife with the housework, the butter-making and the boiling of food for the animals. She drew water from the well in huge buckets until her arms were nearly pulled out of their shoulder sockets. She had to do the work of a man in the fields, and watch herself from the amorous advances of the farmer when they got out of sight of the house. She worked for a whole year for a ten pound note. Of course she had her board and she slept in the loft over the stable. At night she used to pull up the ladder after her so as to be out of reach of her boss and the servant boy. Some of the men took these accounts to be a form of bravado because I saw them winking at my father.

Despite the hardship of the few years she gave in service she wouldn't exchange her young life for that of Queen Victoria. She relished the memory of her days at school. Her mistress was a real lady and her father used to doff his hat to her the same as if she was the priest. Her youthful days before she went out working were all sunshine. Strolling by the river bank, gathering hurts (whortleberries) in Merry's wood in October or courting on the grassy slopes of the railway on a Sunday evening fair; Sunday nights too at the dances in a neighbour's kitchen. The tapping on the flagged floor to the music of the Kerry slide and the mad wheel at the end of the hornpipe. She was back in those days again as she lilted or sang a verse of one of the songs which used to punctuate the set dances:

> When the roses bloom again down by the willow,
> and a robin redbreast sings his sweet refrain,
> For the sake of auld lang syne,
> I'll be with you sweetheart mine,
> I'll be with you when the roses bloom again.

When her brother married in his small farm the dowry his wife brought him came to her and enabled her to marry into this house, where she met a lovable man, God be good to him, and where she never saw a hungry day.

When I looked around the old kitchen it reminded me of the house where my grandfather was born in Gallaun. The same small window in a wall that seemed three feet thick. The open door to allow in the light, and the closed half-door to keep the small animals and the fowl out. Two hens and a cock perched on the half-door as we were eating on the first day and seemed to complain bitterly that they were hungry and why weren't they getting something. With a 'hurnish' from the woman of the house and a flapping of wings they were gone. About three feet out from the fire wall and at a person's height there was a round beam, the thickness of a telegraph pole, extending from side wall to side wall. Over the fire and resting on the beam there was a six-foot wide wickerwork canopy tapering up to the chimney outlet. It was plastered over and whitewashed like the beam and the walls of the kitchen. At each side of the canopy the beam was boarded into the fire wall so that there was a place to store things. On one side was the donkey's tackling and on the other side the harness for the horse. The door to the bedroom was at the side of the fire and at the other end of the kitchen in the middle of the wall was the door to the second room very often used as a dairy. High up on the same wall was another door reached by a ladder, to the loft where the son slept.

The settle, which was a bed at night, was placed by the back wall a little down from the fire and below it the dresser. These were brightly painted in blue and white and the dresser, even with the dinner plates and drinking bowls in use, carried a fine array of shining delf. Between the window and the front door and high on the wall was an open-shelved piece of furniture called a clevvy. A hanging piece, it carried a display of tin mugs, lustre jugs and highly polished saucepan covers on hooks. Directly under it stood the separator, screwed down to the gravel-filled box in which it came from Sweden. Alpha was the name at the side. There was a large bowl at the top into which the new milk was poured and as the handle was turned the milk went through the machine and cream came out one spout and skimmed milk out the other. The separator replaced the broad shallow pans in which the milk was set and left for the cream to come to the top and in a short time it too was replaced by the travelling creamery.

In olden times and indeed still in some houses there was a coop beside the back door in which fowl were kept at night. It was a splendid piece of furniture, painted the same as the dresser and the settle. It had two compartments into which a dozen hens could be packed, six above and six below. The shutters were slotted and through them the hens poked their heads and carried on a constant cluck-cluck until the lights were put out and everyone went to bed. The cock was never cooped up. He sat on top or perched high up on the cross-beam. At the crack of dawn he flapped his wings and crowed and the hens clucked so that there was little peace in the house until someone got up and released them into the yard. The rafters were blackened from maybe a century of smoke but for three feet before they entered the walls they were whitewashed. These were the rafters that echoed to the loud cries of sorrow when there was a tragic death in the family, or in happier times to the sound of music at a wedding dance or to the tingling of the consecration bell at the station Mass.

There was a notion creeping in lately of having a cup of tea after the dinner. The older men wouldn't hear of this. They preferred to wait for the tea break at about four o'clock. I drank the tea and so did my father, while the masons smoked their pipes. After a suitable lapse of time to allow the food to settle, one of the masons, much to the farmer's relief, got up with a 'This'll never pay the rent' and the men walked back to the building site and my father and I went to our temporary workshop in the hayshed. Everyone was in good form after the dinner. We could hear the masons singing as they worked. They were expert tradesmen and in a matter of days they had the walls high enough to receive the joists for the upper floor. When the walls reached the eaves and the two gables were built, my father put on the roof. The rafters, each two coupled, had been made on the ground and hoisted into position with a bird's beak shape at the end of each rafter finding a resting place on the wall plate. With the slating machine I punched holes in the bluish-purple Bangor slates. The men tending drew the slates to my father and with some help from me he covered the two sides of the roof in one day. The chimneys were lead-flashed, the roof ridged and the eaveshoots and downpipes fixed in position.

We glazed the sashes and put them in the window frames. I loved pressing the soft putty between my hands and if it got too soft I added whitening to bring it to its proper consistency. My mind often wandered and, making small animals with the putty, I populated my corner of the bench with cows, horses and sheep. A shout from my father would bring me back to reality and I would proceed to bed the sash rebate with soft putty to receive the glass. With the sashes glazed, the weather was excluded from the house and the woodwork of the inside began. First the timber floors were put down. I became an expert at driving black brads shaped like a 7 with a long leg into the boards. The last blow of the hammer had to be so timed that the head went below the surface without leaving the mark of the hammer on the board. If I did this I'd get a rap of my father's hammer handle on the knuckles. He hated slovenly work. He was a kindly man and lost his temper only if I did something extremely stupid like this. He expected me to learn the trade by watching him rather than telling me or demonstrating the work like an instructor. Only if I persisted in doing something wrong would he take the tools from me and show me how to do it the correct way. But Rome wasn't built in a day and it took much practice and hours of hard work before I achieved proficiency in the use of the wood-working implements. I often spotted him watching me out of the corner of his eye and if I got something dead right a smile of satisfaction would light up his face.

When the floors were down we made a workbench inside the house and here we made the staircase. A simple knowledge of geometry was needed to work out the rise and the going of each step. The two heavy string boards which support the steps were marked and chased to take the treads and the risers. My father with the tenon saw cut into the wood and I with the chisel and mallet scooped out the channels. Chips flew before the chisel as I did the rough work. My father finished the channel with the paring chisel to the correct depth. The steps, risers and treads were glued and wedged and with a newel post at the top and the bottom the staircase was manoeuvred into position. I was the first to run up and down. Seeing my obvious delight at treading on my own or partly my own handiwork, my father as he stood back admiring the structure said, 'Will you ever grow up!'

Our next job was to erect the partitions to divide the rooms upstairs. These partitions were sheeted with ceiling boards, four and a half by a half inch and 'veed' and rebated. With the same boards we ceiled the rooms upstairs and the parlour below. The kitchen joists were left bare. From these would hang the flitches of bacon when the farmer killed a pig in October or November. The window-sills were put in and the reveals boarded. With the architraves in position around the doors and windows the woodwork of the house was complete, but before we were entirely finished all the exposed wood was sized, stained yellow ochre and then varnished. The masons had put in the concrete window-sills, put down the cement floor and plastered the walls. When the plaster dried out the farmer and his family left their snug house in the hollow and took possession of their castle on the hill.

The last time we all sat down to a meal in the farmer's old kitchen the talk turned to the new system that was creeping in of building houses with poured concrete. The masons realised that houses built with stone would soon be a thing of the past. There was a sadness in their voices as they spoke of their ancient craft, a trade that went back to the legendary *Gobán Saor* who built the round towers and was so respected that he, the bard and the storyteller sat at the same table as the king.

FUGITIVE

ᕲ

The hayshed in which we had our temporary workshop was built by my father. The rick thatched with green rushes and the round stacks of oats with their pointed roofs looking like an African village were no longer seen in farmers' haggards. Haysheds to hold hay and corn were going up everywhere when I started my apprenticeship to carpentry. My father was in great demand for this type of work and had the reputation of building a hayshed in a day. He had to in order to cope with the call on his services. But he had to have help. The farmer, his sons and maybe a neighbour or two had the holes already dug and were in readiness in the early morning to stand the poles in position and pack the earth firmly around them.

Wall plates were secured to the tops of the poles, the roof couples made and by the break for the midday meal the skeleton of the structure stood in place, crying out to be covered with corrugated iron. It was a very mean man who wouldn't have a few dozen of stout in the house for an occasion like this. The men had a bottle each with their meal instead of a bowl of milk. After we had eaten our meal the sheets of zinc were stretched on the purlins and I helped my father nail them down. For the next few hours an almighty din of metallic sound filled the countryside and before the sun sank at the end of a long summer's day the roof was capped and two sides and one gable were sheeted and secure. When my father had driven the last nail home he threw down the hammer and struck his hands together as much as to say 'I've done it again!' If there was a bottle of stout left he got it and the men praised him and said no other man alive could have accomplished what he did in one day. When the farmer gave him the money which was agreed to, after a little bit of humming and hawing, my father put it in his pocket and when we came home he

131

gave it to my mother and she put it in the small box with the sliding top. When he was paid for a smaller job in the workshop he kept the money to buy a half-quarter of plug tobacco, or for the security of feeling a pound or two in his pocket if he met a man in town and they went for a few drinks.

Haysheds weren't long up when they became trysting places for courting couples on their way home from all-night dances. Indeed they often housed two or three couples locked in fond embraces. We were told that a farmer in the dark of a winter's morning, collecting an armful of hay for his cows, unknown to him pulled the slip-on shoes off a young woman's feet and carried them buried in the hay to the cattle shed. She uttered no syllable of protest because she and her partner were afraid of being caught in such a place. The owner would go out of his mind if he knew the hayshed was being used for such a purpose. Morals didn't trouble him. What did bother him was the lighting match of a cigarette smoker. The winter feed of corn and hay for his stock could go up in flames. When the coast was clear we presume the lass and her lover stole out, very careful not to arouse the dog, and she went home barefoot.

I slept in our hayshed for nearly a week one time and my parents didn't know I was there. This is how it came about. After a few years working with my father and doing a man's share I was in my view a man and should be doing the things young men were doing. One of these was going on Sunday nights to house dances. My mother, who was the boss in these matters, didn't mind but she objected to my staying out until three or four o'clock in the morning at all-night dances. Dancing in an overcrowded, unventilated kitchen with a blazing fire in the hearth and coming out into the freezing winter air covered in perspiration could result in a very bad cold. Getting wet going to a ball night and leaving the clothes to dry on my back often gave me a cough so severe that my mother likened it to the sound of two stones striking together. Many people died of consumption around where we lived. In one case a whole family was wiped out.

'You'll never stop,' she used to say to me, 'until you bring it into the house to us.'

Her brother Mike had died of tuberculosis a few years before and my racking cough filled her with horror.

But I went against her wishes. I had met someone for whom I had a true wish, and she was the attraction which drew me to any dance where I thought she might be. Because I was a good dancer she liked being asked out in a set dance with me. There were two kinds of set dance, a jig and a polka. Each comprised three figures and a slide, but the jig set ended with a hornpipe tune and the polka set with a reel. I used to whirl my girl like mad in the wheel of the hornpipe, but I never lost my footing as I did the first time I went dancing. Jude was slim and fair-haired and her blue laughing eyes were before me every waking hour. It took a long time before she agreed that I could walk her home, but at last when she fell in with my wishes I was in the seventh heaven. Holding hands was the only liberty she allowed and after a few words at her father's gate she was off like lightning into the house.

She kept me on tenterhooks for ages. The more she resisted my well intentioned advances the more my heart ached to hold her in my arms, if only for a single minute. The more I thought about it the more I feared the muddle I would make of the whole thing if it ever came to pass. I wasn't eating, my mother said, and my father had to call me from my daydreams to attend to the work in hand. Walking in the pitch dark one night coming from a dance, Jude and I bumped into a horse that was standing stock-still in the middle of the road. She held on to me because of the fright she got and I threw my arms around her to comfort her. The horse trotted off and my mouth found hers, and oh glory, the blood surged through my veins and bells and gongs and a delightful commotion took over my head. She was taken aback at my ardour but it was the start of many a blissful sojourn as we backed an oak tree close to her father's house. She would never go into a hayshed or lie on the soft grass on the slope of the railway. We met on Sunday evenings and walked the quiet stretch by the river or picked whortleberries in Merry's wood in October whose juice stained our mouths a bluish purple. I loved her but I was never sure if she had a true wish for me.

One night the stepping stones were dry as we crossed the

wide river to a dance at Griffiths, but it rained so heavily during the night that they were covered when we were coming
back. By the mercy of heaven the sky had cleared and the
moon shone brightly, and we could see the tops of the stepping stones under maybe three or four inches of water. Rather
than go the long way around by Gortacoosh we decided to
cross the river. We took off our shoes and she gave me her
stockings to put in the pocket of my body coat. I put my socks
in the other pocket and we set out. The water was freezing
cold and we doubled back a few times. Finally taking courage,
we faced the river. I went first and when I reached a step I
helped her to gain a foothold beside me. Halfway across, the
surface of the stepping stones became very uneven and it was
harder to get a firm footing. Nervousness on her part turned to
sheer fright when she saw how far more we had to go. I had
often seen the river when it was nearly dry and I knew the
height of the stepping stones. If we fell off them, I told her, we
wouldn't drown only get very wet. The river was fordable at
that spot and didn't run very swiftly. We were quite safe. By
the dint of assurance and reassurance she soldiered on from
step to step until we reached the other side. What were tears
on her part turned to laughter. We threw back our heads and
roared merriment into the night. We ran barefoot up and
down the bank till we got the blood in circulation again. As
our feet were wet we put on our shoes barefoot and strolled
along. We stopped and hugged and talked and hummed and
sang till we came to her father's gate. I doubled back home and
the cock crew as I went in the door.

My mother was awake and scolded me severely for being
out so late. She lost her temper as she was wont to do when I
came in at what she called an unearthly hour. My smaller
brothers and sisters woke and began to cry, and my father, ever
a man of peace, pleaded with my mother to wait and thrash it
out in the daytime. Half of my mind was savouring the happiness I had experienced walking from the river with Jude in the
moonlight and the other half was revolting against a scene
like this which was ruining the memory of that enchanted
hour. My temper was as quick as my mother's. Everyone said I
was taking after her. I shouted back that I was a man now and

that I would come in any time I liked. This unexpected outburst made her cry bitterly. To think that the son she had reared would shout at his mother. To think that he had so little
respect for her and for his small brothers and sisters to stay out
all night God only knows where, or in what company, and to
come home now at cockcrow and turn the house into a place
of turmoil.

'Do you hear him?' she said to my father. 'He'll come in
any time he likes. He can come in any time he likes but it
won't be into this house!'

Now that her temper had taken possession of her she was
in full flight vocally, her language almost poetic as she assailed
me for being an ungrateful son. A son, for all she knew, lost in
the depredation of sin. How could there be luck or grace in a
house where a son had turned his back on God and succumb-
ed to the temptations of the devil! I hung my coat on the
newel post of the stairs and the daylight poured through the
window as I climbed up to bed. Even as sleep claimed me I
could still hear my mother sobbing and speaking to herself and
praying the verses she often prayed:

Angel of God my guardian dear,
To whom God's love commits me here.
Ever this night be at my side,
To light and guard, to rule and guide!

As I fell asleep, a resolution was forming in my mind. I would
leave this house ... yes, I would leave ... I would go ... I was
dreaming and a torrent was raging in the river and sweeping
my loved one from my arms. I struggled to save her but my
head went under and the water poured into my lungs. Slowly
darkness filled my head and the world slipped away from me.
My mother was there in my dream. She stretched out her
hand to me. She was smiling. 'A *leanbh*' (my child), she said,
'I love you!' Then through my open mouth my soul in the
shape of a butterfly escaped from my body and hovered over
the river. I could see the body my soul had left drifting with
the flood. Beside it was the body of my sweetheart, Jude, her
fair hair flowing with the stream. And as I called out to her a

white butterfly came out of her mouth and fluttered up towards me. We winged our way to paradise and strolled together through flower bedecked fields. We had shed our wings and walked again with earthly bodies. We saw the bearded saints and St Joseph was making a wheel, our Lord a young man holding the spoke as St Joseph drove it into the stock. Mary brought tea to them in the workshop. Angels flew overhead and God when he appeared was a dazzling light ...

The sound of the blind going up woke me and the sunlight flooded into the room. 'Are you going to get up at all today?' It was my father and he didn't sound cross as he added, 'You'll be the death of your mother!' And, I thinking of the resolution that was forming in my head as I went to sleep, said, half under my breath, 'I won't be troubling her long more!' As I dressed and went downstairs I recalled the strange dream I had and the vision of my mother smiling and holding out her hand to me as I drowned. She was standing in the middle of the kitchen floor holding out a pair of girl's stockings which she had found hanging out of the pocket of my coat. My whole being went into a jelly at the thought of what she and my father would think. There was a look in my mother's face I had never seen before.

'What have you done?' she demanded. 'Have you shamed us?'

My love for my mother was stronger than that for my father. I treasured every thought of how she cherished us when we were young. I couldn't live under the same roof with a mother whose love had turned to ice, a mother who believed that I had done something that was terrible to her way of thinking. These thoughts went through my mind in a flash as I explained to her what had happened.

'Coming home from Griffiths' dance,' I told her, 'the flood was over the stepping stones and we took off our shoes and she put her stockings in my pocket.' My mother wanted to know who I was with and I told her it was Jude Scanlon. 'Our feet were too wet to put on our stockings when we reached the bank. We laced on our boots and forgot to put on our stockings after. If you don't believe me, see in my other pocket and you'll find my socks.'

She gave me a look and I didn't know whether it said, 'I believe you,' or 'I don't want ever to see you again.' I went back upstairs and put a few things together and threw them out the window. On my way down I took my coat, then went out of the house, hopped on my bicycle and rode away. As I pedalled on, tears of temper blinded me and I had no notion of where I was going. What was driving me on? Was it the bitter pang inside of me of being rejected for something I didn't do? I knew from my catechism and from the sermons of the holy fathers at the missions what was wrong, but I hadn't done anything. Jude Scanlon and I were as pure in our love as the driven snow. I thought again of the dream I had of being in heaven with her. To be dead and that dream a reality was what I wished for now; to go on forever walking hand in hand through the flower-filled fields of paradise.

A magpie perched on a birch sapling let out a raucous screech at me. Mocking me. It was unlucky to see one magpie. One was for sorrow. I cycled on through the next village and the next. I had had no breakfast and I wasn't hungry. I stopped in Millstreet, almost twenty miles from home. The church was being repaired. I left my bicycle against the gate and went in to look at the work. Who should I see but Dan Cronin, who used to build houses with my father. He was surprised to see me and wanted to know where I came out of. I told him that there was a row at home and that I ran away. He laughed. 'All part of growing up,' he said. 'I ran away from home myself but I was soon back when the hunger picked me.' The hunger was beginning to pick me now.

'Was it a woman?' he asked. 'Ah, but you are too young for that caper!'

'Maybe it was!' I admitted, a manly tingling surging through my boyish frame.

'I'll ask the boss if he has anything to do for you and maybe you'd be over your *tormas* (sulk) in the evening.'

He went and asked the contractor and I was taken on to help a carpenter who was making a framed and sheeted door for the sacristy. I had no tools and he was lazy enough to let me use his. Tradesmen are noted for their attachment to their implements and stonecutters have been known to bury their favourite chisels in the mud floor of the workplace if they are going away for a few days.

I mortised the stiles of the door and the carpenter cut the tenons on the cross pieces. He was pleased with my work. He wouldn't let me bead the sheeting as I hadn't used a bead plane before. The top of the door had a Gothic head and I had a lot of sawing to do to shape the head from a wide plank. I did the rough work and the carpenter finished it. At the mid-day break Cronin remarked that people who run away from home don't have any money.

'I have a ten bob note that's in two halves. I don't know how I tore it. If you can fix it,' he said, 'you are welcome to it.'

I was at my wits' end to know how I could piece it to-gether until I thought of the gummed strips torn from a stamp sheet. I went to the post office and there on the window-sill were plenty of them. I licked a long strip and put it at the back of the ten shilling note with half the strip protruding. Then very carefully I matched the two pieces of the note together. It looked perfect on one side and that was the side I kept up when I paid in a small café for tea, bread and butter and a plate of ham. The whole thing came to a half crown. I brought the change back to Cronin. He took only the price of two pints and left me the rest.

That evening with the door nearly finished, there didn't seem to be any more work for me. The contractor gave me five shillings. I got on my bicycle and without thinking I headed for home. It was dark when I got near the house but I couldn't get myself to go in. The *tormas*, as Cronin called it, hadn't worn off. I hid my bicycle in the lime kiln and went into our own hayshed. Even though it was late spring there was still a pole of hay there. After being at an all-night dance the night before, I was worn out for the want of sleep. In no time I was fast asleep and it was the cock crowing in the morning that woke me. I stole out in the half dark and cycled away. Passing a neighbour's house I saw that they were up and I went in. Paddy, the man of the house, was someone I could trust and I told him that I had left home and asked could I lie low for a few days. I stayed, and as I was in the house and idle he went to town and got ceiling boards to ceil the room. The stations were due next month. He had a good sharp saw and a hammer and that would do me to carry out the job. When the boards arrived I fell into work, Paddy tending me and holding up the board at the far end until I had nailed it in place. In my innocence I told him and his wife Mary about my trouble at home and the situation that led to it. Paddy had often crossed those flooded stepping stones himself when he was courting Mary and they had often taken off their shoes and stockings. Paddy thought it a very comical occurrence going in home with the stockings of the girl next door in my pocket. He laughed heartily at it but it was no laughing matter for me. Still his attitude helped to thaw out the ice of ill-feeling between me and home just a small bit. I took my time with the job of ceiling the room. There were a few more things around the house which needed the attention of a tradesman and I did these as well.

Each night I came back home but as I couldn't face in I slept in the hayshed. There were small insects in the hay which worked their way inside my clothes and irritated my skin. How I longed for my own bed and the pleasure of changing my clothes and putting on a clean shirt. When I was sitting by the fire in Paddy's kitchen the heat aroused the insects next to my skin so that it was a torture to keep from scratching myself. I made excuses to go out and rub my back to the cornerstone of the house and give myself a good shaking.

Paddy pulled my leg about Jude Scanlon and it was a nice sensation hearing her name mentioned. She was never for one moment out of my thoughts. As Paddy said, 'You have it bad! You are only a *garsún* (boy) yet. You will put many more women through your hands before you settle down.'

I was seventeen and I hadn't my trade fully learned but no matter how long I had to wait to marry, Jude would be the woman I'd choose to spend my life with. I was firmly convinced of that.

'If you went knocking at Scanlons' door looking for Jude's hand at your age old Scanlon would put the dogs after you,' he laughed. Then he talked about Jude's father, in his lighter moments as comical a man as there was in the parish. I knew him well. He was the life and soul of any house where people gathered. Paddy heard him say that when he was courting Jude's mother he went to ask her father for her hand. He boasted that his was a love match, which was unusual at the time. Her father offered him a drink and a pipe of tobacco, and Scanlon in an effort to make a good impression said, 'I don't drink, smoke, play cards, go with women, bet on horses or take an active interest in politics.'

'Tell me,' the girl's father enquired, 'Do you ate grass?'

'Oh no, I don't,' said Scanlon.

'In that case,' he was told, 'you are not fit company for man or beast!'

Scanlon, reaching out his right hand for the glass and his left one for the pipe, said, 'Now can I marry her?'

Suddenly Paddy changed his tune and said that Mary and he had humoured me along for most of a week and that it was time for me to go back home. 'I am a friend of your family,' he told me, 'and I would be failing in that friendship if I didn't urge you to return to your parents. Your mother will be out of her mind wondering what has happened to you. The *tormas* [Cronin's word again] should be worn off you by now.'

I thanked him and his wife for their kindness to me and went out into the black night. I took my bike and instead of riding off I walked with it through the dark, mulling in my head Paddy's words. I wasn't a man yet, no more than a boy trying to come to grips with growing up and coping with the miracle of being in love. I thought of what my father and mother must have felt all the days I was away. A warmth for my mother was burgeoning in my breast. The *tormas* was wearing off. I could go back tonight and sleep between clean sheets. I hopped on my bike and rode like a madman through the dark till I came to our own gate. I put the bicycle in the hayshed and went to the door of the house. Passing the window I saw that the men, the nightly ramblers, were still sitting in the kitchen. This would be the wrong time to go in. I waited in the hayshed until I heard them going. At the sound of the last 'goodnight' I went and opened the door and peered into the kitchen. There was no one there but my father. He had his boots off and was hanging his socks on the crane. As he reached for the tongs to rake the fire I said 'hello' very softly.

Without lifting his head he took the red coals and half-burned small sods and buried them in the ashes.

'I came back,' I said, in an effort to fill the painful silence. 'If you were younger,' he replied, 'I suppose I'd have to take the stick to you. Have you anything to say for yourself?' 'I'm very sorry,' I blurted out, 'for upsetting you and my mother. Where is she?'

My mother was in bed. I lit the butt of a candle, put it in the sconce, and went into the bedroom. I put the candle on the chimney-piece and, seeing me, she sat up in bed and looked at me for a while. I expected to get a telling off. But no. Suddenly her face softened and she smiled. 'A chuisle mo chroí!' (my heart's pulse) she said. 'A leanbh bán!' (my dear child). Irish often came to her lips like now when she wanted to express her love.

'A chuisle mo chroí,' she said, 'I believe what you told me the morning you ran away. I believed it then but I was in too much of a temper to admit it.'

She reached out her hands and I went and knelt by the bed. She put her arms around me, a thing she hadn't done since I was a small child. I was overwhelmed by the suddenness of finding myself being embraced by my mother. She held me close and an uncontrollable spasm seized my body and I began to shake. I cried and buried my face in the blankets so that she couldn't see me. Thousands of thoughts milled around in my head. Things I wanted to say to her, but when I raised my head all I could say was, 'I'm sorry!'

I sat on a chair and she told me that she was worried to death while I was away. Expecting every minute that the door would open and I would be standing there. She spoke of my father, who had never uttered a harsh word to me. It was hard on him working alone and trying to cope with all the extra jobs that were coming his way lately.

'Tomorrow,' she said and she was in her old form now, 'he is going building a hayshed for Scanlon.'

She looked at me to see what effect the name would have on me. I thought of Jude as she said it and I suppose I reddened up.

'You are too young,' my mother said, 'to take a thing like

that seriously. Your father was twenty-seven before he met me. Take your time, the world is wide. You'll find that Miss Scanlon has other things on her mind. It's only a couple of years since she was going to school. She's too young to take on the cares of life. You wait. She has other plans, you'll see.'

The episode of my running away was at an end and I was happy to be back. I would have dearly loved to talk to my mother as I sat there. To ask her how she met my father and what life was like when she was my age. I wasn't able to bring myself to do it. Somehow some sort of barrier came down when I felt like talking about things like that to her or to my father. We thrashed out the ordinary everyday matters about the house. But when it had anything to do with the heart we were trapped in a web of silence.

'Will you have anything to eat?' she wanted to know.

'I'll have a cup of milk,' I said, 'if it's there.'

'There's plenty of milk,' she assured me, 'and before I forget it. I put them in a paper bag. It's there on the top of the press.'

I looked in the paper bag. It contained Jude's stockings. I put them in my pocket and to cover my embarrassment I went out of the room. 'Good night!' I said to my father as I crossed the kitchen and climbed the stairs to bed.

Strawboys Come Dancing

❧

The day we went building Scanlon's hayshed was a joyous day for me. I saw Jude going about her household duties, feeding the calves, giving mess to the fowl and drawing water from the well. She drew my mind away from my work and my father had to call on me to pay attention to what I was doing. At about eleven o'clock Jude and her mother brought out two bowls in which there were beaten-up eggs in steaming hot milk with sugar, and a few spoonfuls of whiskey in my father's bowl. It was a drink my father loved; maybe Jude's mother heard somewhere of his liking for it. He thanked the women and told Jude's mother that she had a big heart to go to so much trouble.

'It was no bother at all,' she said. 'You deserve it. Good tradesmen are to be cherished.'

She remarked then that she was related to my mother. Consanguinity again! She and my father began tracing relationships and I was praying that the connection wasn't too near and that it wouldn't be an impediment if Jude and myself ever thought of getting married. 'This boy is your eldest, Ned?' she said to my father, and without waiting for an answer she went on, 'He is a great help to you. Shake hands with him, Jude. Maybe ye know each other already.'

I shook Jude's hand and taking the hint from the gleam in her eye we both acted as if we were meeting for the first time. I was reluctant to look at my father in case he'd spill the beans, but on second thoughts I knew he wouldn't, though my heart missed a beat when he said, 'Nearly all young people know each other now. They get around more than we did, ma'am. The bicycle was a great invention.' Though I was only seventeen I could hardly remember the first time I rode a man's bike; it was so long before. When I started my apprenticeship

I got a new model and my father and I cycled everywhere to work.

Dinnertime came and Jude came out to call us. I waited to talk with her until all the men had gone into the house. There was a small moment of embarrassment when I gave her the paper bag with her stockings. Blushing, she concealed the bag under her apron and when we talked about the night of the stepping stones, I never mentioned about my mother finding her stockings in my pocket. We both went into the kitchen. All the places around the large deal table were filled but mine.

'*An té a bhíonn amuigh fuaireann a chuid*,' Jude's mother said (He who is out his portion cools). Old Scanlon sat at the head of the table, a big red-faced man with a sandy moustache and a good cover of thatch on his head. All the talk among the men was about a marriage that was taking place some distance away in a few days' time. Getting married outside Shrove was very rare, but the groom, who had spent some years in the city and was home on early pension from the prison service, had drifted a little from the old customs. It was a made match and he was marrying one of the Galvin girls of the Knob. There was no son in that house and the gaoler was getting the land.

'She's a prisoner now for life,' Old Scanlon laughed.

'And there will be hard labour too,' managed another.

'That'll do,' Jude's mother said, drawing a rein on the conversation before it went too far. 'It will be a great wedding. The Galvins always had the big heart. There'll be no shortage there.'

'What good is that to us,' Old Scanlon replied, 'when we won't be invited? Unless we'd straw. Did you ever straw, Ned?' he asked my father.

Strawboys were the uninvited guests who went to a wedding in disguise for a short visit. They were given a drink and a chance to dance a set, and many groups of them called in the course of a wedding night.

'Many is the time,' my father told him. 'But strawing was an art in the old days. A week would be spent making a straw suit, complete with skirt, cape and high-caul cap. Our faces were blackened or covered with a piece of lace curtain. There was always a captain over a group of strawboys. He was the

144

only one who spoke and the others had to obey him.'

'Surely the girls went strawing as well,' Jude's mother asked. 'We didn't have the custom up our way.'

'Of course they did,' my father replied, 'Where would we be without them!'

'Strawboys in the old days were an orderly enough crowd,' Old Scanlon held. 'They added a bit of variety to a wedding dance. Was our wedding strawed?' he asked Jude's mother.

'By the way he doesn't remember!' she laughed. 'Maybe you were too far gone guzzling Ballyvourney poteen to remember anything.'

'I had a few jorums all right,' Old Scanlon admitted. 'But where's the harm in that. It's only one night in a man's life. My match was a love match, so I had something to celebrate.'

There was talk then of matchmaking. The men said it was a good system and only for it many would go unmarried. It was a way of bringing people together, especially shy people, and it made sure that the dowry which enabled the groom's sister to marry another farmer was paid. Often the same dowry went the rounds of the parish. Even though those getting married did not know each other until they were brought together some weeks before, they all seemed to get on very well. The men could only think of one case out of all those who had matches made for them which broke down. The woman returned to her own people the morning after the wedding and if the groom shook gold under feet she wouldn't go back to him. Two lives were ruined for neither could marry again. The fortune she paid was never given back to her, and the men from the two sides belted one another black and blue with ashplants over it every fair day.

In the conversation we heard of a man who was going with a farmer's daughter. They were always together at house dances. The young girl had no brothers and her elder sister, no oil painting, was to get the farm. When Shrovetime came round an account of a match was sent to the elder sister by the young man's parents. The match went ahead and he married the elder sister and lived in the same house with the two women until the young girl went away to America.

'The land he loved and not the woman,' Old Scanlon remarked. 'It was often a man with a big farm and an unpresentable daughter got as fine a man as was going for a son-in-law. The craze for land is great. It is indeed!'

'Men and women,' he continued, 'having spent ten years in America working hard, came back with dowries in their pockets and were in great demand when Shrovetime matches were being made. They settled into new homes with partners they barely knew. With their Yankee clothes and New York accents they were conspicuous for a while, but in a few years, except for the gleam of gold in their teeth, you wouldn't know them from those who never went away.'

Jude had heard all that was said and when I got a chance afterwards I put forward the idea of strawing the wedding on the Knob the following Tuesday night. She was excited about the notion and there and then we decided to get a crowd together to make up a group of strawboys. Six would be enough; three boys and three girls, as many as would make up a set dance. Some evenings before, we came together and with wisps of straw made ropes to put around our lower legs like army puttees. We fashioned bands of straw to place about the waist and shoulders and plaited shorter lengths to decorate out caps. We, the men, turned our coats inside out and the girls, borrowing their fathers' or their brothers' coats did the same thing. With the straw leggings on and our bodies festooned in straw and our faces covered with pieces of old lace curtain, we defied anyone to recognise us. The kick we got out of helping each other to dress and seeing the end effect was tremendous.

We marched together to the house on the Knob, and hung around outside for a while listening to the music and the jollity from within. Then, summing up courage, our captain knocked on the door and chanted:

Strawboys on the threshold,
Strawboys at the door.
Keep a place for strawboys
On the dancing floor.
We wish the bride and groom
The very best of cheer.
May they have a son or daughter
'Ere the end of the year!

The bride's father, old Galvin, came forward and made room for us in the middle of the kitchen floor. The men accepted a bowl of porter from a large bucket. There was a tint of wine for the ladies. It was my first time tasting strong drink. I kept my confirmation pledge until that instant. When the porter touched my tongue I nearly gasped at the sourness of the mixture. It was as bitter as the gall which was given to Our Lord on the cross. The second sup tasted a little better and I finished the bowl in time with the other men. Then we lined out for a set dance. The captain spoke to the musicians and called for a polka set. We tapped the floor in unison, waiting for the opening note in the music. When it came we started out around the house. Early in the first figure one couple danced to the centre while all the others stood by. Guests at the wedding moved forward and playfully tried to remove the disguises from our faces. We fought them off and I had a hard job protecting Jude from the inquisitive advances of a large man with hands as big as a hayfork. Our costumes and disguises were much admired as we heeled and toed to the lively music. There were cheers and much applause at the antics of some of the dancers. At the end of the last figure we all wheeled together, our arms encompassing each other in a tight bunch in the middle of the floor. We swung until the house and people swung with us and when we came to a halt our heads were still spinning.

'A song! a song!' the crowd demanded and the captain called on me to sing 'My Mary of Loughrea'. I held on to the frame of the room door to steady myself and get my breath back and then I gave what I considered was a good blast:

> The youths will miss you from the dance
> On Sunday evenings fair.
> The grass will miss your fairy steps
> To wash the dews away,
> But I will miss you most of all
> My Mary of Loughrea!

It was an emigration song and on the last line, which was always spoken, Jude caught and squeezed my hand.

'I have something to say to you tonight,' she said. 'Not

now.' I had bent eagerly towards her. 'Later on.'

We said goodbye to the bride and groom and wished them luck. Our captain thanked them for having received us. On our way out there was another group of strawboys. They were admitted and as we crossed the yard a third group arrived. We waited until the second group came out, only to find that the third batch was refused admission. The people of the house, I am sure, thought they had enough of a good thing for one night.

This last bunch proved to be of a very unruly element and cut up rough, shouting, name calling and casting aspersions on the family. They lifted loose stones from the fence and began throwing them on the corrugated iron roof. The din was earsplitting and drowned out the music. The door opened suddenly and young men from the wedding party rushed out. They waded into the strawboys and there was the father and mother of a fight, lit only by a watery moon. We and the second group made ourselves scarce as we didn't want to be identified with a pack of blackguards. As we legged for home, we could hear those who were refused admission taking to their heels as well. I couldn't help thinking that whichever rogue strawboy met up with the large guest with the hands as big as a hay fork must have come in for a fair hammering.

We got rid of the straw at the next hayshed, turned our coats the right way back and put the lace masks in our pockets. We walked to the oak tree where Jude and I always rested and talked and laughed and courted and kissed. Many were the outlandish things we talked about. I told her about the strange dream I had the night we crossed the stepping stones. There was a silence and a turning away of her head as if she doubted my sanity. We talked of mundane things too like would it rain tomorrow? No. It would be fine. There was no cap of clouds this evening on the twin mountains. The breasts of Dana were clear and plain to be seen. Of course I didn't dare call them that, but I called her Dana, my goddess of the mountain. She laughed, and said I was turning into a prime eejet.

'And don't be associating me with a mountain, two mountains in fact!' she said, pushing me away from her playfully.

We walked the last steps to her father's house. She went

inside the small wicket gate and closed it, and with the gate between us she said, 'You remember me mentioning that I had something to say to you tonight?' I waited. The dog barked.

'I won't be seeing you again. I am going to England tomorrow.'

A lump rose in my throat and I couldn't speak. Tonight had been so wonderful. The dressing up, the music, the dance, and Jude and I had been so happy together. The dog barked again. She became uneasy.

'My sister Mary is nursing in England,' she said, 'and I am going over to her. When I am gone, it'll be out of sight out of mind. You'll find someone else.'

I couldn't ever forgive her for saying that. The bottom had fallen out of whatever little world was mine. Her hand was resting on the gate. I placed mine on it and caressed it for a second but no words came and as I turned away she said, 'Goodbye.' I kicked the rambler stones before me on the roadway with temper and disappointment. In anguish I bit my lip and the blood tasted salty on my tongue. The suddenness of her announcement that she was going away really floored me, left me without words. But now phrases and sentences raced through my mind as I realised how bleak my life would be without her. I thought of how she squeezed my hand at the end of the emigration song I sang at the wedding. How sweet that memory was. How sweet was every memory of every moment since the first night I summed up enough courage to ask her to allow me to convey her home from Bryanie's dance.

Even though it was early they were all in bed when I went in home. I went lightly up the stairs but my mother heard me and called me in to my parents' room. She wanted to know how things went at the wedding. She and my father had strawed weddings when they were young. I told her that we were well received and that it was very enjoyable. She was interested in the names of people I saw at it. I thought it better then not to mention about the ferocious fight. Maybe tomorrow.

'I'll be home early every other night,' I told her. 'Jude is going to England.'

My mother must have noticed the sadness in my voice for

she said, 'You'll get over it; there are as good fish in the sea as ever were caught. Don't get so involved the next time. It will be many a long day before you settle down. You'll soon forget this canter. Time is the great healer.'

But I would never forget and each disconnected sentence of my mother's echoed in my head as I tried to sleep. I longed for this day to end. To entice the cloak of sleep around me I thought of the first time I laid eyes on Jude, and I recalled each time we met and walked and talked and sang and kissed, our backs to the old oak tree by her father's house. Gradually her face faded and music took over. We were dancing, not at the wedding on the Knob, but on a dancing deck on a Sunday afternoon in Shronaboy. Lough Guitane lake was down below and Lough Léin was in the distance. The mountains were coloured brighter than I had ever seen them. Everything was bright and the light was dazzling. Jude and I were doing the solo piece in the second figure of the dance. It ended in a wheel. The music raced and so did we. I lifted Jude off her feet. She was so light and as we spun the dancers cheered us. There was laughter and loud clapping and then someone shouted, 'the Priest!'

The parish priest drove his car on to the dancing deck, scattering the dancers in all directions. The girls screamed as we barely got out of the way of the Ford car with spurts of steam coming from its radiator. We hid behind the bushes while the fiddler, who was blind, played on. As the priest step-ped on to the deck the car began to dance to the fiddler's tune, the wheels in turn lifting off the platform, the horn crazily blowing. Waving his blackthorn stick the priest danced madly, wisps of straw circled his biretta, and he wore a stole of woven straw around his neck. The blackthorn blossomed in his hand and his vestments fluttered wildly in the breeze. We emerged from our hiding place and cheered him on as jets of steam coming from the radiator kept time to the music. Steam soon enveloped the car and the priest's mad, laughing face got lost in the fog. Down below us Lough Guitane lake bubbled and boiled and fish put their heads out of the water and screamed, 'We're scalded!' It must have been the end of the world for the Punch Bowl on Mangerton overflowed its brim and water cascaded down the side of the mountain engulfing us. As we fought our way through the flood I sat bolt upright in the bed, and ended the madness that was churning in my brain.

'You're to be pitied,' my mother said, who had been wakened by my shouting. 'Is there any other boy whose head is so crazed by nightmares? That Jude'll be the death of you!'

Goodbye to the Hills

❦

Concrete was the new building material and the construction of stone houses was becoming rarer as time went on. My father had gained much experience in the use of concrete while building bridges for Singleton after the Civil War, and the making of boat piers in Ballinskelligs and elsewhere. He built the first concrete house in our district. It was for the Galvins on the Knob. The new man, the ex-gaoler, had modern ideas and engaged my father to do the building. I helped to make the casing from the new floorboards to hold the poured concrete. When one layer of cement and gravel mix extending right around the house was set, we undid the bolts, raised and re-bolted the shutters and poured another layer. The house went up as quickly as if four masons were building it in stone. People came and watched the job in progress and the more cynical predicted that the walls wouldn't keep out the damp nor the chimney pull the smoke. In a short time the house stood waiting to be capped with a roof and the dark windows like blind eyes waiting for glass lenses to be put in. When the last stroke had been struck my father went down the field to admire his handiwork. From the laying of the foundation to the turning of the key in the front door he had, with a little help from me, done it all himself. He had been mason, carpenter, joiner, slater, plasterer and glazier.

The family moved in and the cynics were proven half right. The walls were as dry as pepper but the chimney had not as good a draft as a masonry house. The ex-gaoler got over this drawback by installing a turf-burning range, and my father, by studying the work of the old masons, mastered the art of chimney making. In subsequent concrete houses he built, the draft was so great he used to remind the woman of the house with a half-smile to keep the small children back from the fire in case they'd be sucked out the chimney. He was now on his way to becoming, in the eyes of those who begrudged him his success, the concrete king.

We were engaged in the enlargement of an hotel in town, an all-concrete job. One day the proprietor asked me if I intended giving my entire life sawing boards and grouting concrete. I told him that I had every notion of improving myself and that I was taking a correspondence course with the Bennett College in England. He laughed at that. 'Learning carpentry by post!' he said. 'And a fine technical school inside in your own town.'

The building and craftwork teacher at the technical school was the architect of the hotel enlargement project, and the next time he came to the site in his capacity as clerk of works, the proprietor introduced me to him and I said I would like to join his class when it opened at the technical school in September. Meeting this man, Micheál Ó Riada was his name, was the means of changing the direction of my footsteps and putting me on the first mile of a journey that would take me far from my own parish. He taught me and others the craft of wood and in time we passed examinations set by the technical branch of the Department of Education in carpentry, joinery and cabinet making. He taught the theory of building and how to draw and read plans; he taught solid geometry which holds the key to the angles met with in the making of a hip roof or a staircase.

Two nights a week, no matter how far from home my day job was, I cycled to the tech. We, Micheál Ó Riada's students, soon discovered that his interests were not confined to the bench or the drawing board. His passion for music was great, though he didn't like jazz; he thought it a very primitive sound. When his demonstration lesson was over and we were busy sawing and chiselling he put on classical records on an old gramophone in the classroom. Books and writers he talked about, and the theatre.

On the head of this I went one night to see Louis Dalton's company at the Town Hall in *Juno and the Paycock*. It was my first time seeing actors on a stage and the humour, the agony and the tragedy of the play touched me to the quick. I laughed and cried and when I left the hall I walked a mile through the dark, coming to terms with the plight of the Captain's family. O'Casey's characters kept me from sleep that night and I envied the actors their power to draw me away from the real world and almost unhinge my reason long after the curtain had come across. I told Ó Riada about my visit to the town hall. He was interested in my reaction to the play and after class that night he talked to us about O'Casey's other plays. He mentioned the works of J. M. Synge and Lennox Robinson and advised us if ever we were in Dublin to go to the Abbey Theatre.

Ó Riada didn't tell us, but we discovered that he had been interned in Ballykinlar Camp during the trouble. While there he made an illuminated book in Celtic strapwork design in which were the names of all the prisoners. This book is in the War of Independence section of the National Museum. His interests were even out of this world, and one night when there was an eclipse of the moon he populated the blackboard with planets in their courses, and illustrated how the eclipse came about which was taking place over our heads in the sky. The different timbers he taught us to cherish – from Honduras mahogany to the pale beech of our own woods. The furniture of the fields he called the deciduous parkland trees, and following his illustrations on the blackboard we grew to know these from their outline and the shape of their leaves. We could, after a time, readily recognise the timber that came from them by its colour and the grain of the wood. He could carve, inlay and French polish. He talked to us about nature, and when a class was over and the tools stored away we remained behind discussing with him whatever was the whim of the evening until the caretaker came along jangling his keys. By the time we got our bikes out of the shed he was in the street. He always dressed as if he were heading for some formal occasion. As we put on our bicycle clips we watched him for a moment as he set out in his soft hat and long brown overcoat, carrying a walking stick as he walked with a limp. Before we overtook him and waved 'goodnight' he had passed many shopfronts which he had designed himself. His Celtic strapwork was a feature of fascia boards in our town and as far away as Listowel.

One evening Mr Ó Riada mentioned to me that if I kept making headway in my studies and passed the senior grade in the practical and theory papers he would enter me for a scholarship examination to train as a manual instructor in Dublin. In the meantime, as well as the theory of building and craft work I would have to study English, Irish and maths. I would need a good grounding in these subjects as I had left the national school when I was fourteen. Since then my secondary education had been taken over by the editor of a daily newspaper.

I wasn't long working with my father when the *Irish Press* came out. It was a bright paper with news on the front page instead of advertisements. Newsboys, the first we had seen in town, were on the streets with it on fair and market days. Later during the economic war which raged between Ireland and England and which was brought about by de Valera's withholding of the land annuities, the English put an embargo on our cattle and small farmers had their backs to the wall. Animals were brought to the fair so often that they knew their way in and out of town. In the middle of the Fair Field a newsboy said to a dejected farmer standing by a cow he had failed to sell, '*Press*, Sir!'

'Be off,' the farmer replied. 'We have presses at home and nothing in 'em!'

But still the bulk of the people stood behind de Valera in his fight with the British. On his second or third election victory I marched with those same farmers to the village. Each man had a two-pronged hay fork on which was impaled a sod of turf steeped in paraffin oil. At the outskirts of the village the sods were set on fire and we marched down the street in a torchlight procession, stopping and jeering outside the houses of those we knew didn't vote for de Valera. An older man in the company, who had fought against the Tans and the Free Staters, carried a shotgun. Under the light he dismantled the firearm and gave me the stock to conceal inside my coat in case the guards would spot it. But the guards, drawn from a pro-treaty background, kept well out of sight this night. Later on when we had left the barracks behind us, the old IRA man reassembled his gun and discharged both barrels in the direction of the residence of a well-known Cosgraveite. The band played more loudly, smothering the report.

A large bonfire was lit by the ball alley which, with the torchbearers ranged about it, made a memorable scene in the surrounding darkness. There were speeches and tributes to the tall gaunt man with the foreign name who stood against the might of the Empire. Amid the wild cheers and cries of 'Up Dev!' a poor travelling woman, the worse for drink, threw her black shawl on the bonfire. It spread out in the air before landing, then for a moment the fire was blotted out. Soon the flames came through the shawl and a shower of sparks went up. Hannie, for that was the woman's name, pulled out her combs so that her long grey hair fell down over her face, older than the Hag of Beara's. With her arms raised as if in supplication to some strange god she danced around the fire as the Millstreet fife and drum band struck up another tune.

The blood coursed warmly through our veins. There were shouts of 'Up the Republic!' and 'Smash partition!' Stones were thrown into the fire and sent up sparks. The band marched off and Hannie's ancient feet grew weary of the dance. As the music died in the distance the hilarity subsided. Gradually the sods of turf on tops of the pikes burned out and so did the fire. As the light faded from the faces of the crowd anyone who had the price of a pint went with the old IRA man to John Dan's public house. There he demonstrated again, as he had done many times before, the correct way to dislodge a horse policeman, and told how with an old cannon mounted on a railway wagon he and his comrades captured Rathmore RIC barracks. He called for a glass of whiskey for Hannie. The artist deserved her fee. She sang a verse of 'When Sandy Heard the Rifle Fire', but tomorrow without her shawl she would feel the cold, and the small farmers would feel the pinch of the economic war.

Whenever we worked in town or passed through it, I spent a precious penny on the *Irish Press*. At night I read it from front to back. The sports pages, the book page on Saturdays and the daily contributions of Roddy the Rover which had characters like the garda called Sergeant Gasta MacCliste. There was a section devoted to the Irish language and it galled me that I could not read it as well as I could the English. I was embarrassed by the fact that as a young Irishman my own language was almost a closed book to me. I went back to my old teacher at the national school one night a week to study Irish for the examination. Micheál Ó Riada asked me to come to his house another night to study maths. He gave me some tips on how to write an English composition and helped me with grammar.

All this extra interest outside my work, going to the tech two nights a week, a night studying English and maths and a night at Irish helped to heal the wound caused by parting from my sweetheart Jude. But she remained forever in my mind and in the mornings when I met the postboy I saw him as a link between us. I always expected him to have a letter from her but one never came. I hadn't much time for dancing but I did go to the local house dance on Sunday nights. But the dancers were drifting away. A new dancehall had been built in Barraduv village, a concrete affair with a corrugated iron roof and a boarded floor. The dancers seemed to glory at the effect their dancing feet had on the timber. It sounded like a drum and was a change from the stone-flagged floors of the country kitchens. Visitors from the town introduced old time waltzing. It took some time before I had the courage to venture out in that. When I did we waltzed to the strains of 'Oft in the Stilly Night' and the sound of our feet was quieter than the pounding we gave the floor when out in a set dance. The hall of laughter and music was directly across the road from the church and was the subject of many a sermon by Fr Browne.

'The house of God,' he thundered, 'is on one side of the road and the house of Satan at the other!'

A mature spinster from out the Bower claimed as gospel truth that while dancing with a stranger in the house of Satan she looked down and saw a cloven hoof and his hands, she said, were burning hot. The dancehalls were licensed by an Act of the Oireachtas and that notice was prominently displayed above the door. The halls in time sprung up everywhere, putting an end to the house dances which the clergy themselves had been trying to do for years. Many is the time the parish priest and his curate raided the houses where Sunday night dances were held. And even though scouts were posted outside to watch for the beam of the headlights those headlights were turned off at a distance from the house and the raiding party was down on top of the dancers before they knew where they were. One night when the curate stood in the front door the back door wasn't wide enough to take the outflow of dancers into the dung-stained yard in front of the cowhouse. The women, fearful of being recognised by the priest, in an effort to retrieve their coats and shawls from the room got caught in the narrow door. The last lady was so dazed after leaving the light that she ran straight into the parish priest who was coming in the back way. To save himself from falling in the dirty yard and ruining his new top coat he had bought in Hilliard's cheap sale, he put his arms around the young woman and she, struggling to free herself said, 'Bad luck to you! Isn't it hard up you are for your hoult and the priest coming in the front door!'

One young man, our famous full-forward in the football team, remained oblivious to all this. He was courting in a dark corner under the stairs. He never felt a bit until the curate shone the flashlamp on him. He got such a fright it was said that he never scored after!

I never heard of a dancehall being raided by the clergy, but the priest in our neighbouring parish succeeded in per-suading the dancehall proprietors in his jurisdiction, as you might say, to close their premises during the hours of darkness. Béalnadeega hall, the nearest one to us until Barraduv hall was built, opened only on Sunday afternoons. We flocked there and danced until it was time for the farmers' sons and daughters to go home for the evening milking of the cows. As well as the economic war, de Valera had another thorn in his side in the shape of the Blueshirts. These followers of General Eoin O'Duffy arrived in force at Béalnadeega hall one Sunday. They were dressed in their military type shirts and were ac-companied by their women, the blue blouses as we called them. Young men of the new IRA and members of Dev's political party resented this intrusion into what they held to be a Re-publican stronghold. They jostled the blueshirts and the blue blouses while dancing. One provocative shoulder borrowed another, tempers frayed, and while you'd be saying Jack Robinson fists started to fly. The blueshirt women screamed as strong daughters of the Republic tore the blouses off their backs. The blue army retreated, leaving behind the torn shreds of their fascist uniform. Despite what seemed like a murderous onslaught, no blood was spilled and no bones broken. The musicians struck up a dance tune called 'The Cat Rambled to the Child's Saucepan' and with order restored, the dancing continued till the cows came home.

On Monday morning it was back to work for me and that night to my lessons in English and maths at Micheál Ó Riada's house in Rock Road. Wednesday night was given over to the study of Irish and on Tuesday and Thursday nights I went to the tech. I worked hard for the next two years until the time came for me to sit for the scholarship examination. I did my best when the day came and finished the practical test on time. I had to make a joint used on a stairs landing known as a tusk tenon, an intricate affair. Time went by slowly until at last the results came out. I was over the moon. I had got through the test and passed the interview in Dublin as well.

September was now approaching when I would be going from the valley where I grew up. My father was sorry to lose me when I could be of most help to him. But the third son in the family, Laurence, was working at the trade and showing a real talent for the job. The second son, my brother Tim, who was always better than me at school, was in a seminary in Cork and going on to be a missionary priest.

The night before I was due to leave for Dublin I went around to all the neighbours' houses. In each house I sat by the fire and everyone's attention was on me; a kind of curiosity as I was the one going away. We talked about the little incidents, that for us loomed large, incidents that had happened in the district in the twenty odd years of my life. Then it was a hearty shake hands and a good wish for my success. Next morning my mother and father went with me in the pony and trap. I had a new travel bag, a valise my mother called it. The last time my father had driven me to the railway station was when my brother and I were going on the school outing to Rossbeigh. From the platform where we now stood I had seen many young men and women leave for America and I recalled the tearful partings. From here Jude went out of my life. But now as the train from Tralee reversed into the platform I put mournful thoughts aside and got into high spirits, thinking of the new life that lay ahead. No need for fond farewells, my mother said laughingly. I would be home on holidays for Christmas. My father fell silent and, noticing him, I fell silent too as the reversing train blotted out my last look at the tower of the friars' chapel. The guard's green flag was waving as we warmly shook hands. I stood by the carriage window of the moving train until my parents turned to go. I watched them walk slowly away.

We passed under the Countess Bridge where Nelligan's soldiers blew my countymen to bits. Soon we were in the open valley and I could see houses built by my father and myself. I could see houses where I had danced all night and I could see the river Flesk where Jude and I crossed the stepping stones. Things to remember in my old age, and fresh in the mind's eye forever would be that half-ring of hills like a ground row on the stage where my youth was acted out. Nearing Millstreet I put my head out the window and looked westwards towards home. In the distance I could see the twin mountains, *An Dá Chích Danann*, the Olympus of Ireland. And as the train sped on, the glorious breasts of the goddess Dana gradually sank out of my view.

SEA SHANTIES, SHAKESPEARE AND POITÍN

☙

'Little paint and many waters!' the Dutch professor who gave occasional lessons on furniture design advised us when he wanted a transparent colour to wash over a pencil drawing. Mr Romein was a big man with large hands, yet with a few deft strokes of the brush he coloured in a sideboard or a Chesterfield suite in a jiffy. His English was as colourful as the paints he used, but he had a good sense of humour and smiled with us when he made a language blunder. One day as he came in and found us in a merry mood in the classroom I saw him cry.

'How can you laugh, gentlemen,' he said, 'when my country was invaded by Germany this morning!'

We calmed him down and said we were sorry. To see this huge man so distressed had a sobering effect on us. His tears brought me back to the time when as small children we dived under the table at night when we heard the Tan lorries approaching. I could visualise the German tanks thundering over the Dutch border and people who yesterday were free now looking for some place to hide. I was twelve months in Dublin and the Second World War was raging. The windows of the College of Art, where we were housed, had had dark blue shades recently fitted and these were drawn when darkness fell, so that no light filtered through to the sky to tempt the Nazi warplanes to release their deadly cargo – as they did later on the city's North Strand.

There were twenty of us, trainee woodwork teachers on a course in the National College of Art which was situated between Leinster House and the National Library. Military stood sentry by the Dáil, and on our way to and from class we often paused to watch the changing of the guard. In the college two large rooms had been set aside for our training course. One was the workshop where the sound of saws, planes and hammering often disturbed the quiet of the place. The other room was the drawing office where we learned draughtsmanship. The personage in charge of us was J. J. O'Connor. A large man too with a pockmarked face and a bulbous nose, he was bald with a straggling wisp which never remained plastered across his head, and stood up like an off-centre cockscomb.

He was wall-eyed, with a short upper lip from which sprung a bristly moustache. In class he was a strict disciplinarian and had a tongue so caustic it would nearly take the paint off the door. On a bad day when his temper got out of hand he hissed like a rattlesnake and could get much venom into a word like 'lout'. But on a good day his face lost its bulldog appearance and became soft and almost comic as he reminisced about the characters he knew in the trade in his native Cork. It was there J. J. and his assistant, Nicky Hartnett, started their working lives as carpenters, and fine craftsmen they were. J. J. had good stories about his apprenticeship and told of the man who when making a lavatory seat from a plain board marked the hole by drawing a line around his hard hat. He then auger-holed it, cut it out with a lock saw, and rounded it off nicely with a spokeshave.

J. J. read widely and often talked about Frank O'Connor and Sean O'Faolain, whom he said he knew. Like Mícheál Ó Riada, my teacher in Killarney, he talked to us about the theatre and was stone mad on Shakespeare. When a backward student mutilated a job of work, J. J., taking the damaged exercise, would intone:

> O, pardon me thou bleeding piece of earth,
> That I am meek and gentle with these butchers.
> Thou art the ruins of the noblest man
> That ever lived in the tide of times ...

and standing back from the bench, and in the best tradition of a Fr O'Flynn loft player, he would continue Mark Anthony's speech, and when he came to view the wounds on Caesar's body:

> Which like dumb mouths do ope their ruby lips
> To beg the voice and utterance of my tongue.
> A curse shall light upon the limbs of men;

162

Domestic fury and fierce civil strife
Shall cumber all the parts of Italy ...

he would raise his voice to such a terrifying climax that passing professors would open the door and look in to see if all was well.

One day he made a collection and put in some money himself. I was dispatched down to Fred Hanna's to get twenty-one copies of *The Merchant of Venice*, which cost sixpence each and were in the Penguin series. Woodworking came to a halt and in the midst of wood-shavings, sawdust and chips we settled down to read the *Merchant*. I remember reading the part of the elder Gobbo, while two refined Corkmen were cast as Portia and Nerissa. Portia describing one of her suitors says: '... he doth nothing, but talk about his horse, he can shoe him himself. I am much afeared, my lady, his mother played false with a smith.'

The reader made a bad fist of the speech. What he read was 'I am much afeared me mother played false with a smith.'

'Judging from the way you are stuttering over the text I don't doubt but she played false with a forge full of smiths!' J. J. said.

When the mood moved him, whatever work we were engaged in, J. J. got us to read Shakespeare. He fancied himself as an actor and often, as one of the lads used to say, he gave us a 'blaist' of Falstaff. Of course reciting Shakespeare was a useful exercise for young men who would yet have to stand before a class. To improve the voice he also got us to sing. In the storeroom where our stock of timber was kept he installed a piano; we paid the rent. One of the students was a good pianist and once a week J. J. herded us in there to sing sea shanties. He sang shantyman himself in as deep and salty a voice as ever came from a man of the sea. We joined in the chorus.

J. J.:	*King Louis was the King of France*
	Before the Revolution.
Students:	*Away! Haul away! Haul away, Joe!*
J. J.:	*King Louis had his head cut off,*
	Which spoiled his constitution!
Students:	*Away! Haul away! Haul away, Joe!*

Each student in his turn became shantyman and we sang such songs as 'Blow the Man Down', 'In Amsterdam There Lived a Maid', 'Johnny Come Down to High-lo' and 'What Shall We Do with the Drunken Sailor', which had the chorus of:

Put him in the long boat till he's sober,
Ear-ly in the morning.

Out of the classroom J. J. dropped his stern attitude and one night a student met him in a pub in the company of a professor from St Patrick's Training College in Drumcondra. The professor was a fellow Corkman and they both came back to our digs. They were well in their cups and sang 'The Banks' and a snatch of:

The stench at Patrick's Bridge is wicked,
How does Fr Mathew stick it?
Here's up 'em all, says the boys of Fair Hill!

J. J. played the cello. He gave us a short recital once in the storeroom after a sea shanty session. His assistant Nicky Hartnett played on a violin he had made himself. With the sound of music and song one day and hammering and sawing the next, we livened up the quiet atmosphere of the College of Art.

When the Free State government made Irish obligatory for technical school teachers, J. J. was sent to the Ballingeary Gaeltacht in west Cork to learn the language. A teacher accustomed to standing in front of a class finds it difficult to sit in one. The recitation of the Irish tenses bored J. J. and at the break he took his cello to a neighbouring meadow, and with his back to a haycock played a lugubrious tune much to the amusement of the cattle in the next field. Gradually they stopped their grazing and in ones and twos drifted towards the fence, where they stood enjoying the music to the accompaniment of much tail-wagging.

J. J. claimed that the Irish he learned on these visits stood him in good stead afterwards. A man called Lang came from Austria to teach woodcarving at the College of Art. He and J.

J. became firm friends. Lang used to take part in the famous passion play at Oberammergau, which was performed periodically by the villagers in thanksgiving for being saved from the black plague of 1633. I think he played the role of Christ. He invited J. J. to Austria one year and J. J. was never done telling us about it. Because J. J. spoke English, the local people took him to be British, which offended him very much, and when he was asked to sing at a party, to put some sort of seal on his identity he decided he'd sing in Irish. But he knew no song in the language, so what he did was to put together all the phrases he had learned in Ballingeary and sing them to the air of 'An Droimeann Donn Dílis':

Tá an cat ar an urlár.
Tá sé fliuch, fan go fóill ...

(The cat is on the floor. It is wet, wait a while ...)

'An Droimeann Donn Dílis' is a haunting air and, being a good singer, J. J. brought down the house. The trouble was when he was asked to repeat the song he had difficulty in getting the Irish phrases in the same sequence.

We trainee teachers serving our new apprenticeship didn't mix very much with the art students of the college, but we did go to their professors for special subjects. The Dutchman, Mr Romein, was one and we also went to Mr Golden who taught freehand and object drawing. I remember for our first lesson he arranged a number of two-and-a-half-foot cubes in a certain order in the middle of the floor and added his overcoat, soft hat and walking cane. Bit by bit we got over our initial tinkering and learned to use quick confident strokes to complete the picture. To be able to sketch freely on blackboard or on paper is an important asset for a craft teacher.

A man came in to teach us Irish and another to take us for maths, but the person we looked forward to most was an instructor from Bolton Street Technical School, who had been a cabinetmaker in James Hicks' famous workshop in Pembroke Street. I have never forgotten the thrill of watching this man, Tom Mitchell was his name, make a mahogany drawer for a writing bureau. The precision with which he cut and fitted the dovetails was worthy of a watchmaker, the eye, brain and skilled fingers working in unison. He talked as he plied the dovetail saw, and related that James Hicks once had a commission to fashion a doll's house for the King of Sweden's daughter. When making the miniature furniture for the interior Hicks flattened a packing needle and sharpened it to cut the tiny dovetails for the drawers of the dressing table.

J. J.' knew Hicks very well and, one time when the old man was ill, he went to see him only to find the patient sitting up in bed, a piece of mahogany between his knees, while with a spokeshave he fashioned a cabriole leg. The shavings curled from the spokeshave and spilled from the quilt on to the floor. In the midst of this highly inflammable material Hicks chain-smoked, the cigarette always in his mouth, and when he threw the spent butt into the grate the nicotine from constant smoking had turned the centre of his moustache to amber. J. J. had the same reverence for a craftsman as the Pope would have for a saint, and he took great pleasure in telling us that examples of Hicks's work were in the National Museum.

Because of his arresting appearance J. J. didn't escape the eye of the artist, and Seán O'Sullivan painted his portrait as J. J. posed in a *súgán* armchair he had designed and made himself. The picture used to hang in the Crawford School of Art in Cork, and very impressive he looked, warts and all. Remembering the conversations he had with the artist as he sat for his portrait, J. J. told us that Seán O'Sullivan was one day walking through Stephen's Green. He was carrying a portable easel and a drawing pad. Suddenly he saw a scene he wished to capture. He hastily set up the easel, put on the drawing pad, and in a fury of creativity his hat blew off and sat upturned at his feet. As his pencil flew over the paper he was too engrossed to retrieve the hat. A gentleman in spats and morning dress paused and, seeing the upturned hat like a begging bowl, said, 'You ought to be ashamed of yourself! An able-bodied man like you should be working!'

J. J. claimed that Dublin was awash with philistines, and so as to rescue us from that sad state he constantly guided our reading and sent us to good films and to the theatre. He said he didn't want us to be the intellectual inferiors of BAs and BComms in our after-years of teaching in vocational schools. He made us aware of what was going on in the visual arts, and we had a private viewing of the Royal Hibernian Academy exhibition which was held annually in the college. He shepherded us upstairs to the exhibition hall before varnishing day. Having had a training in draughtsmanship and the application of colour, we had a fair appreciation of the pictures. We were often the first to see the paintings that Seán Keating and Maurice McGonigal brought out of Connemara.

To sharpen our wits J. J. encouraged debate, and warned us against wilting alone and going to seed on a diet of fried bread in a dull digs. My lodgings were in Adelaide Road, and with me were two students from Cork, one from Kerry and two from the west of Ireland. Willie Gannon, a Dublin student, left his parents' house in the suburbs and joined us. The Adelaide Road address had once been the residence of Dr Douglas Hyde and sometimes circulars in his name sat on the hall table. The rooms were huge. There were three single beds in my room, and it was still large enough for a table in the centre where the two sharing with me and myself could study. Around it we learned to play a hand of bridge. The landlady, Mrs Harrison, had over a dozen lodgers under her care. They were all students except for one civil servant who occupied a single room at the top of the building. He came out on the landing every morning and shouted down the well of the stairs to the maid in the kitchen, 'Annie, I'll have tea, lightly browned toast and a boiled egg, please!'

As a digs it would have measured up to J. J.'s ideal of what a student's lodgings should be. After we got to know the young men from the university, arguments often raged into the small hours, and those of us from rural parts had our horizons broadened in matters of sex, socialism and almost every aspect of human activity. At night in the sitting-room when it came to us trainee teachers versus the university students, Willie Gannon was our star turn. He had read widely and knew something about everything. One medic admitted that Gannon's knowledge of medicine would get him through the first-year paper on the subject. He rattled off the parts of the body with the fluency of an Order of Malta first-aid man. At the slightest hint of indelicacy in Gannon's enumeration the two female students who made up our company betook themselves to bed. Later when voices were raised in the heat of debate, Ma Harrison would knock at the door and politely ask if we intended keeping everybody awake.

We affectionately called her 'Ma' but not to her face. She was like a mother to us and the only time she lost her temper was when some lout threw his empty cigarette packet into the lavatory bowl and blocked the system. We had a chronic medical student – he must have been thirty – and when he and his family went broke, it was said that Ma paid his fees and kept him gratis in the hope that he would pay her back when he qualified. He was still there when we left two years later. We thought that her love for him was a little more than motherly – she was still a young woman – because he spent much of his time in the family sections of the digs.

Mrs Harrison had a ramshackle country house in Shanganagh and any six who volunteered were welcome to spend the weekend there. When she knew who was going she bundled their bedclothes and night attire into the back seat of her old saloon car. One Saturday when I was walking down Merrion Square to get the Bray bus, Ma flew past with one leg of my pyjamas dangling out the side window. Because of the shortage of staff at Shanganagh we all helped in the kitchen under the direction of the senior medic who was always there. Once he accompanied us to the pub and, despite our country curiosity in such matters, he revealed nothing of his family background.

The open spaces around the house, the trees and the Wicklow Mountains to the south reminded me of home. With the busy routine at the college and the liveliness of the company in Adelaide Road, it was only now that I reflected on the life in Kerry which I had left so recently. I longed for the peace and even tenor of that time when life seemed to take its tempo from the slow gait of the cow chewing her cud as she walked home to be milked. I had the image too of the stonemason unhurriedly going to the heap of rubble, selecting a stone, eyeing it and dressing it, almost caressing it, with the hammer, before he placed it on the wall where it would sit in memory of him long after he had taken his rest in Killaha churchyard. That leisurely rhythm changed only when the sluggish stream grew to a torrent in a thunderstorm, or in the dance house on Sunday night when the music accelerated into the mad swing of the hornpipe. Then with a pang of regret I realised that that was all in the past – and a good job too maybe. Still, as I sleepily turned in my bed in Shanganagh and sagged into the foetal posture of slumber, I longed again for the times that were gone. I missed the company of the people I knew then, I missed the certainty of everything, I missed my family, and above all I missed my father and mother. At twenty-three I was too old for tears, but they weren't far away as I escaped into the land of nod.

There I was happy again on my way to school or working as a young apprentice in my father's workshop. Different aspects of my youthful past occupied my sleeping hours: the rounds on the pattern day, or walking in the inch by the *glaishe* with my love Jude on a Sunday evening fair. In time, back in Adelaide Road, my new lifestyle took over. When I slept, I stood in my dreams as a shantyman in the storeroom singing 'Johnny Come Down to High-lo' or 'Oh, You New York Girls, Can't You Dance the Polka?'

Of the twenty young men on our course all had started their working lives as carpenters or cabinetmakers. The skill in using tools they had acquired over five or six years at the bench was indispensable to their work as manual instructors. Practical experience in the handling of sharp tools was essential when it came to teaching young boys how to use these implements. Some of the men on the course had had a secondary education, but others like myself had left school at fourteen and depended on night classes at the tech to get to a standard sufficient to pass the scholarship examination. Those with a post-primary education liked to lord it over us, displaying their knowledge of Latin and Greek and quoting widely from Milton and Eoghan Ruadh Ó Súilleabháin. But we who left school early were longer at the bench and that training was what mattered in the job ahead.

As well as the subjects of Woodwork, Drawing and Maths,

we were expected to have a good knowledge of Irish. To improve that knowledge, at the end of our first year, we were sent for two months to the Gaeltacht of Carraroe in Galway. Two or three students stayed in each house and with our basic Irish, very basic in some cases, we managed to carry on the essential conversation of making our needs known. The local people had years of experience in dealing with the *lá breás*, as learners of the language were called. The phrase *lá breá* (fine day) was as much Irish as beginners could muster when they met a native speaker on the road. The family, as was expected of them, spoke only Irish to their visitors and went to a lot of trouble explaining words and phrases.

Two pounds ten shillings was our weekly scholarship allowance in Dublin, which was reduced to two pounds in Carraroe. The Department of Education believed it was cheaper to live in the country. A guinea went for our board and lodgings and the rest was ours to spend. The woman of the house washed our shirts, socks and underwear. Most young men smoked and a few of us drank the occasional pint, which if I remember cost eight old pence. We managed, and were able to afford to go on the odd outing.

One Sunday we went by hooker to the Aran Islands, Inis Mór to be exact. The hooker, a fishing vessel, was often used to bring turf to the islands. It was my first time in a boat as big as this, and it took a while before I got my sailor legs. We docked at Kilronan and set out on the long walk to Dún Aengus but were driven back by the rain. We took shelter in a public house, where most of the day was spent. A storm blew up and we thought we'd have to spend the night on the island. But the men in charge of the boat, having spent the day drinking, knew no fear and decided to set out for the mainland.

We were nervous enough going on board and those who enjoyed the trip standing on the deck coming over now crowded into the hold. There wasn't room for everyone and I and many more remained on deck. It was plain sailing until we got out of the shelter of the island, then the sea rose mountainous high. The ship bounced on the brine like a cork, and when it was carried high on a mounting wave we could see a great valley of water below. We held on to anything we could grasp

170

while the waves washed across the deck. As the ship swayed, Barbara McDonagh, a young teacher from the college, stood with her back to the mast, her arms enfolding it behind her. As she sang her dark hair streamed in the storm. The inland women screamed in the hold and huddled together as they prayed to God to bring them safely home. Barbara's summer dress clung to the outline of her body as each successive wave washed over her. She was one with the mast as if sculpted, like a mascot on the prow of a viking longboat. Water spilled into the neck of my open shirt and ran down my body and into my shoes.

The skipper, showing his drink, shouted and argued with the men at the tiller, disputing which way the ship should go. In the gathering gloom there was a mighty shout. 'Na carrig-reacha! Na carrigreacha!' ('The rocks!'). The ship swerved and we could make out the sharp ridge of rock now visible, now covered by the surging sea. The wreck of the Hesperus came to mind, 'impaled on the horns of an angry bull!' Soon we saw the dark mass of land at both sides which meant we were in the bay leading to the pier. Gradually the water calmed and the frightened people emerged from the hold as we docked safely in the little harbour of Calladh Thaidhg. Those of us who had stayed on deck were drowned wet. The clothes stuck to our bodies as we walked the distance to our lodgings. My wardrobe was not very extensive but I was lucky enough to have a change of trousers, a dry shirt and a pullover. The sea air whetted our appetites and we were ravenous for our supper. Afterwards we set out for the Sunday night céilí in the college. With the help of an Irish dancing teacher we were already able to make a fair fist of 'The Walls of Limerick', 'The Siege of Ennis' and 'The Haymaker's Jig'. The dance steps came easy to me as I had plenty of practice at set dancing at home in Kerry.

Local girls as well as visitors came to the céilí, and Barbara, she of the mast, advised us to dance with the local girls. We'd be killing two birds with the same stone, she claimed – improving our dancing and perfecting our Irish. I asked Barbara what I should say to my partner if I felt like seeing her home. She told me. After a few dances I met up with a young lady who was warm, friendly and attractive. When 'The Siege of Ennis' was over and the 'Soldier's Song' played, marking the end of the night, I summoned up enough courage to ask my partner, '*Bhuil tú a' dul ann?*' (Literally, 'Are you going there?') She drew herself up to her full height and said with what I thought was more than a modicum of disdain, '*Bhí mé ann cheana!*' ('I was there already!'), and flounced off.

It happened one time that we organised a céilí in the house where we stayed. The local people danced the Connemara set, where at the end of a figure all the dancers grasped each other around the waist and went into a wild spin, chasing the mad, galloping music until, exhausted, they came to a halt. In the pause after the dance a man came from the shadows, and with his eyes closed sang in the old way. His neighbours listened intently, their eyes fixed on the fire, the dresser, or on some object like the lamp, as the rise and fall of his voice searched out the nooks and crannies of the room. The soft words cloth-ed in sweet melody flowed from the singer's mouth to a hum-ming accompaniment through his nose. It was lonely, eerie and enchanting. It was the cry of a young lover poisoned by a meal prepared by his sweetheart. The song was a conversation between him and his mother:

Cad a bhí agat dod dhinnéar a bhuachaillín Ó?
Sicín go raibh nimh ann a mhaithirín Ó,
Ó cóirigh mo leapaidh, tá mé breoite go leor.

What had you for your dinner my own darling boy?
A poisonous chicken. Oh, dress my bed soon,
I've a pain in my heart and I want to lie down.

An elderly man was called upon to dance. It was easy to see that as a performer he was held in high esteem.

'What way will I give it to you?' was the accordion player's tentative question in Irish.

'Give it to me now,' the dancer said, 'according to the way you think I'll want it!'

He took his place on the flagstone in front of the fire fac-ing the crowd. He waited with the toe of his right shoe resting on the floor. When the music struck up he sprang into action.

Well, sprang is the wrong word, because unlike the stepdancers of my native place, his feet were hardly ever raised more than a few inches above the flag. He made an intricate movement with his feet using heel and toe and dancing out to fill the floor space available to him. Now and again he gave an involuntary little hop which brought a reaction from the crowd.

In one of these departures from the routine of the dance there was a commotion in the room off the kitchen. As voices were raised and as people turned in their direction, the dancer came to a halt and the music trailed away. In time we found out the reason for the disturbance. It seemed that visitors had brought a bottle of illicit spirits into the house. The abuse of poitín had been so bad in that district that the clergy encouraged families to have their houses consecrated to the Sacred Heart, at which ceremony a vow was made that poitín would never enter the homestead.

The woman of the house was devastated that the family should have broken its vow to the Redeemer. She cried openly, her lament having many echoes of the *sean nós* song we had heard a short time before. When the people responsible for bringing in the drink had been ejected, neighbours explained to her that the pledge had not been broken by a member of her family but by strangers over whom she had no control. She calmed down and after a while the céilí was resumed, but the spirit had gone out of the night and the family was glad when the affair was over.

Poitín-making, despite the efforts of the police to bring the illicit distillers to justice, was widespread in Connemara. Church and state were opposed to it and when the mission came every five years the Redemptorist priests preached on the evils of poitín. Fr Conneely in the course of one of of his sermons asked the sergeant – a dark, swarthy Kerryman with a pair of enormous eyebrows that would nearly fence cows out of cabbage – to sit outside the altar-rails. The priest praised the sergeant's efforts to quell the evil practice, and likened his work to a crusade. And indicating the sergeant he said, '*Breathnaigí air, nach naomh é!*' ('Look at him, isn't he a saint!') Two old ladies in the congregation did as the priest bade them. Then one said to the other, '*Ní fheadar mé. Tá cuma a' diabhail*

173

air!' ('I doubt it. He looks like the devil!').

Fr Conneely was a thundering great preacher, a native speaker who could reduce his congregation to tears or fill their hearts with terror. He pleaded with the poitín-makers to bring their stills to the chapel yard. At first there was no response, but then a man giving in to the pleadings of his wife came in the darkness and placed his still by the chapel wall. Egged on by this headline and promises of glory in heaven or everlasting torture in the flames of hell, a few more stills arrived, until by the end of the week there was a great mound of corkscrew pipes in the chapel yard. Sunday night was the closing night of the mission. With lighted candles the faithful renounced the devil and all his works and pomps. Fr Conneely led them out into the yard. The great heap of metal had been drenched with petrol. With a prayer he threw his lighting candle into the heap. There was a sudden blaze that reached as high as the eaves and was reflected in the church windows, giving them the quality of stained glass. The corkscrew pipes glowed red in the blaze and from the scum of alcohol secreted in the tubes a black pall of smoke with a blue-purplish flame at the centre rose to the sky. It was a dramatic moment. As the people gazed at the psychedelic design in the midst of the smoke, the priest, his arms upraised, shouted, '*Breathnaigí, a phobail Dé! Tá an diabhal ag eirí as!*' ('Behold, brethren! The devil is rising from it!')

174

A Change of Name and a Job

We left Carraroe on a bright September morning. It was 1939 and coming through Galway city we heard that Hitler's army had invaded Poland. Having learned about Pádraic Ó Conaire, the writer, in the Irish classes in Carraroe, we set out to see his statue. We found him in Eyre Square sitting with his hat on in the attitude of a *seanchaí* telling a story. I thought it a pity the sculptor hadn't depicted his *asal beag dubh* (small black donkey) standing beside him. Pádraic was happy looking, forever sitting there, and the war wouldn't worry him. Nor did it worry us. We went and drank a few pints to kill the time before the train left. The crowd of us almost filled the small pub, and much to the amusement of the local clients we sang the songs we had learned in Carraroe. '*Maístir bád mór ag dhul ród na Gaillimhe*' ('Skipper of the big boat on the road to Galway') and many others like '*Bíonn caipín bán ar amadán, 's púicín ar mo ghrá*' ('A fool wears a white cap and there's a mask on my lover's face').

It took some time for the signs of war to appear in Dublin but the dark blue shades I mentioned earlier were fitted to the windows of the College of Art. Wide cowls were put over the streetlamps to keep the light on the roadway and out of the sky. It would be a while yet before food and clothes rationing was introduced. One more year was all we had to go before we qualified. That year we worked hard. We cut down on the number of times we went dancing to the Teachers' Club in Parnell Square or to Barry's Hotel. No more fly-by-night relationships with young civil servants in their first year up from the country.

The extra attention we gave to our work paid off and everybody got through the final exams. Some weeks before that testing time an advertisement for a vacancy for the post of

175

woodwork teacher in Kerry appeared in the papers. I applied for it and I was advised by Paddy Mawe, a Corkman, that as county Kerry had two Gaeltachts I should make my application in Irish. This I did and got the post. I found out later that the head man in the Kerry Vocational Committee hadn't a word of that tongue. He used to wait until an Irish teacher called to the office to translate any correspondence in the old language. He, the chief executive oficer, wrote back to me in English to say that I had been appointed, but when he came to my name Éamon Ó Ceallaigh he half translated it to Éamon Kelly. I was so happy to get the job that I let things rest so and the name Edmund which I had received in baptism became a part of my past life and my new name Éamon Kelly was emblazoned in the records of the Kerry Vocational Committee and in the Department of Education in Dublin.

My first job in Kerry was that of an itinerant teacher, giving a course of six weeks in woodwork in a village and then moving on. Posters with my new name writ large appeared in shop windows and in advertisements in local papers, so that everyone called me Éamon when they got over the 'Mr' stage. In time I got used to it. Ardfert outside Tralee was my first stop, and I stayed in the lodgings of Mrs O'Leary. The hall where the classes were to be held was a short distance away beside the ruins of the ancient cathedral. My first night was given over to the enrolment of the students and their introduction to the woodworking implements. I talked about what was involved in the course and gave a lesson in planing, sawing and chiselling. I found a place to crack a few jokes with them as there is nothing like laughter to break the barrier between strangers.

The next day I put a drawing of the first lesson on the blackboard, sharpened the tools and had the wood ready on which each student was to work. It being my first time going before a class, I was determined that everything should be right and of course very anxious to make a good impression. The class was at 7.30. I left the caretaker to open the hall and I made my entrance at the exact time to find the men, young and not so young, all assembled. I walked up the aisle between the workbenches with a 'good-night' left and right and went straight to the blackboard to begin the preliminary talk.

I was a little nervous as I removed my overcoat. I put it on a hook and when I turned to survey the class with all the assurance I could muster, I was greeted with a burst of laughter. My confidence received something of a dent. I couldn't imagine the cause of their hilarity until I noticed a ladies' silk stocking draped over my shoulder. I managed a weak smile and then a fit of laughter to cover my confusion. Slowly I removed the stocking and, as I folded it, I painted for the class a picture of Mrs O'Leary's kitchen, with a shoulder-high clothesline between the fire and the front door. I demonstrated to them how easy it was for the stocking to fall on my jacket as I went to put on my overcoat.

'A good story!' one man said, while Brendan Scannell NT took the harm out of it by saying, 'It could happen a bishop'. I rocked on the rails but in an instant steadied myself and, with confidence restored, my first teaching lesson was a great success. There was a feeling of a bond of friendship being forged between teacher and pupils by the sharing of an unexpected experience.

Our first two weeks were spent acquiring the skill of using the carpenters' tools, and the last four in making an article of furniture of the student's own choice. Small tables were made, a *súgán* chair, presses and a meat safe. One student made, as a surprise for a devout wife, a miniature portico of a Grecian temple with a tympanum supported by four Doric pillars to hold a statue of the Sacred Heart. It had steps going up and a platform in front to hold the small red lamp. In complete contrast another student made a harrow to break up the earth of a ploughed field. The class consisted mostly of farmers and farmers' sons, with a few shopkeepers from the village and the schoolteacher, Brendan Scannell. Rich pastures and fertile tillage acres abound in North Kerry and Brendan reminded me of a verse from a poem in Irish which ran:

> Tá an talamh comh maith san
> As so go Cillmhaoile,
> Go bhfásfadh garsún ann
> Comh fada le stípil!

(The land is that good
From here to Killmoyley
That a young lad would grow there
As tall as a steeple!)

I had a junior class for boys of fourteen-plus each day, Monday
to Friday at four o'clock. I taught them freehand and mech-
anical drawing and they learned to do woodwork exercises
from drawings they had prepared beforehand. By the end of
the course each student was able to take home a small medicine chest, a cutlery tray, book-ends, a toy wheelbarrow or a
wall bracket to hold a Sacred Heart lamp. I had the weekends
off and after a few pay cheques I bought myself a bicycle and
cycled all the way to Killarney to see my parents. There was
great excitement at home now. At Christmas time my brother
Tim would be ordained a priest in Moyne Park, Tuam, county
Galway. He had spent the years of his novitiate at Gerdingen-
Bree in Belgium, and he would have been ordained in the
summer, but he contracted tuberculosis and had to spend six
months in a sanatorium. That he survived this dreadful disease
pleased us all, but my mother more than anybody.

The ruined cathedral was near my lodgings in Ardfert and
for anyone interested in craftwork there was much to be seen
in the cut-stone window jambs and arches. The west doorway
was Hiberno-Romanesque and in its heyday had beautiful
carvings, but because they had been executed in red porous
sandstone the weather of the centuries had softened and almost obliterated their definition. Around the ruin, and even
within the walls, there was a graveyard with a few enormous
tombs.

As they worked in class the men talked about a landlord's
tomb being desecrated by vandals in search of valuables buried
with the dead. In olden times, they told me, a round tower
stood sentinel beside the ruined church. Because soil had been
drawn away from one side of it, the tower was blown down the
night of the big wind, and tradition has it that it was so well
built it remained on the ground in one piece like a fallen tree
trunk. They said the round tower was broken up and the
stones used to build the curved entrance into Crosbie's, the

landlord's place. I picked up a lot of lore in Ardfert, made many friends and downed a few pints in Flaherty's public house.

D. W. Quinlan, the chief executive officer, paid me a surprise visit in class one night and said that my next course would be in Causeway. 'You'll be in the courthouse, Mr Kelly,' he said. I had visions of an imposing Grecian-type building with Ionic or at least Doric columns supporting a sculpture-filled tympanum. When I got there I found that the courthouse was a large room in a house, a one-time parlour off the grocery shop. The space was bare except for a few chairs, a rostrum and posts set into the floor with a rail on three sides to form a witness stand. With the help of the men who brought my equipment in the lorry, I had the furniture moved out to make room for the workbenches and the tool racks. With the blackboard in place I was ready for business that evening.

The course proved as popular as it had been in Ardfert. I had a full complement of boys over fourteen in the afternoon, and every bench was occupied by adults for the night class. The room wasn't very well lit and when we got down to serious work, one student brought with him a small pocket torch, which he shone on the dovetail markings with his left hand while he sawed with his right. There were many faces at the street window at night looking in. I also had an audience at the other side where there was a cow byre. Contented cows chewed the cud as their large eyes caught the light from the paraffin lamps.

When we got over the early training stage and each man was working on the project he would bring home to show his wife or his mother, many students sang as they worked, such was their enjoyment and total immersion in their new pursuit. The snatch of a love song or a whistled jig sounded pleasant over the sound of hammer and saw or the banshee wail of a pine board under a sharp plane.

I lodged in the same house and my bedroom was directly over the courthouse. As always, I found it difficult to sleep the first night in a strange bed. I was twisting and turning, dropping off and dreaming and waking up with a start. I read for a while, and before quenching the light, instead of counting sheep I counted the religious objects in the bedroom. I had never seen so many in one place except maybe in a huckster's stall at a mission. There were pictures of all shapes and sizes, statues large and small, a crucifix, a rosary, a scapular on a nail and a little glass cylinder with liquid around the figure of the Virgin. When I shook it before going to bed it filled with snow.

One picture had just the crown of thorns with globules of blood dripping from it. In the normal course of events I probably wouldn't have given the image a second thought, but now longing for elusive sleep I found the crown of thorns without the Sacred Head discomfiting. A terrifying instrument of torture, and all that blood! Blood too on the Sacred Heart, both the statue and the picture, and on the crucifix where the lance had speared His side and the nails had pierced His hands and feet. There were plenty of religious objects in my own home and in the houses in which I worked with my father, but not until tonight did something which I had always accepted become disturbing. The eyes of the pictures became riveted on me, or so it seemed, and to avoid their accusing stare I put out the light.

In time I fell into a troubled sleep. I have a knack of recalling bad dreams and that night I dreamt of ancient druids slaughtering animals and offering them as sacrifice on a stone altar that looked like a Mass rock. The celebrant, as gaunt as El Greco's St Francis, raised his eyes to heaven while the congregation in biblical-type dress beat their breasts and lifted their arms in prayerful supplication. Ferocious acolytes pounced on me and dragged me body and bones towards the altar as my clothes were stripped from my back. A knife was poised over my throat and as it came down I bawled like hell and when I woke I was sitting bolt upright in the bed with sweat streaming down my face.

There was a loud knock on the door. It was the landlady. 'It's half past ten,' she said. 'Are you all right?' 'I am,' I replied. 'I'll be down in a minute.' She must have heard me shout. Goodness knows what she thought of me. I lay on for a little while thinking of the strange dream I had, and looking at the religious objects which I assumed caused it. I thought I heard murmuring in the room below me punctuated by an occasional cough. I dressed quickly and went downstairs. I looked into

180

my classroom of the night before to find the district court in session.

Some of the workbenches were stacked at one end of the room and some were put out in the street. The closed tool racks by the wall acted as seating for the small crowd. A half-dozen uniformed gardai stood in front of the rostrum where the district justice sat. One guard was giving evidence of catching people in a public house after hours. He claimed that when he entered the premises the bar was clear, but he found a number of men in the back yard drinking. He went upstairs to the bedroom and when he opened a wardrobe a man who had been leaning against the door fell out. In the bed two more men were sleeping. He looked closely and their eyelids fluttered a bit. They had the blankets pulled up to their chins and their feet were sticking out at the bottom.

'Did they not feel the cold?' the justice said, enjoying the scene.

'How could they, your worship,' the guard said, 'when they had their boots on!'

The landlady tapped me on the shoulder. 'Your break-fast'll be going cold,' she said.

I followed her into the kitchen and never found out how the men and the publican fared in the justice's judgement. A fine is all he could put on the men but the publican could end up with an endorsement on his licence.

A Spell in Ballybunion

I spent a whole year on the road and visited all the villages of north and mid-Kerry. Often when the lorry with the equipment drew up in front of the parochial hall, youngsters would gather around chanting, 'The play actors are here again!' But when they saw the blackboard being unloaded they changed their tune to 'Come on away, lads, 'tis only an ol' school he's starting!'

In Ballybunion my classes were held in the large dining-room of Beasley's lodging house opposite the garda barracks. It was springtime and the holidaymakers hadn't yet come. Wielders of the knife and fork in that dining-room in the high season never enjoyed themselves as much as did the wielders of the chisel and saw in my class.

It is heart-warming the avidity with which men take to carpentry. There is a longing in all of us to make, to create. The way they admired the revealed grain when a sawn board was planed. They would take it up and smell the lath that came from the jack plane and fondly crush the shavings in their hands. The countryside around Ballybunion is bare of trees and the students fell in love with the different timbers they met with in the course of their work. When we talked of sycamore, ash, elm or oak, I showed them illustrations of the trees from which the wood came, or drew the oak leaf and acorn on the board, a small seedling carrying in its womb a baby king.

We remembered talk of ancient times when trees grew almost down to the seashore and Ireland was a great woodland, where squirrels could travel from Antrim to Cork without touching the ground. I cited the poet's lament for the fallen forest. '*Cad a dhéanfaimíd feasta gan adhmad/Tá deireadh na gcoillte ar lár*' ('What'll we do now without timber/The last of the forests is down').

I made many friends in Ballybunion. I almost became an alcoholic in that place. When the class was over at night I went with Jackie Beasley on a pub crawl, as much for the craic, as they say now, as for the booze. After-hours drinking was part and parcel of the nightlife there, a legacy of the high season when the Irish seaside resorts were packed with roisterers. Holidaymakers were confined to Ireland because of the war. Publicans were anxious to keep the beer flowing. In one establishment if we dawdled over our pints the proprietress would admonish us with a 'Gentlemen, your conversation is interfering with your drinking!' The pubs were often raided after closing time but the guards didn't always prosecute. I remember one night Jackie Beasley and myself standing inside the window curtains until the sergeant had cleared the bar. When he left we emerged, called for another drink and resumed the argument which had been so rudely interrupted.

It was in Ballybunion I met Bill Kearney, an army sergeant in charge of training the Local Defence Force. We both stayed in Beasley's when he visited the place. His night-time course of training ended about the same time as my class, and he, Jackie Beasley and I often had a few scoops. Bill was a fine singer, his favourite being 'Santa Lucia', and you could hear a pin drop when he sang. When I followed with a Tan war ballad the assembled clientèle shouted, 'Will you shut up, or do you want to bring the guards down on top of us!' Bill enrolled me in the LDF, but because of my night classes I was excused from training. I had a feeling he put me down as being connected with intelligence! I did attend one church parade. I borrowed a uniform and fell in – the very last man in the line. After a while the drill sergeant bellowed, 'Will the second last man in the rank change step.' The order was for me, but how was I to know that a latecomer had fallen in behind me.

Jackie Beasley and I were detailed to stand guard one night over the LDF arms depot in a room in the barracks. We had only to cross the road. We took up duty at midnight and Jackie gave me a rifle. I wasn't too sure which end the bullet came out, but I sat there, the rifle between my knees, the muzzle pointing towards the ceiling. A civic guard slept in the room directly overhead. Before retiring he looked in on us, regarding me with a little suspicion and noting the direction in which the gun was pointing. He closed the door and a short time afterwards we heard movement upstairs. It turned out that he was taking the sandbags from the windows and putting them under his bed.

Ted Houlihan was the local officer commanding the LDF and his strategy in case of an invasion during the hours of darkness was to ring the church bell to call out the troops. When we were all in our cups one night in Gabrielle's hostelry, the son of a prominent citizen and a comrade in arms thought it would be a damn fine lark to ring the bell just to see how many would come out. Though our reasoning powers were sadly undermined by alcohol, Bill Kearney, Jackie Beasley and I persuaded him against taking such an action, which would bring us into conflict with the law and the Church. He seemed to agree but later that night as I was going to bed the bell rang out loud and clear. He had done it! I expected an immediate commotion with voices raised in the street. No. There was a deadly silence. Then the sound of doors opening in the house. Steps on the stairs and on the road outside. The fumes of the alcohol were rising to my brain. I had drunk too much that night. I became drowsy and lay back in the bed. Bacchus rolled me into the arms of Morpheus, who lolled me into a deep sleep where a tolling bell tore cracks in the silken fabric of the sky. Bright streaks ran down to earth as if made by fork lightning.

I was in the open space outside Riverview with Jackie Beasley and Bill Kearney. We were getting our rifles out of the armoury in the guards' barracks. Everyone was talking. Rumour had legs. Ballybunion was full of Germans. Hitler was seen drinking with Lord Haw Haw in JD's and Bridie skimming the froth off the pint with a white-handled knife. We'd meet the enemy, we bragged. We'd meet him on the beach. As we marched down the street, window sashes were thrown up and women in their chemises cheered us on to battle. Pat Crowley's band left the ballroom and played 'The Minstrel Boy', leading us on to the Castle Green.

Standing behind the ruined walls of O'Connor's stronghold we peered nervously in the direction of the strand. Blessed hour! What was this? In the moonlight we saw that there was nothing to battle against but the waves of the incoming tide. We cheered and let off a volley into the night air. From the sober element came a call for silence. A sound was heard high up in the sky. We listened, but it wasn't the Luftwaffe, just the *gabhairín rua* – the jacksnipe – crying for his lost lover. The band struck up a wartime ditty, and I woke up singing:

> *Bless 'em all! Bless 'em all!*
> *The long and the short and the tall.*
> *Bless de Valera and Seán McEntee,*
> *They gave us brown bread*
> *And a half ounce of tea ...*

In the morning the talk of the town was the ringing of the church bell. The clergy at Mass likened it to a sacrilege, and the Local Defence people were livid at bringing part-time soldiers on to the street. If real danger ever came, what would be the use of ringing the church bell? In time the name of the campanologist got out. We in the know never opened our beaks. He himself must have boasted in his cups. But when it transpired that he was the son of a rich burgher closely affiliated to the powers that be, no word was said.

When I had courses in the nearby villages of Asdee and Lisselton I still lodged in Beasley's of Ballybunion. I was there in June when the holiday season was getting under way. Pat Crowley and his band were in residence and the strains of their music came from the ballroom a little after eight in the evenings. I perfected the old-time waltzing I had learned in the Teachers' Club in Dublin. Before each dance in the ballroom, soap flakes were scattered generously on the floor, which made us glide over it like sailing ships on a still ocean. One night I saw a svelte, lissom creature, divine and beautiful, and I summoned up enough courage to ask her to dance. She accepted my invitation and when the music struck up she moved with grace and rhythm. With my heart in my mouth and schooling myself to take care of my accent I was about to utter some pleasantry when she said, 'Isn't de floor awful skeety!' My Killarney patois wasn't entirely out of place that night.

Local people of the old school never wet themselves in

the brine except maybe to take a hot sea bath. Ted Houlihan who lived down on the brink of the tide told me over a pint one night in Mrs Scanlan's that he was only once in the sea and that was twenty-five miles away in Ballyheigue. On fine Sundays in summer, Ballybunion beaches were black with people. I was a poor swimmer but had enough courage to dash into the huge incoming waves where the legs were taken from under me and I was carried inshore and deposited on the sand. It was an exhilarating experience being rolled about in the water as the waves broke and crashed on the shore with the sound of thunder.

Ballybunion had two bathing places, the men's strand and the women's strand, and largely the sexes kept to these places from force of habit going back to the days of Victorian prudery. But the way of youth is to turn its back on the customs of the old, and now there was an outcry by the powers that be against mixed bathing. Brendan Behan on hearing of it said the next thing to be banned would be mixed dancing. The parish priest, a man of his time, paraded the beaches after last Mass on Sundays, and people on seeing him approach repaired to their respective places. One Sunday he accosted a middle-aged man and a young girl coming in from the sea. He admonished them for bathing together. The gentleman told him that he had been teaching his daughter to swim.

In Beasley's lodging house they talked of the day when a busload of visitors arrived from somewhere inland. Ignorant of local custom they trooped gaily down to the men's strand. The ladies, when they didn't see any other ladies about, drifted towards the women's beach. All but one; she sat among the men and was preparing to divest and take to the water when the PP arrived. Politely he requested her to move away. Very politely she told him that the man sitting next to her was her husband and that her place was at his side. The rules would have to be observed, she was told. Getting a little bolder, she said wasn't it a queer pass when husband and wife couldn't enjoy a day at the seaside together. Her husband, who was embarrassed at the attention the scene was attracting, collected up their belongings and said, 'Come on away, Mary, if he finds out we're sleeping together we'll be excommunicated!'

After Ballybunion and Asdee my travels brought me to Tarbert and Moyvane, where I had to call on the parish priest Fr Danny O'Sullivan to get permission to use the parochial hall. The housekeeper showed me into the parlour, and in an adjoining room there were people talking. This lasted for some time and when they left Fr O'Sullivan came into the parlour with a soda siphon hanging from one hand and a whiskey decanter in the other. When he saw me he swung them both behind his back, making a loud clatter. Thinking he had some damage done he turned them around quickly, examined them and put them on the sideboard.

I explained my business. The hall would be all right. He had let it to the Vocational Committee previously. I thanked him and was about to go when he eyed me up and down and said abruptly, 'Where are you from?' My parents, I told him, were born in the parish of Rathmore, but I was brought up near Killarney. That interested him. Rathmore was his native village, where his people owned the well known public house, the Southern Star. I told him a little more about my family. The men were carpenters, I said. He remembered my grandfather, Brian Kelly, and often saw him lift his elbow in the Southern Star.

'A little dram,' he continued indicating the siphon and the decanter, 'helps to drive a bargain' and he mentioned that his visitors were arranging for a wedding, part of which proceedings was deciding the amount of the marriage offering. The offering is calculated on so much per cow, he said, and fixing me with a doleful eye he sighed, 'Farmers have many cows when they want a new creamery but very few when it's money for a marriage offering!' Then he said with a smile, 'A little drop of Robin Redbreast softens their hearts and I made a good bargain.'

Having explained away the presence of the siphon and the decanter he asked another abrupt question: 'Were you in Ballybunion?' I told him I had spent a few months there. 'Well,' he said, 'the good man who was parish priest in Ballybunion when I was a young curate told me that he was once discussing a marriage offering with a farmer. Five pounds is all he could get out of the man, so he went to the sideboard and produced the bottle. After a glass of whiskey the farmer went up two pounds ten shillings. He filled the glass again and the man went up to ten pounds! The next day the parish priest was walking in the village and there was a publican standing at his door. "Tell me, John," the priest said, "how much are you getting for your whiskey?" "Ten pence a glass, Father!" the publican said. "Ah John, you are a poor salesman!" the priest laughed. "I got two pounds ten a glass for mine last night.'"

There was one last question. 'Have you brothers?'

'I have,' I told him. 'Four, and one of them will be ordained at Christmas time.'

He reached for the decanter and poured a stiff one for himself and a modicum for me.

In the Mail Car to Waterville

❧

Around this time a letter came from the CEO to say that my post as itinerant teacher would end at the summer holidays, and in September I would take up duty as manual instructor at the Vocational School in Waterville. The only way of getting from my home to Waterville was by mail car, in which there was room for maybe a half dozen passengers. It passed by our place at the unearthly hour of 6.30 a.m. and I would be in Waterville before the school opened on the first morning in September 1941. I was the only passenger for ages. We drove by the Robber's Den, where the Black Rogue of Glenflesk had a school for thieves. Some of these emigrated and their descendants, for all we know, could have been implicated in the St Valentine's Day Massacre in Clarke Street, Chicago. Through the Roughty Valley we went, by Kilgarvan and Kenmare and then on to Sneem where John Millington Synge's blue bull came from.

The mail car was filling up now and there wasn't really room for a party of three young girls at Lohar. The driver asked me if I'd take one of them on my knee. I did, and this made for a little hilarity among the others. She was a frolicsome damsel, very shy at first on having to sit on a strange man's lap. I was a little embarrassed myself at all the attention we were getting from the passengers, the driver saying what a fine match we'd make. 'Hold on to him, girl, maybe he has money!' She had to hold on to me because of the bumping of the car on the rough road – an altogether refreshing experience. Ballinskelligs Bay came into view and I asked her if she had ever been to the Skelligs Rock.

'She might have to go there yet,' one of her friends remarked, 'if she isn't married before Shrove Tuesday!'

The young lady was echoing the stories of her father's fireside. The monks on Skelligs Rock monastery didn't recognise the Gregorian calendar of 1582 and Shrove Tuesday fell eleven days later. People who weren't wed by the Shrove Tuesday deadline before Lent on the mainland, could go to Skelligs and be spliced on the Rock. At home when I was a youngster if people eligible for marriage hadn't taken the plunge before Lent, their names, often matched with the most unlikely candidates, were penned in rhyme and pushed under the doors of the laggards on Shrove Tuesday night. The document was called the 'Skelligs List'.

We were in Waterville and the young lady, giving me a playful 'dunt' of her elbow, eased herself and her belongings off my lap and alighted. I went to the lodging house I had booked. Muiris Mac Gearailt, the teacher of Irish and Maths, was staying there. Having made the acquaintance of mine host and his wife, I had a cup of tea with Muiris, then together we went to the school to meet the other two teachers, P. B. Breathnach, the headmaster, who taught Rural Science and English, and Maura Thompson, the Domestic Economy instructress. Maura knew J. J. O'Connor, my old teacher in the College of Art, which gave us something to talk about. I was told that the headmaster was a stickler for discipline. He had a goodly amount of white in a flashing eye which made him stern of demeanour, but he turned out to be witty and had a wicked sense of humour.

He had to work hard to keep up the numbers in a catchment area which was but a narrow inhabited corridor between sea and mountains on the road between Sneem and Cahirciveen. He and the school became known beyond the village because of a scheme he initiated to bring boarders from beyond cycling distance. The students lodged in the village from Monday to Friday and had a system of bringing their week's food supplies, which the landladies cooked for them. Making second-level technical education available to those who would otherwise have been deprived of it brought P. B. Breathnach to the notice of the press, and Keys Von Hoek, the popular columnist, visited us and devoted his entire article to the school in the much reduced wartime *Irish Independent*.

My first class on the morning I arrived was freehand drawing with the senior Domestic Science ladies. I made off my classroom and put out the drawing boards, pencils and drawing pins. As the young women were taking their places I went to the blackboard with a 'Dia's Muire dhíbh ar maidin' ('Good morning, everyone') to write a few notes on the rules of perspective. I turned around to face the class and there in the second row was the young woman who had been sitting on my lap in the mail car.

I must have lit up like benediction for a titter went through the class. Shades of my first evening in Ardfert; but they had been men. I suddenly realised that with these young women I was in entirely different territory. I had to think of something quick. I drew a duck, comical but recognisable, on the board. There is something mildly ridiculous about a duck, and I told them that when God had finished making the animals at the creation of the world the angels asked Him to make a duck. 'For goodness sake,' they said to Him, 'give us a laugh!'

'He made a duck ... well a pair, and when they waddled away' – I did a waddle – 'the angels went into kinks of laughter,' and so did the class. I drew a rooster as if in conversation with the duck and said, 'A cock made fun of a duck and mocked him about his droll waddle and the way he is always nodding his head. "I'm as good as you any day," the duck said, "and to prove it I challenge you to a race!" "Game ball," says the cock. "But I'll have to pick the place," says the duck. "All right," says the cock, "but I'll have to pick the time." "Come on!" says the duck. "I'll race you across the river!" "OK," says the cock, "when there's ice on it!"'

The two stories worked. The students' laughter and mine restored my confidence. I was in control. I could look them in the eye, even the mail car lady, and the class went ahead in great style. I gradually got into the swing of teaching in a school as opposed to my itinerant courses, and once I had my syllabus made out for each class I grew to enjoy the work. There was a war and there were shortages but we never saw a hungry day. The newspapers, which came in late in the afternoon, were down to seven pages. In the digs a crackling radio brought stories of the fighting, and sometimes the voice of Lord Haw-Haw predicting a victory for Germany. But except for the occasional drone of planes high up in the skies, the hostilities could have been a thousand miles away.

English children were being evacuated from their homes in the big cities and some of them found their way to Ireland. In the first-year boys we had Tony Swatton from London. Tony's sallow complexion and his being in long trousers before his time marked him out from the other boys. The Irish in the language class was too advanced for a beginner. To keep him occupied he joined the first year for woodwork in my room. He had a particular flair for drawing and loved copying pictures or designs which I gave him. In the *Capuchin Annual* of the day, Richard King had illustrated Patrick Pearse's poem, 'Mise Éire', surmounted with the stylised face of the beautiful Mother Ireland, and a design to enclose the words of the poem. Tony copied it to perfection, his lettering faultless, but where the name Padraig Mac Piarais was at the end, he penned 'Tony Swatton'. Years afterwards I was in Edinburgh and in a city art gallery. About to enter one room I noticed a group of navy ratings around a picture. They were being lectured on the finer points of the painting by able seaman Tony Swatton. I retraced my steps, glad he didn't see me but delighted to know that Tony hadn't lost his interest in art.

Practical subjects have such an appeal for students at a Vocational School that they rush into the room at the start of the class, and when the bell goes at the end they are lazy to leave. The girls loved the kitchen classroom where cookery and sewing were taught, the boys the garden where they learned about growing things and how to keep bees. They were happy too in my classroom where they worked at the bench and learned to make things with their hands. Their academic subjects were not neglected. They studied Irish, English, Maths and Civics. They did a play with Muiris Mac Gearailt for the end of term, when those who could dance danced and the musical ones sang or played the fiddle.

As well as the huge garden there was a playing field attached to the school where the boys played football. Muiris Mac Gearailt was the games master and, Waterville being on the edge of the Ballinskelligs Gaeltacht, Irish was the language of the pitch. A field away the cable station was still tapping

out its messages to distant shores. The 'graphers', as the opera-
tors were called, were principally English, and on a fine day
they donned their whites and played cricket. In the still air
you could hear cries of 'Howzat?' and 'Well held, sir!' mingling
with shouts of, '*Buail é!*' ('Kick it!') and '*Téir isteach fé!*' ('Go
in under it!').

Across the road from where Muiris and I lodged was the
Butler Arms Hotel. On nights when we didn't have a class or
at weekends we sometimes adjourned there for a drink. There
was a lower bar, as it was called, opening on to the main street,
where the natives were served. We went there and talked in
Irish to the few who still knew the language, but as often as
not we entered by the gate through the gravelled front to the
upper bar within the hotel proper. The surroundings here were
more luxurious and the drinks priced accordingly. Even in
winter there were guests; some permanent residents included
retired colonels and ex-British military men enjoying the
quiet of neutral Ireland. In the daytime they fished in Lough
Currane. I often saw them set out suitably dressed for the occasion, their gillies walking ten paces ahead carrying the fishing tackle. This apartheid was strictly observed until they sat
in the boat. There was a tiled space by the reception desk
where, in the evenings, the anglers laid out their catch in neat
rows: fish with their mouths open and eyes glazed for all to see
and admire. If they were left there too long the place smelled
like Billingsgate.

In the winter of 1943 there was an occurrence in nearby
Lohar which set the whole parish agog. A man was found dead
in his cowhouse. He had passed out under a cow's head and
the animal was thought to have gored him. But there was
something about the wound that made the police suspicious.
An autopsy showed that the victim had been shot at close
range. The dead man, O'Sullivan, nicknamed *Cá Bhfuil Sé*,
was married but childless and his wife's nephew, O'Shea, lived
in the house. Relations were said not to be so good between
the two men. Suspicion fell on the nephew and on a friend of
his called Brennan. The guards in their investigations found it
very difficult to get information about the murder out of the
local people. They talked Irish among themselves to confuse

their questioners. It was common knowledge that one man heard a shot at a certain time on the night of the crime. The police were wise to this but left it until the end to interrogate him. When the individual was finally asked the question, 'And at what exact time did you hear the shot?' He looked at his questioner in blank amazement and said, 'Fhot shat!'

They were a tight-lipped community. A local shopkeeper, lowering the lid over his left eye, told me that a man working in a field overlooking the Cow and Calf Islands, near the Bull Rock, was asked by a guard, 'What islands are they?' 'God, I don't know,' the man said, gazing at them in astonishment, 'they weren't there at all this morning!'

During the investigations detectives and high-ranking gardai stayed in the Butler Arms Hotel. They were so long there and the food was so good that their cheeks filled out and they had to loosen their belts. On seeing these well-fed sleuths trooping out after breakfast one morning, one ex-colonel exclaimed to a friend, 'Swelling wisably!' Finally the nephew, O'Shea, was charged with the murder, as was his friend Brennan. At O'Shea's trial in Dublin a local witness giving evidence was asked by the judge to speak up. While the witness was still in the box, the lawyers put their heads together to discuss a point of law, whereupon the witness shouted, 'Speak up, I can't hear ye!'

The prosecution failed to make a case and O'Shea was acquitted. Brennan was subsequently charged with the same murder but was also found not guilty. The murder weapon was never found but as was remarked at the time, 'Who in his right mind would go looking for a gun in a church?'

How did the victim come by the name *Cá Bhfuil Sé*? It seems O'Sullivan was a blow-in from beyond Sneem. Before he left his native place he had, as they put it there, 'taken a girl off her road'. When he went back to a wake some twelve months later someone told the young lady that he was in the crowded kitchen. She rushed about excitedly shouting, '*Cá bhfuil sé? Cá bhfuil sé?*' ('Where is he?').

LISTOWEL

ᶜᵍ⊁

You got your wits sharpened in Listowel, where I went after a few years in Waterville. Vocal dexterity was an absolute necessity to parry the raillery of tavern or highway. It wasn't unknown to hear two men, oblivious of the crowds, taunting each other in high good humour across a busy street. There could be a sting too, if your sparring partner thought of taking you down a peg. I was often told to go back to the RMC. To the assembled populace this might be something Royal, Magnificent and Cornucopian. But no. It simply meant the Remote Mountainy Coomb where I first saw the light of day. The people of the parish of Prior in the diocese of Ardfert and Aghadoe were so knowledgeable that it was held that a week spent there was as good as a year at school. Listowel is like that. A year spent there is as good as three at a university.

It is a place of books and ballads, of drama and dance and walks by the Cows' Lawn and around Gurtinard to clear the head. It is a place where the people take a lively interest in the world and a livelier interest in his wife. Ears are forever cocked for the sound that comes on the breeze, and eyes are always peeled for the unusual happening. It is a place never to fall asleep on your feet or someone will build a nest in that unlistening ear. Listowel people love their town as the poets Aogán and Eoghan Ruadh loved Sliabh Luachra. Bryan MacMahon wrote lovingly about the place and his ballad about the Feale, the river named after a goddess, is a favourite song of singer Garry McMahon. John B. Keane describes the town as 'my native beautiful Listowel, serenaded night and day by the gentle waters of the River Feale; Listowel where life is leisurely and beauty leads the field, where first love never dies and the tall streets hide the gentle lovingness, the heartbreak and the moods, great and small of all the gentle souls of a great and good community' (*Irish Times* interview with Eileen Battersby, 4 April 1996).

It was a lucky day for me the day D. W. Quinlan, CEO, directed my footsteps there to take over the post of manual instructor in the technical school. Had I missed out on Listowel, God only knows into what forsaken rural or urban byway I would have walked. One of the first people I met there was Bryan MacMahon. Bryan had a lending library, and taking out a book I gave my name, Éamon Kelly. 'Come here,' he said, 'didn't I hear that name called out on the wireless the other night?' Well, it so happened that he did. Austin Clarke had a poetry competition on the radio and I had entered a poem describing my work as an itinerant teacher of woodwork. I didn't get a prize, but like the mongrel at the dog show, I was highly commended. That gave Bryan a handle on me.

At this time he was becoming well known as a short story writer, and I can still recall his joy on opening the slightly off-white wartime pages of *The Bell* magazine and seeing in print his prize-winning story, 'The Ring'. 'The Good Dead in the Green Hills' was another story of this time about a rambling house in Gleann a' Phúca where the last storyteller was ensconced as the radio pulled his audience away from him. We often met two doors down from his house in Dan Flavin's bookshop. We sat in Dan's kitchen and heard him recite again for us 'The Sally Ring' by Patrick Kelly. 'The only thing he wrote, blast you!'

> Within the Ring o' Sallies
> I'll build a house o' stone
> A little house and white with lime
> And thatched with sedge o' yestertime
> And live me all alone
> Within the Ring o' Sallies
> Where I was sometime known.

Bryan's consuming interest then was the Listowel Drama Group, over which he presided and whose plays he directed. I had been on stage a few times in Waterville and my happiness knew no bounds when he invited me to join the Drama Group. Our rehearsals were in the scouts' hall in Market Street, where I made the acquaintance of the dapper Timothy 'Fitzmarshal' Cotter, who trod the boards with distinction. John Flaherty was another wonderful actor, as were Brendan Carroll and Bill Kearney whom I had met earlier in Ballybunion. Other talented people were Kevin Donovan, Mary Cronin, Marie Keane-Stack and Vera McElligott.

Our writers in residence were Bryan Michael O'Connor, which was the quill name of Bryan MacMahon, Michael Kennelly and Paddy O'Connor. They gave us material which was our own to tease out and put together on the floor. It was the perfect theatrical activity of writer and actor working hand in hand, and we had remarkable local success with titles like *Fledged and Flown* and *The Cobweb's Glory*, which last I found the confidence to direct myself. Next came Bryan MacMahon's own play *The Bugle in the Blood*. For this production I wore three hats, those of set designer, director and actor. Tim Danaher did the lighting, and empty biscuit tins with hundred-watt bulbs inside were our footlights.

I played the part of the strongman, Circus Jack. I had to wear long sleeves so that my unmuscular arms weren't seen when I lifted a cartwheel to balance it on my chin. My memory holds one scene, kept fresh by recurrence, of this memorable play, in which Bill Kearney played the part of an Indian peddler who lodged in the house. He sat by the range in a darkened kitchen waiting for a chicken to cook. With the red glow of the fire on his sheet-draped figure he swayed a little as he sang, half to himself, a lonely Indian song. The lights in the kitchen had been lowered out of respect for the funeral of a hunger striker which would soon pass outside. Already the car lamps were making long ladders of light in the sky over Treen Hill.

When at last the measured beat of footsteps and the rhythmic purr of slow motor engines were heard in the street, the Indian's song gave way to the pipes playing 'The Flowers of the Forest'. Faintly the soul-stirring music faded in on the left of the stage monitor, rose to a climax and faded out on the right. A light reflection from each passing car lit the set for a while and then the Indian's song was heard again.

Bryan's play had a successful run at the Abbey Theatre.

Along with Sigerson Clifford his name was added to that of George Fitzmaurice as playwrights representing the Kingdom. Bríd Ní Loinsigh, the Kerry actress, played the part of the mother and Jack McGowran sang the Indian song.

I was every day of thirty-five years when I took the part of Christy Mahon in *The Playboy of the Western World*. But I was thin and spare and a Kerry cap – Christy came from there – covered a receding hairline. Characters in the play talked of Christy as 'a small low fellow, dark and dirty, an ugly young streeler with a murderous gob on him!', though in the love scene Pegeen Mike tells Christy that he is 'a fine handsome young fellow with a noble brow!' If nature hadn't supplied some of these attributes I could fake them. Dress might make the man! John Flaherty, a tailor in real life, made a jockey's colourful coat and knee-breeches with suitable headgear for me to wear at the races 'on the sands below'. I strutted the stage in this finery to see if I could ever give the impression of 'a young gaffer who'd capsize the stars!'

The Playboy of the Western World is nowhere without his sidekick, Pegeen Mike. Maura O'Sullivan, new to the company, and who had been described as a breath of fresh air by adjudicator Mícheál Mac Liammóir when we took *The King of Friday's Men* to the Kerry Drama Festival, was cast in the part. From the first reading she was simply glorious and went on to win the best actress award in Limerick. Maura and I threw our whole being into the playing. We gloried in Synge's beautiful language, so in keeping with the rise and fall of the lilting Kerry speech in lines like:

Pegeen: *And it's that kind of a poacher's love you'd make, Christy Mahon, on the sides of Neifin, when the night is down?*

Christy: *It's little you'll think if my love's a poacher's or an earl's itself, when you'll feel my two hands stretched around you, and I squeezing kisses on your puckered lips, till I'd feel a kind of pity for the Lord God is all ages sitting lonesome on His golden chair.*

Pegeen: *That'll be right fun, Christy Mahon, and any girl would walk her heart out before she'd meet a young man was your like for eloquence, or talk at all.*

Christy: *Let you wait, to hear me talking, till we're astray in Erris when Good Friday's by, drinking a sup from a well, and mak-*

*ing mighty kisses with our wetted mouths, or gaming in a gap
of sunshine, with yourself stretched back to your necklace in
the flowers of the earth.*
Pegeen: *I'd be nice so, is it?*

Synge's words would coax the birds from the trees, and Pegeen's speeches wove a mesh of love to capture Christy Mahon's heart. Love that was make-believe on the stage became real in every waking hour. Marriage was proposed and with her father's blessing I married Maura in Killarney's tall cathedral. We went to live in a house in the Bridge Road in Listowel, but not for long. *The Playboy* won many awards. It was broadcast from Radio Éireann when radio was a power in the land, and if you walked down Church Street in Listowel that Sunday night Synge's gallous language came floating from every casement. Maura and I were asked to do an audition for the Radio Éireann players. This we did. We were successful and came to live in Dublin.

Before I leave that hallowed ground I must tell of a man I met who made a lasting impression on me. He was Maura's father Mícheál Ó Súilleabháin, a Maths and Irish teacher in St Michael's College. Mícheál came from a background in West Cork similar to my own, a place of rambling houses, endless talk and stories that went back to Conán Maol and the Giolla Deachair. He had grown up on a farm there during the last stages of the transition from spoken Irish to English. Like the Tailor Buckley of Gougane Barra, he knew the names in the old language of every flower, shrub and tree; every prominent rock and stream; every field and lake and the story behind them. *Loch an Dá Bhó Dhéag*, the Twelve-Cow Lake, was associated with *an Ghlas Ghaibhneach*, the celebrated grey cow of mythology. The field where she grazed and slept was forever more fertile. She gave an unending supply of milk for the needy, but the evil Balor stole her and sold her milk for profit. She escaped, and with her twelve daughters jumped into the Twelve-Cow Lake and left a greedy land behind her.

Mícheál carried in his head a now forgotten world. He drew me into this eldorado, where at night-time when stories were told in his father's house, *An Peacach 's an Bás* took the floor. The actor playing the part of Death took the scythe from

199

the hedge outside and entered. The Sinner cowered on the settle, imploring the reaper to leave him for another while in this vale of tears. But Death persisted in his requisition and despite the Sinner's pleas for mercy and those of his neighbours, Death won the argument and took the Sinner into the outer darkness.

That was followed by *An Siota 's a Mháthair* where a patient mother tried to placate a gluttonous lump of a son who had her beggared providing him with food. The actors walked around the kitchen as if they were on a country road. The mother first, saying, '*Téanam ort! Téanam ort! Téanam ort!*' ('Come on! Come on! Come on!'). And he lagging behind like a snail going to Jerusalem, smelling the flowers, listening to the birds singing, picking blackberries and eating crabapples until he was fit to burst. She threatened him that if he didn't control the hunger demon in his belly, when he died he'd roast in hell. But if he ate in moderation and fasted during Lent, he'd go to heaven where he'd live in a splendid house with flower-bedecked fields in front and back, and the air forever filled with music and the swish of angels' wings.

'Wisha, Mother,' he'd say, 'if there's nothing in heaven only angels and music what am I going to fill my belly with?'

On St Bridget's Eve the young men and women of that locality dressed in the most outlandish clothes they could find, the men often in women's attire and the young women maybe in their fathers' Sunday suits. To make recognition more difficult they masked their faces with pieces of old lace curtain and pulled their hats down over their eyes. The evening before, they had sculpted a face on a turnip, with the eyes and the mouth deeply incised and the inside of the turnip scooped out. They put a lighting candle into it. In the dark the light coming through the eyes and the mouth looked eerie. The sculpted head was fixed on a broom handle with a bar across to hold a coat, and with a headscarf and a skirt the effigy of Bridget called an *Brídeóg* was taken from house to house. When the mummers and the musicians came to the storyteller's house the floor was cleared, the music struck up and they danced *Gáirdín na Nóinín* ('The Garden of Daisies'). The *Brídeóg*, not the Christian Bridget who built the church in Kildare, but a priestess of the ancient druids, was held high and money was collected.

In the house that night you had all the rude elements of the theatre. The storyteller provided the comedy and sometimes the tragedy, for he could bring a tear as well as a laugh. All the basic ingredients were there: the music, the dance and the dressing up.

Mícheál is now with all his neighbours in that eldorado in the skies, but the Irish spoken in his native Coomerkane is still to the good in his translation of A. E. W. Mason's novel, *Clementina*.

On the second day of February 1959 all heaven broke loose in Listowel with the production of a new play, *Sive* by John B. Keane. At first people didn't know how to pronounce the word. They weren't sure if it rhymed with 'give' or 'hive'. It was of course the lovely Irish name Sadhbh, of which the diminutive is Saidhbhín, as in the town Cahirciveen. In the play the young schoolgirl, Sive of the title, is being traded off in marriage to an old toothless hill farmer. It is a tale of poverty and greed, of humour and tragedy, and has a show-stopping duo of travelling folk, Pats Bocock and his son Carthalawn – a singing and *bodhrán*-playing Greek chorus.

The play was given a splendid production by Listowel Drama Group, directed by Brendan Carroll and with new people like Nora Relihan and Hilary Neilson. It won all before it at drama festivals and, because it was an all-Ireland winner at Athlone, the group was invited by the Abbey to play for a week at the National Theatre then at the Queen's. Like the plays of Bryan MacMahon, Pauline Maguire and Sigerson Clifford, *Sive* drew crowds as Kingdom residents in the metropolis dipped into their savings and bought tickets to the theatre. If you had lost track of a Kerry relative, the Queen's in Pearse Street was a likely place to meet him that week.

Maura and I, who had come to Dublin seven years before, invited them all to our house one night after the show. Players and crew and friends filled our semi-detached in Coolock to bulging point. There was only one house of lords, and the gentlemen, considerate as ever, left that for the use of the ladies, while they, when the need arose, retired to the back lawn. They brought their conversation with them as they stood in a circle under a watery moon. In the weeks that followed, the wetted grass grew tall, lush and a shade of dark green, so that a little patch of Dublin was forever Listowel – maybe not forever, but for very many moons.

On the Radio

When Maura and I came to Dublin to join the Radio Éireann Repertory Company in July 1952, we first stayed in an upstairs flat at Mountshannon Road in Rialto. The little kitchen where we cooked and dined overlooked the canal, and at that time boats drawn by horses on the tow-path passed by fairly often. Many is the morning, as I watched the lazy gait of the animal and the slow progress of the boat, I listened to Denis Brennan read the 9 a.m. news. It was Radio Éireann's first venture into early morning broadcasting, brought about by a newspaper strike in Dublin. The radio was all right, one Dublin lady said, but you couldn't put it around chips.

The old couple who owned the house hadn't an idea of where Maura and I worked, and when we were in a Sunday night play we rehearsed the script in the flat. Sometimes, carried away by the drama, we raised our voices, often in acrimony. We were once cast as the servant boy and the servant girl in a play, Michaelmas Eve by T. C. Murray. The characters had fallen in love but the servant boy through the scheming of his mother married the daughter of the house, no oil painting. Because of this the servant girl was livid, and when the pair were alone she gave full vent to her fury. Her language, often intemperate, contained threats like: 'I could choke and strangle you!' Hearing that row overhead the old couple were in trepidation, convinced that murder would soon be done under their roof!

Finding them anxiously listening on the stairs when I opened the door one night, I thought I had better explain the situation. I felt that it strained their credulity quite a bit to hear that we were actors on the wireless, and that our raised voices meant that we were practising our lines. Going to the studio that Sunday evening, I left the radio page of the Sunday paper with the play and the time of the broadcast marked on it on the hall table. When they heard the key in the door on our return that night the man and his wife were in the hall to greet us. They brought us into the sitting-room and made coffee. What they couldn't get over was that the voices they were listening to now had been on the radio a short time before. They were thrilled, they said, but I think what pleased them most was that the voices they had heard raised in anger upstairs weren't real after all.

We had two ardent fans while we were in that house. Of course they were sometimes disappointed because we didn't always have as big a part as we had in *Michaelmas Eve*. Sometimes, as in rep work, it was only a walk-on. The man of the house, after he had heard me in a few bit parts, advised me when I was next on the radio to hold my place at the microphone and not let the Dublin lads shoulder me off it!

Radio Éireann at that time occupied the attic of the General Post Office overlooking Henry Street and Moore Street. Through sound-baffled windows you could see the great mounds of oranges and cabbages in the traders' stalls below. Seagulls sat on the window-sills, and by the vigorous movements of their beaks they seemed to be protesting loudly at the content of the material being broadcast. There were two studios, one large and one not so large, with drapes sagging from the rafters and collar braces to improve the sound. Here all our work as actors was done, Sunday night and midweek plays, short stories, reading the linking scripts in music programmes, G. O. Sherrard's gardening account, and *Sports Stadium*. I figured prominently in this last, giving voice to the report from the south. Reading the Dublin report one evening, an actor not fully au fait with GAA clubs called the Faughs 'the Fucks', which made for no mean hilarity in the Green Room and red faces in the balance and control. The balance and control was the large glass box between the two studios, where the sound engineer, the discman and the producer sat to regulate all activities in the studios.

To get to these halls of merriment you entered the building at Henry Street, went up in the lift to the third floor and walked through a long corridor known as the 'Wood of the Whispering' (from a play of that name by M. J. Molloy). The administrative offices opened off each side of this passageway and heads of departments met there to discuss business. They lowered their voices as you approached in case they gave away any secrets. At the end of the corridor a narrow stairs brought you to a sort of lobby leading to the two studios.

In this space there was always a policeman on duty during broadcast hours to guard against IRA infiltration. A monitor brought him the programmes as they went out. Thomas Studley, a leading actor in the Rep, was one night reading a very funny short story. He came out of the studio afterwards to find the guard in contortions of laughter. Beating his thigh in paroxysms of merriment he said to Tom, 'In the Abbey you should be putting it over!' Other guardians of the law took their duties a little more seriously. The newscaster Tom Cox told me that he had started the 8 a.m. bulletin one morning when a young man walked into the studio, sat down and put a revolver on the desk in front of him. In the best traditions of the business, though the words were hopping off the page, Tom carried on and finished the news. Then on enquiry the young man told him he was a detective from the Special Branch sent to prevent the news being taken over by subversives. No standing outside for him. There is a saying in Irish, 'If a goat goes to church, the altar is his destination!'

Around this time, or maybe later, a very posh announcer came to Radio Éireann. The imperial timbre of his voice evoked echoes of the ascendancy calling from their carriages to the tradesmen in country towns. He was so grand that he put the cream of BBC newscasters in the shade. People protested. It was claimed that it wasn't our own radio station any more, that it wasn't redolent of its surroundings. Eventually the announcer left and became the presenter of a dry-cleaning-sponsored programme. The radio director, Maurice Gorham, was asked why the man had been relieved of his post, to which he replied, 'We always send our best things to Imco!'

Rumour had it that a newsreader went to confession in the Pro-Cathedral. She had been partying the night before. She knelt in the box, and because the penitent at the other side had such a long story to tell, she fell asleep. Suddenly the shutter came across with a clatter. She woke up and said, 'Radio Éireann. Here is the news!'

A newsreader in Irish placed his hat on the desk beside

the microphone as he read and when he announced the death of a prominent citizen he raised his hat as he said, 'May God have mercy on his soul!'

Around 1954 we actors left our old haunts in the attic, came down the stairs, through the 'Wood of the Whispering' corridor, and turned the corner into new quarters facing O'Connell Street. The people who paid 3d to go to the top of Nelson's Pillar could look in the windows at us going merrily down the passageway to the new studios. There were two, one large and one middle-sized, and several smaller cubicles for reading short stories, chat shows and disc jockey programmes. In contrast to the attic, everything was new except the floor-boards, which creaked through the carpet and the sound was picked up by the large kidney-shaped microphones.

We got to know where the mighty creaks were and avoided them. Sometimes in the run-through of a play one would forget, and producer Séamus Breathnach would shout from his glass box, 'Merciful hour! Will you get off that creaking board!' When actors in high spirits indulged in a little horseplay at rehearsals, Séamus once gave vent to an expression which has gone into radio folklore: 'Will ye stop the acting and get on with the bloody play!'

Mícheál Ó hAodha was head of drama and variety in the station and also produced plays. He was the first to use the new studios. And it was from them he directed the poetic plays of Pádraic Fallon. *The Vision of Mac Conglinne*, which had a Munster king with a hunger demon in his belly, I remember best. Sides of beef, legs of lamb and roasted piglets were washed down his gullet with churns of buttermilk. His queen, as odd as bedamned, swallowed a fly in a cup of whey and became pregnant. Fallon's plays were an undoubted success, his language matching the outlandish imagery of the folktale.

Mícheál produced a strange play called *The Paddy Pedlar* by M. J. Molloy. It was a one-act, meant for the stage, in which a near-demented man, the Pedlar, carried his dead mother on his shoulders in a sack, bringing her across forbidding land-scapes to find her family burial place. A promise to the dead must be fulfilled. He talked to his mother in the sack and his cry of love for her was soul-searing, as was his simmering hatred for his cruel father who had brought her so much pain. In his voice the Pedlar endured again his mother's suffering as he described how his father 'fisted her down on the mouth!' The part of the Pedlar was beautifully and frighteningly played by Éamon Keane. I was Uaisle, owner of the house where the Pedlar sought shelter on his journey. Uaisle was a step above his station, a man who put his words on edge, mimicking the verbal precision of his betters.

Julia Monks, writing in the *Irish Press* on 22 November 1954, said, 'One of the most remarkable things about the production – apart from the incandescent acting of Messrs Keane and Kelly – was the fact that if ever a play was written for the stage and not for radio this was it ... How Mr Ó hAodha worked the trick of making us see – almost smell – what was going on defeats me. For it was by no means an acting, or "effects" job alone. It was let's say, just magic – ever so slightly off white magic. Whatever happens don't miss the repeat. And turn down the lights and hold on to your seats!'

Radio drama in the days before the goggle-box took the spotlight off it!

There were over twenty actors in the Rep, falling, because of their stage experience, into what I'll call Gate and Abbey traditions. We had our Lady Bracknells and our Queen Gertrudes, our Bessie Burgesses and Widow Quins, our Ophelias and Pegeen Mikes. We had too our Joxer Dalys and our Old Mahons, our Mark Anthonys and Brutuses, our White-Headed Boys and our Playboys of the Western World. We were virtually an All-Ireland side, with actors from the city and from the regions, so that drama of town and country was presented with a deal of authenticity.

Two actresses did their work in Irish and English, Maura O'Sullivan and Neasa Ní Annracháin. Eight actors appeared in plays and features in Irish, but in my opinion by far the most accomplished of us men was Niall Tóibín. Niall was a scholar of the language. He spoke mellifluous Munster Irish, and was equally at home in the other three dialects of Ireland. His mimicry in either language was only delightful. The bilingual actors were the hardest worked in the Rep. Frequently an actor who played the lead in the Sunday night play in English would appear again in the same role in the mid-week play in Irish.

But for pontifical and dogmatic intonation, when God sat on the clouds and spoke in English to the universe, it was in the voice of Joseph O'Dea.

As well as our own producers, outsiders came in. Frank O'Connor came to do a trilogy of his short stories which he had adapted for radio. A resident producer sat with him in the glass box to attend to the technical details. Frank took his eyes off the script and listened to the actors' voices. He noticed that players picked up the pace from each other and tended to sound alike. He got an individual pace from each actor so that their characters were distinguishable to the listener. Because it was his own work the words were never frozen on the page; as new ideas and new ways of saying things struck him, he altered the text, even coming dangerously near broadcasting time. Before Frank came in, the actors had already been cast in their parts by the station. Listening to them speak he saw that some were more suited to other roles. I, who had a walk-on part in *The Luceys*, found myself playing the lead. Other actors had the same experience in the other two plays, *In the Train* and *The Long Road to Ummera*. In this last Pegg Monahan created the part of the old woman living in the city who got her wish to be buried in west Cork.

Denis Johnston came in to produce his own plays and in particular I remember him doing a work of great imagination and humour, *The Old Lady Says No!* Mícheál Mac Liammóir was guest artist in the role of Robert Emmet, a part he had created many years before at the Gate. Though he was older now, Mícheál's voice was still young and my fresh green memory is of the way he used that beautiful voice to create a memorable portrayal of an actor in the part of Emmet, who because of a fall on the stage continues through Dublin in the same role, reliving the days before he met his fate in Thomas Street.

One day at rehearsal Niall Tóibín, with his back to the studio door, was regaling a group of actors with a delectable impersonation of Mícheál. The door opened noiselessly behind him and there stood the great man himself. Unaware of his presence, Niall carried on, and the actors facing Mícheál were glued to the ground fearing an outburst of vexation. Mac Liammóir's face clouded momentarily, then cleared, as he realised, I suppose, that imitation was a form of flattery. He gripped Niall's hand and said, 'Dear boy, you are a very good actor, but don't let me ever hear you do that again!' And with a joyful hum through his nose, which was slightly in the air, Mícheál strode out into the corridor.

Many people came in. We rubbed shoulders with the famous – Bridges Adams, Hilton Edwards. But the most notable was Tyrone Guthrie, a man of international repute. He came to produce *Peer Gynt*, which went out live on two Sunday nights. As in Frank O'Connor's case, the play had already been cast for him, but on hearing the actors' voices he recast it. Cyril Cusack was to play the title role, but as he wanted some days off to finish a film, Guthrie dropped him in favour of Chris Curran. Guthrie didn't like the acoustic in the large studio. He wanted a livelier, crisper sound, and the carpets were taken up. Now the sound of the actors' shod feet was picked up by the microphones so he asked them to remove their footwear. Doing it with our boots off was new to us. Most actors brought in their bedroom slippers the next day.

Sound effects on disc he dispensed with. The actors had to produce them vocally. For camels trotting in the desert we hit our open hands against our pursed lips making a pop-pop sound, which seemed to tickle him immensely. Howling winds were a kind of banshee sound. With bass, baritone, tenor, soprano and contralto voices, the winds high and low had great variation.

For a sinking ship there was a large bath of water in which we sloshed about with our hands to give the effect of men struggling in the brine. Drowning sailors filled their mouths with water and gurgled their way to Davy Jones' locker. Guthrie's ideas were so new, so inspired and came so rapidly that you'd swear the Holy Ghost had descended on him. But he was a rigid disciplinarian. His voice had the hard edge of that of a British officer and aroused in my memory cells echoes of peasants being made to toe the line. He was a stickler for punctuality. At ten o'clock he stood at the studio door and tardy arrivals had to answer for themselves. One morning a principal actor was some minutes behind the time and was asked what had delayed him. He replied that he had had a nosebleed.

'Show me your hankie!' Guthrie demanded. The actor did and the rag was red enough to stop the traffic.

At ten past ten Guthrie saw through the glass Roisín Ní Shé, who provided the harp music, arrive. Putting down the talk-back button, he shouted, 'Mrs Harp, you're late!'

Lionel Day (Lal O'Dea in real life), Arthur O'Sullivan and I were cast as a kind of ancient chorus. If we weren't on the mike dead on cue Guthrie wanted to know what had happened to 'these three old drearies'. He was quite uncomplimentary in his references to the men, and the women too, and had no compunction in using the soldier's word in front of them if things went wrong. But nothing did … on the night. The two shows went out on consecutive Sundays and were rightfully acclaimed.

After the second show we had a party in the studio where we all became very pally. Because of a shortage of containers, Guthrie and I drank out of the same glass, what he called 'sup chum'. I remember him telling us that he had been connected with a radio production of *Journey's End* for the BBC. It was before the days when effects were put on disc and all sounds had to be manufactured in the studio. The producer wanted the tramp of marching men for a few seconds at the opening of the play. Extras were employed to mark time in a gravel rectangle in another studio. The red light went on, they were on air, the men were cued and began to march. At the end of the show the producer went to the other studio and there were the men still marching! He had forgotten to cue them out.

Actors are the worst in the world to do party pieces, but that night Arthur O'Sullivan prevailed upon me to tell a humorous folktale I had heard in Kerry. I don't think it meant a lot to Guthrie but he wasn't dismissive. He pronounced it a prime piece of clowning. Mícheál Ó hAodha was at the party and asked me if I had many more stories like that. I had, and he gave me a spot on Din Joe's *Take the Floor*. Like Guthrie's *Peer Gynt*, it was a success and that was the start of my storytelling career.

THE RAMBLING HOUSE

ᐧᓂᶬ

Din Joe's *Take the Floor* was the only radio programme with dancing. Dancing on the air seemed in no way odd at the time. The rat-a-tat-tat sound of the Rory O'Connor troupe was refreshing, and was achieved by the tapping of well-shod dancing feet on thin wooden laths backed with strips of canvas – a little like an extended roll-top desk cover. The laths moved under the dancers' feet and made an unbelievable clatter lifting off the floor. Rory O'Connor was the foremost dancer of his time and had the doubtful distinction of having danced for Hitler during the 1936 Olympics in Berlin.

One night in 1956 I had a story in *Take the Floor* about the Killarney man who fell into the bottomless Devil's Punch-Bowl and came out in Australia. To which Din Joe added, 'He walked down the road to Melbourne and was just in time to enter for the swimming competition in the Olympics!'

By this time, 1956, electricity on tall ESB poles had marched into the remotest valleys and people were able to dispense with their (only for the news) dry battery sets. On the new plug-in radios *Take the Floor* had a huge following in the country, and every new show brought me a sheaf of stories in the post. Not all of them were suitable for the microphone, but many came up trumps in the retelling.

I became so well established that Mícheál Ó hAodha gave me a programme of my own. It was called *The Rambling House* after the houses I knew in Kerry in which people collected at night for news, stories and entertainment. Donnchadh Ó Céilleachair wrote the script and the occupants of the house were singers Teresa Clifford and Seán Ó Síocháin; Éamon Keane recited poems from *Around the Boree Log* and the ballads of Sigerson Clifford. Maura O'Sullivan and Kevin Flood were the son and daughter in the family, who welcomed and chatted with the performers as they entered, exchanging the news of the day and the happenings of the locality. With them I was the man of the house, the *seanchaí*, sitting in the corner adding gems of wisdom to the general conversation and telling a story when my turn came. Albert Healy provided the music on the accordion. As with *Take the Floor*, we had listeners throughout the land and across the sea in Wales.

Because of our radio popularity we actors were invited to perform at functions in Dublin and elsewhere. Ulick O'Connor introduced me to the Bohemians, a brotherhood who met in Jury's Hotel in Dame Street every Tuesday evening. A condition of one's membership was the ability to sing, make music or otherwise entertain. There I learned to work with a live audience and endeavoured to perfect the art of timing. Éamon Keane was invited to the Donegalmen's Association one night and in the course of his party piece Neil Blaney, the then Minister for Posts and Telegraphs, passed some remark about Radio Éireann at which Éamon took umbrage. One word borrowed another and the upshot of it all was that Éamon was dismissed from the Radio Éireann Players and ordered to go back to the civil service from which he had been seconded.

Éamon refused and went missing. Somebody wrote somewhere that his associates didn't stand up for Éamon. Nothing could be further from the truth. *The Rambling House* was taken off the air as a protest at his treatment. Conor Farrington and I searched Dublin for him and finally found Éamon in An Stad, a Republican lodging house in Frederick Street off Parnell Square. We gave him his weekly cheque, which had lain uncollected in the Green Room.

We advised him that the best thing to do would be to rejoin the civil service and, when the storm blew over, wheels could be set moving within wheels to get him back to the Rep again. He wouldn't hear of it. He was angry at his treatment but he didn't blame Neil Blaney. He thought the decision to sack him was that of some official in the government department showing a little muscle. The next thing we heard was that Éamon had gone to England. He remained there for a while until he came back to Cork to take part in his brother's play *Sharon's Grave*. He worked on the stage for a time and then, as Conor Farrington and I had predicted, he was taken back in the Rep where he remained until he retired.

Without Éamon Keane *The Rambling House* was not revived. Later Mícheál Ó hAodha had the idea of bringing together Seán Ó Riada with his famous orchestra, *Ceoltóirí Chualann*, the singer Seán Ó Sé and myself in a programme called *Fleadh Cheoil an Radio*. The music, singing and storytelling proved a successful combination and it ran for ages. We taped the programmes in the O'Connell hall opposite the Gresham Hotel and if we had some minutes to spare between rehearsal and the time of recording, Seán Ó Riada and I went across to the hotel and had a cup of tea – nothing stronger before a performance. Seán, who gave a new lease of life to Irish music, was one of nature's gentlemen. He was high good company, a keen observer of humanity in all its moods and ridiculous tenses. He had stories he had heard from his mother and in the Coolea Gaeltacht where he lived. I was welcome to use whichever stories of his suited my book, and very welcome they were, for at this stage I was running out of material. And I told him so.

'When hard pressed,' he said to me, 'why don't you do what de Valera does – go to the country!'

I took to the roads and of all the places I halted, Gougane Barra in West Cork was the best. It brought flooding back to mind all that went on in my own district when I was growing up. Dinny Cronin, the proprietor of the hotel of that name, sent out word when I was in residence, and the neighbours arrived at night and sat in the big kitchen behind the bar and in front of a roaring fire. They were, as the man said, taking the legs off one another to tell me stories. Dinny, rising after putting a sod on the fire, would set the ball rolling.

'There were these two women west here in Kerry. One of them was going to town and the other one was coming from town after a heavy night's rain. This was away back in 1922 when the I. R. aye were fighting the I. R. ah and all the bridges were blown down, and people had to ford the river to go to town.

'The woman going to town said to the woman coming from town, "Were you in town, what time is it, what price are eggs, is the flood high?"

'The fleetness of a woman's mind when it is in top gear!

And as quick as lightning the woman coming from town answered, "I was, two o'clock, one and fourpence, up to my arse, girl!'" – at which point Dinny would hit the patched backside of his trousers a most unmerciful wallop.

Dinny claimed that the Free State soldiers were the first to bring bad language to Kerry. 'They were billeted in a certain village not a million miles from where I'm sitting, and a private soldier took a woman's bucket without her permission. He wanted it for drawing water from the well or something. An officer saw what happened and, wanting to keep good relations between the military and the community, ordered the private to return the bucket to the lady and apologise for taking it. The soldier took the bucket back to the woman and said, "Here, Mrs Tuckett, here's your bucket and fuckit I'm sorry I took it!'"

One night as the rain came down in bucketfuls the conversation turned to St Patrick. According to one man, when the saint had converted the Irish they became curious as to how the world would end. St Patrick told them it would go up in a ball of fire. His listeners didn't like one bit the idea of being burned alive, and they wanted to know if the saint could save them from such a catastrophe if the end of the world came tomorrow. (Still the rain came pouring down, which drove one wag to remark that if the end of the world came tomorrow the place'd hardly light! He was called to order and we got back to the narrator.) The holy man pondered the people's question and after some consideration told them he would give them a pledge that God would drown Ireland a year before the end of the world. The people were pleased with that. If they had to go, drowning was a better end than being burned alive! At this point the wag got up to go home and when he opened the door you could hear the rain lashing down on the corrugated iron roof of the cowshed. He poked his head back into the kitchen and said, 'It looks like as if St Patrick is keeping his promise!'

The cottage where the famous Tailor Buckley and his wife Ansty once lived was only a short distance from the hotel, and Dinny had many of the Tailor's stories. According to Dinny, a wealthy farmer put an overcoat making to the Tailor. The farmer after a few days came for a fitting. He liked the way the job was turning out, and as he had the money handy, he paid the Tailor. When the coat was finished the rich farmer didn't come for it. The weeks and the months went by and winter arrived and at last the farmer came for the coat. But there was no coat. The Tailor had given it to a raggedy poor man going over the hill into Kerry on a cold night. 'It struck me,' the Tailor told the farmer, 'that he needed it more than you! Didn't our Lord say to clothe the naked!'

'A man died sitting on a chair,' Dinny said one night, remembering a Tailor story. 'Dammit if rigor mortis didn't set in, and when it came to waking him he couldn't be straightened out on the table, and a sitting corpse could look bloody awful comical. One neighbour thought of a plan. He tied down the corpse's feet under the table and put another rope hidden by the habit around the dead man's chest. A couple of men put a good strain on the two ropes and secured them well. When he was straightened out if he didn't look as fine a corpse as you'd see in a day's walk. As the night wore on people came to the wake. There was plenty to eat and drink there. Too much drink, maybe, for in the middle of the rosary a blackguard got under the table and cut the rope around the dead man's chest.

'The corpse sat up like a shot, saying "Ahhh" as the wind escaped from his stomach. There was a gasp of horror from the mourners and they skidoo-ed out the door the same as if the plague had hit the place!'

Even though the people in the kitchen had often heard the story before, there was a big hand and praise for the storyteller. Listeners often joined in with words of encouragement during the story such as 'Maith thú!' ('Good on you!'). On his uttering a truism they'd say 'Is fíor dhuit!' ('True for you!'). Or telling of some terrible tragedy someone'd say, 'Dia linn go deo!' ('God be with us forever!'). When the storyteller made a very telling point the audience would all chorus, 'Go mba slán an seanchaí!' ('May the storyteller prosper!').

To Dinny I was always the seanchaí, and he'd greet me when I arrived with one of the jingles which used to introduce my own programme on the air:

Lift the latch and walk straight in,
There's no better place for glee.
You are welcome to the Rambling House
To meet the seanchaí!

The first night I came to Gougane Barra he brought my bag
upstairs. There was an occupant already sleeping in the room.
Throwing down my bag, Dinny said, 'That's your hammock
and that's a hoor of an Englishman in the other bed!' To call
me in the morning Dinny threw pebbles from the loose gravel
of the yard at my window and shouted, 'Get up, *seanchaí*!'
Dinny was as famous a character as the Tailor Buckley. He
hadn't as many stories as the Tailor, but he felt that his mission in life was to put me in touch with those who had. He
took me in his car at night to farmers' kitchens all over the
parish where people gathered to talk after a day's work. I was
as welcome as de Valera, a small God there then, and who had
had a safe house in nearby Gortaphludig during the civil war.
I told tales, some tall tales, and heard tales, some taller. I had
to cast a sprat to catch a salmon. I came home with my head
bulging with stories and ideas for many more.

I went to Dinny's mostly in the winter when there were
no tourists to distract the locals or take up Dinny's time. He
had no staff in the winter and he and his wife Nellie saw to my
simple needs. Seamus Murphy, the sculptor, told me that he
took Milan Horvat down to Dinny's hotel in the middle of
winter. Horvat, a Hungarian I think, was the conductor of the
Radio Éireann Symphony Orchestra. It was playing in Cork
and Seamus was given the job of showing the conductor the
hidden Ireland so he brought him to Gougane. Dinny showed
them into the sitting-room. He knew Seamus well. Seamus
had been to the Tailor's cottage and had made a now famous
bronze bust of that storyteller. Seamus introduced the conductor to Dinny without mentioning the man's occupation.
Dinny sensed the imperial foreignness of Milan Horvat and
was as curious as hell to know 'where he came out of'.

He set about putting down a fire, a gesture of welcome,
spattering talk all round him as he brought in papers, sticks
and sods of turf. Every now and then he cast an eye in the

direction of Horvat, who was standing by the picture window: a tall, aloof man in a long black coat, holding a fairly wide-brimmed hat behind his back, his eyes taking in the treacherous and dramatic sky tinged with red, the mountains, the lake and the monastic ruin on the island, seeing them we may presume in musical terms. The fire wasn't lighting for Dinny and he took off his cap to blow it as Seamus sat beside him. Finally Dinny's curiosity overcame him and nodding towards the window he said to Seamus, 'Who's this hoor?' Seamus, grateful that Horvat didn't get the significance of the word, explained that he was a conductor. Dinny eyed the stranger, and with a modicum of incredulity enquired, 'On the buses in Cork?'

In Milan Horvat's eyeline across the lake was Timmy Callaghan's house. During my visits to Gougane, Timmy and I became firm friends and I was invited to his house. I am still not sure whether he expected me to believe all the things he told me. Timmy didn't fight for freedom when his age group was out in the hills, but he carried dispatches hidden under the saddle of his bicycle. He was, as he said himself, a handy footballer and played in every position in the field including the mark. Because of a falling off in speed as the years went by, he found himself in the goal.

'We were playing in the final of the parish league,' he told me, 'and the opposing team knowing my weakness placed all the good looking women they could find at the two sides of the goal. Blast it,' he said, 'watching the women I left everything in, and we lost the match!'

Timmy believed in fairies and told me that if you met them they looked the same as you or me. You wouldn't know the difference. Then he continued: 'I went with my own horse and butt to Bantry for fish. I set out the night before, so as to be among the first at the market in the morning. The night was bright except when great banks of cloud scudded across the face of the moon. After some time on my way I put my hand in my pocket and found I had no matches to light my pipe. Around the next turn of the road I saw a fine house all lit up. It must be new, I said to myself, for I hadn't noticed it going to Bantry before. Maybe an ex-policeman built it.

'I tied the horse to the butt of a whitethorn growing on

the ditch and went in. A great crowd inside; all strangers to me and they made no wonder of my presence. There was music playing and young men and women dancing as wild and as airy as they would be at the pattern below in Gougane. I filled my pipe as I watched them stepping it out. With the crowd I couldn't get near the fire to light it so I put the pipe on the table in front of me. When the quadrille was over the lady in charge asked for a donation for the piper. I put what loose change I had, a couple of pennies and a threepenny bit, on the table. Some men were slow in parting with their money, and some refused to give anything. An altercation arose and while you'd be saying trapsticks fists began to fly. Women screamed as someone blew out the lamp. I gathered my legs out of the place as quick as I could, ripped the cob from the whitethorn and drove away.

'Halfway down the road to Bantry I put my hand in my pocket and found that I had left my pipe behind on the table in the new house. There was nothing for it now only grin and bear it. I'd call in on the way home and ask for the pipe. I did my few commands in Bantry, bought the fish and hit for home. When I came to the turn in the road, that I may be as dead as my mother, but there was no house there. And I couldn't mistake the place. There was the whitethorn tree where I tied the cob, there were the fresh horse-apples and the mark of the cob's hooves in the mud. I went in the gap I had gone in the night before and there on a flat stone was my pipe and the two pennies and the threepenny bit.

'Who were they, those people I saw dancing in that house? Were they the fairy horde? Or the people who have gone before us? Or did I for a short time visit the afterlife?'

Timmy believed in a hereafter for animals and he often told me about the man who had a grey horse: 'A spirited animal with a ferocious amount of white in his eye. A high stepper that left all the traps and sidecars on the road behind him going to Mass. Very well why, the man died and shortly after the horse got sick. People would stay up at night with a sick animal that time. Two neighbouring men were in the stable, one at each side of the horse. With the handle of a broom they were massaging under his barrel to bring him relief from the stomach cramp he was suffering from.

'They were resting from their work when the dead man walked into the stable. One neighbour was stricken with terror; the other fell backwards into the manger with fright. The horse whinnied to his former owner and the ghost put his hand on the horse's forehead. Then he rubbed down along his mane and down his spine to his tail and the horse crumpled up on the floor. The two white shapes of the dead owner and the dead horse floated out the door and away through the night air. A cow in the stall bellowed and the cock crew on his roost in the fowlhouse.'

I left Timmy and walked back to the hotel by the lake shore and thought of the time when the waters parted and revealed another world below. A woman storyteller, according to Dinny, was joined in butter with Timmy Callaghan's grandfather. She was going by the lake with her firkin in the moonlight when she saw the waters part in the middle and lay bare an enchanted land, where the sun shone, the birds sang, the men worked in the fields and there was an abundance of flowers and fruit. She knew if she had a piece of steel to throw into the opening the waters would remain parted, and she could walk down, meet the people, see how they lived, and have another story to tell when she came back.

She remembered the steel tip on the heel of her shoe and she put down the firkin to untie her lace. Taking her eyes off the lake broke the spell and when she looked again the gap had closed. She was left with only what the mind's eye can hold, a picture that would always remain vivid and bright.

It is all of forty years since I first visited Gougane. The men and women who sat in the big kitchen behind the hotel bar and hurried the night are long since gone. They lie in the little churchyard by the lake. May the sod rest lightly on them and on Timmy Callaghan, Dinny Cronin and the Tailor Buckley. Their spirits are somewhere in the skies in a land of fruit and flowers where the air is forever filled with music and the beat of angels' wings.

THE STAGE

Not every actor in the Rep wanted to spend his life behind a microphone, but it was very difficult for us to get permission from the radio authorities to work in the theatre. Stage work could clash with the radio actor's performance at night when almost everything went out live. However, in the late 1950s tape became available and the Sunday night radio plays were prerecorded. On these free Sunday nights, and without the knowledge of the station I am afraid, I went off with a party of singers and musicians who had appeared in programmes like *Take the Floor*, *The Balladmakers' Saturday Night*, *The Rambling House* and *Fleadh Cheoil an Radio*, to distant parts of the country for a one-night stand.

The pay was small but there was the advantage of working with an audience. Before the era of television personalities, we were the attraction of the hour and we played to packed houses everywhere we went. It gave me a chance of meeting people and many of those I met had stories for me. About seven artists filled the bill: two male and two female singers, a musician, a storyteller and a dancer. A male singer did compère and each performer appeared once in the first half and once again in the second half, but in a different order.

The shows were lively. There was a great reaction from the crowd and sometimes people talked back to us from the audience, offering comments on the proceedings. In Killarney an old woman in the front row, agreeing with some sentiment in my story, hit the floor with her stick and said, "Tis true for him!' And in Macroom one of our lady singers wore an off-the-shoulder creation and the other an evening gown showing just as much flesh but with shoulder straps. Coming to the end of the night the compère remarked, 'We have time only for one more item and what better way to conclude the evening than with a song from one of the ladies. Which one will I send out to you?' There was a shout from the gods, 'Send out the one with the galluses!'

After the show there was always a party and whether it was distant Cahirciveen, Ballina or Castleisland, we travelled back through the night to be in time for work next day. Watching the white road lines under the lights of the speeding car meant that a reflection of those same white lines rolled over my eyeballs as I tried to get an hour's sleep before going to work in the morning.

Nearing the end of the decade all the talk in Radio Éireann was about the new television station to be set up. At first it was to be called *Cianamharcaíocht* – a 'distant sighting' – before they hit on Telefís – a 'ghost seen afar off'! Some people, not as many as expected, were transferred from the station to the new Radio Telefís Éireann. Among them was Meave Conway who took charge of children's television. She asked me to do a series of ten-minute stories for young people, and on 2 January 1961, after RTÉ's opening night's festivities, my face was among the first to be seen in the regular television schedule at 5.30 in the evening.

I told the stories live, sitting on a chair, with two cameramen who took alternate shots of me. In time one cameraman was dispensed with and later in the series the other one was also given his walking papers, and I was left with the camera fixed in front of me in a studio so small that it was christened the 'confession box'. The programmes were announced that time, not by a voice-over, but by a physical presence. A lady continuity announcer sat in my chair and told the viewers what they were about to see. Then when the title board came up on the screen – where it originated I don't know – and while the signature tune was being played, the lady quickly vacated the chair and I sat into it. The red light came on and I was talking to the nation!

Our two eldest children, Eoin and Brian, were toddlers at the time. I was told that on first seeing my face in the box, they viewed it with an air of incredulity. Then they laughed and began to talk to me, but when I became stern-faced in the course of the story they thought I was 'telling' them to be quiet. In a day or two they accepted me as part of the normal order of things. Now I often meet people facing middle age who, as children, watched those programmes.

I had a story one evening called 'The Cat and the Splinter'. It was about a carpenter who taught his cat to hold a light for him while he worked at night. The splinter was a long sliver of bog deal used as a light before candles were perfected. I got real splinters from a source in the country and was able to show them on camera. I thought it would be a good idea to light one, and permission to do so was given by the director. It would be an improvement on what was virtually visual radio.

A little way into the story I lit the splinter 'and oh my friends and oh my foes it gave a lovely light!' But when I wanted to put it out, the more I blew on it the more it blazed up. A moment of panic! I thought of throwing it away, but I had visions of an enterprise just opened going up in flames. Suddenly an idea struck me. Maybe I was blowing too hard? I let the light die down a little and then with the slightest puff the flame went out, much to the relief of myself, those in charge and maybe the viewers if they had noticed anything wrong.

Back in Radio Éireann, restrictions on getting off from the Rep were being eased, and actors were let go to do stage and television work. My first television play was *The Weaver's Grave*, adapted by Mícheál Ó hAodha from a short story by Seamus O'Kelly and directed by Christopher FitzSimon. The piece was rehearsed in much the same way as it would have been for the stage, and when it came to the 'take' three cameras photographed the continuous action and the director selected the shots he wanted for the screen. We already had audio tape on radio; now visual or video tape became available for television and shows could be prerecorded. Before that, live plays on the box could be an alarming experience, with the next scene being feverishly set up in a compartment of a revolve, and the waiting actor already up and doing when he was turned into the camera. It was said that an actor who had to do a quick change wasn't fully into his costume when his partly clothed image burst into the sitting-rooms of the country!

Our play was recorded in sections as the tape was twenty minutes long. If for some reason we had to stop, the action could not be picked up again and we had to go back to the top. We were in the last minute of a tape in *The Weaver's Grave* when a camera on a crane hovering to take an overhead close-up crashed into the end of Malachaí Roohan's bed. There was a gasp from actors and crew, and Arthur O'Sullivan who was playing the character of Malachaí, and was in the bed at the time, gave vent to an expletive which almost drowned out the sound of the impact. After a cup of coffee the scene was reset and with our hearts in our mouths we started from the top again.

Hilton Edwards had been head of drama in Telefís Éireann during those early years. One of his first jobs afterwards was to direct Brian Friel's *Philadelphia, Here I Come!* for the Gate. Maybe he was conversant with my work, I don't know, but he sent for me to look at a part in the play. I read it, we talked about it, he gave me the script and said the part was mine. I applied for and got permission from Radio Éireann to absent myself from the station for the rehearsal period only. When the play was running I was to report for work every day. I was often in a live radio programme as late at 7 p.m. and I had to have a taxi ticking over in Henry Street to make a dash for the stage door as near as I could to half-hour.

We rehearsed *Philadelphia, Here I Come!* in the bar space in the Gaiety Theatre for three weeks, which was considered adequate time for the preparation of a show in those days. Patrick Bedford and Donal Donnelly played the public and private sides of Gar O'Donnell. Maureen O'Sullivan was the housekeeper. I was S. B. O'Donnell ('Screwballs' to Gar Private) owner of the shop, county councillor and father of Gar. Éamon Morrissey played Ned, and Emmet Bergin and Brendan O'Sullivan the other two young men who come to say goodbye to Gar on the night before he goes to America. Dominic Roche was the schoolmaster and Alex McDonald played Canon Mick O'Byrne. Later Mavis Villiers joined the cast as Aunt Lizzie, with whom Gar goes to live in Philadelphia.

Hilton Edwards was a director of the old school, a gifted man of the theatre. He heard the play in terms of classical music, and he saw it in terms of the pictorial compositions of the great painters. The movements, positions and business of his actors he had in his head as he sat down to rehearsal in the morning. An actor was free to suggest a change in these and if it was an improvement it was kept in.

'May I stand over here, Hilton?' an actor might say.

'No, dear boy,' Hilton would answer. 'You'll be in that position in Act Two.'

In interpreting the part of the uncommunicative father of Gar, I fell back on old men I knew in our locality while growing up, one man in particular who rarely spoke when with his own family. At first I was making him too old, senile in fact. Hilton said I was creeping around like a troglodyte, and Brian Friel told Hilton when he came to rehearsal that the man was barely over sixty. I was fifty myself at the time, so a little ageing was sufficient. I got inside the skin of the character and rounded him out till he was redolent of his place on the planet in every respect but one.

Philadelphia, Here I Come! is set in Ballybeg in county Donegal, but Hilton didn't want us actors using a Donegal accent. He was totally opposed to what he called 'regional intonations', and he settled for a clear peasant quality speech which I believe was much in evidence in the early days of the Abbey. As Hilton observed, 'If we ever take this property abroad, the punters of New York or Brighton won't know the difference between a Donegal and a Cork accent. Give them a clear speech. They pay their money and the least they may expect is to understand what's being said.' Accents were never my strong point so I was happy enough with that arrangement, as were many others in the cast, to judge by their expressions.

Under Hilton's tutelage Patrick Bedford and Donal Donnelly perfected a wonderful double act. They were the same person: one was Gar's outward manifestation, the other the inner workings of his mind. Gar Private is not supposed to be heard by the other characters in the play as he reveals what the silent Gar Public thinks about them. To the audience this was hilarious when handled by these two talented players. In Act One Bedford sat and felt the lines as Donnelly described my entrance from the shop to sit down to supper with my son on his last night at home. 'And here comes your pleasure, your little ray of sunshine ... ' Donal introduces me to the audience in mockingly glowing terms: 'I give you – the one and only – the inimitable – the irrepressible – county councillor – S. B. O'Donnell!'

He hums a fanfare while I hang up the shop keys, check my pocket watch with the kitchen clock, tilt my hat a bit ... Then in tones reminiscent of the catwalk, he says, 'And this time Marie Celeste is wearing a cheeky little headdress ... The pert little apron is detachable!' I marry the action of removing my apron to his words. 'Thank you, Marie Celeste!' I dust down my trousers. 'And underneath we have the tapered Italian-line slacks in ocelot ... We call this seductive outfit Indiscretion. It can be worn six days a week in or out of bed! Have a seat, Screwballs.' I sit. 'Remove the hat.' This I do and bless myself. 'On again.' I put it on. 'Perfectly trained. The most obedient father I ever had ... But hold it. Hold it.' Here the script says that I take out my handkerchief, remove my upper denture, wrap it in the handkerchief and put it in my pocket.

I had no false teeth to take out and I was in something of a quandary as to how I could make this piece of business look credible. Hilton unknowingly solved it for me. At the time he had put in a set of top dentures, which appeared to sit uncomfortably on his palate. He champed a little in the manner of a horse with an ill-fitting bit. He always had the denture in place, to enhance his smile, when he spoke to us on the floor, but when he went back to his directorial chair, he turned his head a little, holding a large handkerchief over the lower part of his face with his left hand, took out the offending denture with his right, folded the handkerchief over it quickly and put it in his pocket. An altogether slick operation.

I practised this manoeuvre, taking out an imaginary denture behind the handkerchief, and it went well at rehearsal. As I have the knack of appearing gummy with my teeth in, when I did it on opening night it brought the house down.

A delicate thread runs through the bright fabric of the play. It is a memory Gar has of a day spent with his father in a blue boat on a lake when he was a child, a haunting memory of the two of them together. His father sang, and it must have been raining because he put his jacket around Gar's shoulders and gave him his hat. They were happy. So happy that the thought of it keeps recurring. It comes up when Gar's mind wanders during the rosary. Was it a dream? To know for sure becomes an ache in Gar's heart and, through Friel's beautiful writing, an ache in every heart in the audience.

Philadelphia, Here I Come! was presented at the Gaiety Theatre as part of the Dublin Theatre Festival. *The King of the Castle* by Eugene McCabe ended its run on the Saturday. That night the McCabe set was struck even though it contained a full-size practical threshing machine. Hilton's Gate Theatre company got in later and on Sunday morning the split-level scene of room and kitchen by Alpho O'Reilly was erected. Hilton lit it during the day and next morning was the technical run-through. That afternoon saw the dress rehearsal and we went on stage that night – Monday 28 September 1964. To do all that nowadays the theatre would be dark for a week.

Time has washed all memory of the first night from my mind except the curtain call. The first to move down to the footlights were the lesser players. Dividing each way they made room for the supporting characters, and they, dividing again, left space for Donal Donnelly and Patrick Bedford to walk down to thunderous applause. We held the line and bowed until the punters' hands got sore. Some actors don't read their notices until the end of the run. My curiosity gets the better of me. I read them and they were good, with Donal Donnelly and Patrick Bedford being singled out for their excellent work. All the actors featured in the plaudits, with special mention of Maureen O'Sullivan, Alex McDonald, Éamon Morrissey and myself. Hilton was praised for his superb direction and lighting and Brian Friel for giving us a play that marked a turning point in Irish theatre.

There were one or two dissenting voices. The critic of the *London Times*, talking about John Keane (*sic*), who like Friel wrote about rural Ireland, said that Keane's characters could translate to Minnesota or Malmö, whereas he felt that Friel's people lacked this universal quality and that therefore his play might have more significance for local audiences than for people elsewhere. Time has proved this man to be as far out as a lighthouse. Brian Friel's plays have turned out to be top box office attractions on Broadway and the West End.

Seamus Kelly of the *Irish Times* loved the play, but wondered why it all hadn't been said before and at the Abbey. Frank O'Connor writing in the *Sunday Independent* quarrelled with Hilton's direction, saying that the wicked magician (Hilton) turned Friel's gentle play into a rip-roaring revue, all sexed-up, chromium-plated and with anti-clericalism. Your humble servant, according to O'Connor, was the only one who never lost sight of Mr Friel. '... Éamon Kelly as the taciturn father allowed nothing and nobody to impinge on his conception of the play, and by the hokeys in the last few minutes when it was lying dead on the stage didn't he get up and give it the kiss of life. As for my friend Hilton Edwards I could personally have beaten him to death with my programme.' O'Connor praised Friel, faulted Hilton and gave me powers of resuscitation which I didn't have, or didn't need, but he ended by saying the performances were brilliant and the audience adored the play.

Professor Liam Ó Briain, in a letter to the *Irish Independent* on 6 October 1964, defended Hilton's direction and said there wasn't a trace of anything that could be remotely described as rip-roaring in his handling of the play. Naming the principal actors, the professor said that they contributed equally to make it a production which for unity of tone was one of the most noteworthy of Hilton Edwards's many noteworthy productions in Dublin.

BROADWAY

❦

At a street crossing the traffic lights flashed an urgent 'Don't
Walk'. Hilton Edwards, on seeing this, enquired, 'What do
they expect us to do, run?' Presently a friendly white 'Walk'
beckoned to us in a lamp as big as a television screen. We were
in New York and going to rehearsal. *Philadelphia, Here I Come!*
had been revived at the Gate Theatre in 1965, and London
and New York impresarios, seeing it, arranged for its presentation on Broadway and later in the West End. The two
leads, Patrick Bedford and Donal Donnelly, were included in
the deal, as were Maureen O'Sullivan, Mavis Villiers and myself. Éamon Morrissey joined us later.

It was a difficult decision for me leaving Maura and three
young children behind. I was every day of fifty-one and a bit
long in the tooth for haring off across the Atlantic. But
Maura, true thespian that she was, gave me her blessing. We
agreed that if the play were successful she and the children
would join me in the States. I got my passport and visa and
was vaccinated, and in the middle of Christmas 1965, after a
fond farewell, more smiles than tears, I got a cab to Dublin
airport. Hilton Edwards and Brian Friel accompanied the cast
on the flight and to my dying day I'll never forget the sight at
twilight of the New York skyscrapers all lit up like benediction
as our plane circled to land at Idlewild. Christmas at home
with its candles in the windows paled in comparison to the
fairyland that was Manhattan.

All my relations who emigrated came to New York, and
from an early age listening to their letters being read and
hearing them talk when they came home, New York placenames like Hell's Kitchen, the Bowery, Central Park West and
Chinatown were familiar to me. I mentioned this to Brian
Friel on the plane and he drew a map of Manhattan with its

avenues going north and south and the streets running east and west, and indicated roughly the places I had mentioned.

Our spirits soared that morning as we walked along. The New York air seemed more invigorating than that of Dublin. Everything was livelier. The traffic and even the pedestrians were all hell-bent on getting somewhere fast. Flashing advertising lights competed for our attention and tall buildings, their toenails firmly on the sidewalk, stretched away into the sky.

There was no dining-room in the hotel we actors could afford. We had to go to the corner café for meals. I ordered a boiled egg for breakfast the first morning and got it broken up in a teacup like my mother used to give the baby of the family when I was young. One of the many little things that make America different.

New York actors were auditioned by Hilton for the other parts in the play, and after three weeks' rehearsal we opened our pre-Broadway tour in Philadelphia, which town stays in the memory because the streets were named after trees, and a large statue of William Penn dominated the centre of the city. We played in the Walnut Street Theatre, reputed to be the oldest in America. Sheridan's comedy *The Rivals* opened the playhouse in 1812. It was the great impresario David Merrick who put on our play and he, his aides and assessors accompanied us on the tour. Actors who didn't measure up to a Broadway standard were replaced and we lost two players on the way to New York.

'Where are you going, Biff?' an aide enquired of another one night in Boston.

'To dressing-room four to fire Louise,' Biff said, I thought with a little relish.

In a while's time a distraught Louise came down the stairs in floods of tears. Without her knowing it, another actress had been understudying the part. Not until we reached New York were some of us free of the fear of hearing that knock on the dressing-room door.

Television stations in Philadelphia and Boston were wont to place a camera before an audience emerging from theatre productions and ask the punters for their thoughts on the play.

Merrick disliked this type of publicity as some nut was quite likely to say that the show was a load of garbage. To counter-act it he had his crew members, all dickied up, merge with the audience, hog the microphone and offer comments which were laudatory in the extreme. This could only work a few times as the camera people recognised the crew and ignored them. Then Merrick's men played a record from *Hello Dolly*, one of his shows which was running on Broadway at the time, to muffle what was being said. Better still, with a pair of pliers he often cut the leads to the television speaker and left the interviewed playgoers on the screen opening and closing their mouths silently like goldfish in a bowl. He took the pliers out of his back pocket and showed them to us.

David Merrick was described as the *adulte terrible* in *Time* magazine. We were told that once when he got all round very bad notices for a show, he looked up the telephone directory and invited people of the same names as the drama critics to dinner. There were tickets to the panned show, after which he asked the 'Stanley Kauffmanns' and the 'Walter Kerrs' for their views. Quotes from their lavish praise were writ large on the publicity boards in the theatre marquee.

After a week in Philadelphia and another in Boston, where we played in the Wilbur Theatre, we opened in the Helen Hayes on Broadway. There were to be two previews on Mon-day and Tuesday, 15 and 16 February, and the press night was to be on the Wednesday. At this time there was a row going on between Stanley Kauffmann, the new critic of the *New York Times*, and the Broadway producers. Kauffmann insisted on coming to the second preview because he said the time be-tween curtain down and going to press was too short to write an in-depth review. Merrick's and the other producers' argu-ment was that a preview was not the finished article. Even at the last moment changes could be made which would improve the performance. And anyway, a press night opening was at seven-thirty instead of eight o'clock.

We were in our dressing-rooms getting ready on the sec-ond preview night when there was an announcement on the tannoy to get into our street clothes and leave the theatre at once. Outside, a thousand ticket-holders and Mr Kauffmann of the *Times* approached a darkened marquee and a notice saying that the show had been cancelled. Mr Merrick, when pressed for an explanation, said, 'A rat got in the generator.' The cancellation of that night's showing of Friel's play made front page news in New York next morning. Anyone interested in the theatre knew that Merrick had a new play called *Philadelphia, Here I Come!* opening in the Helen Hayes that night.

Being new to Broadway we were nervous, but the excitement of the events of the evening before tended to put us on an all-time high, and we turned in a great performance which received a tremendous reception at the curtain.

Later that night I was walking after Brian Friel on our way into Sardi's Restaurant, a favourite eating place for after-theatre people. When we got inside the door there was a burst of applause. I looked behind to see what famous personality was entering. There was nobody. The applause was for Brian, a warm New York welcome for a new playwright on Broadway.

We sat up in Moriarty's pub and diner until the papers hit the streets in the small hours. Douglas Watt wrote in the Daily News: 'I am happy to report that David Merrick didn't cancel last night's performance of *Philadelphia, Here I Come!* as he did the previous night's.' And he went on to say: 'It is beautifully performed under Hilton Edwards's sensitive direction ... *Philadelphia, Here I Come!* casts an undeniable spell.'

Walter Kerr of the *New York Herald Tribune* wrote: 'This morning the sun shines brighter. Producer David Merrick has gone window shopping in Dublin and brought us back a fine new play ... Author Brian Friel has set all of his cranky, fond and obstinate shy people to searching for the word that is everlastingly on the tip of everyman's tongue, and everlastingly not spoken. He has written a play about an ache, and he has written it so simply and so honestly that the ache itself becomes a warming fire.'

Stanley Kauffmann's review was not so warm, and didn't merit quotation among the thirty-one excerpts which appeared in a full page advertisement in the *New York Times* on 15 February.

We played on Broadway until November. There were many

awards for the play, director and leading actors. Brian Friel received a Tony Award nomination, as did Hilton Edwards for his direction. Donal Donnelly, Patrick Bedford and Maureen O'Sullivan were also named (Maureen had now become Máirín D. O'Sullivan because her name clashed with the famous Maureen in Hollywood), and wonder of wonders, a nomination came to an astonished yours truly. I was pipped at the post for the actual award by Patrick Magee who was playing in Marat-Sade.

Many notable people took in the show during its run on Broadway, and we often had to stay on stage to meet them after the curtain. One night Bobby Kennedy and a family party came. The actors crowded around the Kennedys, Bobby's sisters and his wife, and I, not being of a pushy nature, was left in the background. When the party left the stage, still surrounded by the actors, Bobby was last in the line. He stood for a moment and saw me at the far side. I was going to approach him but hesitated. He walked across, shook my hand and said how much he had enjoyed the play. I was very moved by the thoughtfulness of his action.

But of all the notables who came, I think I enjoyed Paddy Murphy's visits best of all. Paddy had been my next-door neighbour at home in Ireland, and I was a schoolboy the morning he set out for America. I remember going to his house to wish him farewell. His departure was in many ways not unlike that of Gareth O'Donnell in the play. His father, as well as being a farmer, was a building contractor in a small way, and Paddy had been helping him and learning the trade. It was a severe blow to the father when Paddy got it into his head to go to New York. The old man was brokenhearted and refused to speak to his son. As Paddy paused at the door the morning he was leaving, to wish him goodbye, his father's only words were, 'You'll be sorry yet.'

Paddy got on fine in the States. He was a motorman on the subway train from the Bronx to Manhattan. Every morning he brought carriageloads of commuters down to the city and carted them home in the evening. He told me he had never seen a Broadway play and was very curious about them when he heard I was going to be in one. I got tickets for him and he rang me up a few times before he came. He had many questions to ask. How long would the play last? Would there be a half-time?

When he came he was so interested in the activities of the household, the naturalness of the people eating, washing up, playing draughts, saying the rosary, the boys dropping in to say goodbye to Gar, that he had to come again to savour what was being said. He told me that it brought him back to his own last night at home, and that the taciturn father 'was my own old man out of the soot'. He admitted to being close to tears. Gar's alter ego puzzled him. He took it that he was a dead brother who came back to advise the young man.

In the following months Paddy organised parties of Kerry neighbours and friends to visit the play. There were so many that afterwards he drew them up in two lines in the wide corridor outside my dressing-room. Then I was called out and marched up and down the lines like de Valera reviewing a guard of honour. He introduced each person as we went along. 'This is Jerry Sheehan from Knockanimeris! And here's a man from Mayo.' (Paddy's wife came from that county.) He read up everything he could lay hands on about the theatre. He became an authority on what was appearing on Broadway and he had sheaves of newspaper cuttings when I called to see him in the Bronx.

I had two aunts and numerous yankee-born first cousins in New York. Sundays were set aside for visiting them. I first called on Aunt Mary at Dittmar's Boulevard in Astoria. I was treated to the same warm hospitality the settled Irish always lavished on greenhorns on their arrival. There was a sumptuous meal and drink to go with it. Generosity knew no bounds. My jacket was put in the closet because of the central heating. On my way home when I looked in the pockets they were full of dollars. There had been a whip-round, what they used to call a 'shower', for the new arrival.

Nearly all the talk on that first visit was about Ireland. How many of the people my aunts remembered were still alive? Marriages of relations at home were discussed and I was questioned about any contributions to the matrimonial fruit basket. Then I was told how my New York cousins were getting on – where they worked and where they lived. Maria, Aunt Margaret's daughter, was married to an Italian policeman. I knew from listening to American relations that marrying outside the ethnic group was frowned upon. Women like my aunts would ask their daughters who were that way inclined, 'What's wrong with Irish boys?' A father giving away his daughter to a Pole or an Italian might say to her at the altar-rails, 'What's that you said his name was again?'

The policeman son-in-law wasn't present on that first visit and I told his wife Maria that as he was on duty in Manhattan he should call into the Helen Hayes Theatre to see me after a Wednesday matinée. Sure enough he turned up with an Irish cop, both of them bedecked with guns, batons, handcuffs, parking tickets, whistles, notebooks and pencils. They were hardly able to walk under all that paraphernalia. Actors exchanged curious glances as they saw them entering my dressing-room. I kept a bottle of Irish in my locker and there was a drop all round. They turned out to be a good-humoured pair, and I said for a lark, why not slip the handcuffs on me and frogmarch me out when the other actors were leaving their dressing-rooms. This they did, to the open-mouthed astonishment of my colleagues. They deposited me in the squad car and drove off with one or two hoots on the siren. They dropped me safely at my hotel, where the phone was hopping off the hook. News had spread to the staff of the theatre that I had been abducted by the police. I reassured the staff, and they took some convincing that it was all a joke and that I was available for duty that night. My biggest difficulty was keeping the incident from the ears of the PRO, who would have used it for publicity that would have got two of New York's finest into trouble.

LOST IN THE UNDERGROUND

꧁

It was March, the play had been successful and the people were coming in. It looked like as if we'd be in New York for a while, so I sent to Ireland for Maura and the children. My first cousin Bob Rodden drove me to the airport to meet them. It was three months since I had left home, and Eoin, seven, and Brian, five, had not forgotten me, but Sinéad, a little over a year-and-a-half, didn't know me at all. She stood by a railing holding an upright bar, and with her head turned away she cried her fill. Any word of consolation I had to say only made her worse. Then I must have had a nudge from the Holy Ghost or something because I began to hum an Irish lullaby with which I used to put her to sleep when she was smaller. Gradually the crying stopped and gradually she turned her head around, looked up at me quizzically and began to smile through her tears, as much as to say, 'Ah, I have you now!'

When we got into Manhattan we discovered that we had left Sinéad's go-car behind at the Aer Lingus terminal. Next morning I set out with Eoin and Brian on the subway to re-trieve it. Riding on the underground train was to be a special treat for them. We had to change trains at a place called Union Turnpike in Queens. I took Eoin's and Brian's hands firmly when the train stopped. The doors open swiftly and when the people are through they close just as quickly. As we faced the opening door, Eoin, always independent, let go my hand and went towards a door on his right. In a second Brian and I were on the station platform and Eoin, unable to push his way through the entering crowd, was held back by the closing door and left inside. The train sped off and he was gone. The life almost drained from my body with the shock.

My first primitive instinct was to rush after it and try and catch the departing train. There was a coloured man at the window of the carriage and I waved to him and indicated as best I could that I had left the child inside. A lady who had been on our train from Manhattan and noticed the two youngsters with me, seeing my distress, spoke to me very slowly as if I didn't understand English. I was dark and a trifle swarthy and maybe she took me to be Spanish. She asked me to remain exactly where I was and said that she would follow in the next train and see if Eoin had been put out at Van Wyck Boulevard station. She went off and after what seemed like an eternity during which time my brain, veering towards madness, visualised all the dire things that could befall Eoin – would I ever see that dear child again? – the down train drew up and there she was with Eoin by her side. She had found him in the safe keeping of the coloured man. God be praised, I was in the seventh heaven with delight. Eoin, afraid I would tell him off, was inclined to hang back, but I rushed forward, swept him off his feet and embraced him, and when I put him down, my benefactor had gone. On our journey to the airport and back home in the train Eoin clung to my side like a barnacle to the black rocks in Ballybunion.

When news of the incident broke in the theatre the publicity man put me in the hands of a journalist, and a photograph of Eoin and myself appeared with an article in the *New York Herald Tribune*. Heading the article was a verse which read:

> Has anybody here seen Kelly,
> The kid who was lost and found?
> Blessed be the souls who retrieved him,
> All in the underground.

Not great. It wouldn't have rated a mention in Radio Éireann's *The Balladmakers' Saturday Night*. There was an appeal in the paper to the lady who found Eoin to come forward. Eventually she turned up and David Merrick hosted a dinner in her honour in the Rainbow Restaurant nearly a mile up on top of a skyscraper in Manhattan. Her name was Mrs Francis Koschir and she was the wife of a Jewish doctor from Long Island. She and Eoin were photographed and he had a present for her – an Irish linen tablecloth which Maura found in a New York shop.

I had rented a housekeeping apartment in the Excelsior Hotel at 81st Street and Central Park West. When Donal Donnelly's wife Patsy and their little daughter came to New York they stayed in the same hotel, as did Brian Friel, his wife Anne and their family. We, the Kellys, had two bedrooms, a sitting-room, dining space and a small kitchen. The apartment was cleaned every day and, as ever in America, a mountain of fresh towels put in. We were fourteen storeys up, and when the window-cleaner came I had to close my eyes. He went through the casement and slipped an S-hook from his tackling into a staple on the outside of the frame. The sight of him leaning back into nothingness, singing as he cleaned the window, sent a nervous tingle through my wrists and ankles.

There was a park in front of the building with a planetarium in the middle where we sometimes went to view the stars. During President Kennedy's time a scheme was brought in to cater for preschool children. As Brian was only five he qualified for this and went to the nearest public infant school, where he made friends with kids of every colour in the human spectrum. For his birthday he invited a bevy of them to the apartment and had the time of his life.

Eoin, seven, had been going to school in Dublin and I found a place for him a few blocks away where a one-time Irish parish had flourished, with church and schools all built with the cents and dimes of the emigrants. The neighbourhood was now deepening from white to brown and black, while the stained glass windows in the church still carried an appeal for prayers for the soul of a John O'Brien or an Elizabeth Reidy. Many years later I went to Mass there and the notice on the door said Misa en Español. The Irish had gone.

New York streets were very unsafe in the 1960s and children were never left out on their own. I accompanied Eoin and Brian to school every morning and collected them again in the afternoon. Maura did the later chore when I had a Wednesday matinée. Because Eoin would be back in Dublin again to resume his studies, I was anxious that he didn't lose touch with the subjects taught at home. I spoke Irish to him on our way to and from school. After a month or so when he had become accustomed to his surroundings he said to me one morning, 'Dad, I think we shouldn't talk Irish any more.' 'Why so, Eoin?' I asked. 'Because,' he answered, 'people might think we are Puerto Ricans!'

The children enjoyed the strange city although they were too young for any abiding memory of it to stay with them. Because of their skin colouring as against the pallor of American white children, they caught the eye everywhere they went. Women stopped Maura in the street, curious to know what country they came from, and admiring Sinéad's rosy cheeks they exclaimed, 'Isn't she a doll!' Eoin became very patriotic in the States and hated having to stand in front of the star-spangled banner before class every morning as they all sang 'America the Beautiful'. He told the teacher that it wasn't his flag. I had to traipse around the Irish shops of the city until I found a tricolour for himself and Brian. I have a photograph of the two of them with the Irish flag firmly planted in the ground. With toy guns they defend it against all comers on a small knoll in Central Park.

If Maura and the children enjoyed New York it was a new lease of life for me. In my first days I liked to sit in Schraft's café near Broadway and watch the passing crowds while I partook of a dish of ice cream with scalding hot butterscotch poured on top of it. In these cafés at mid-morning groups of older men with their hats on sat at tables and talked. One day I heard them mention our play and discuss the part I was taking in it. At that time I wasn't hooked on the pint and didn't go to pubs much except to Eddie Downey's of 8th Avenue where showpeople went after the theatre. Eddie had a corner where he displayed pictures of the greats of Broadway and we of *Philadelphia, Here I Come!* figured prominently there.

I rode the subway down to the theatre every night, but when money was plentiful I hailed a cab and asked to be driven through Central Park. The fare was eighty cents and you left the driver the dollar. On the east coast of America spring follows swiftly on the heels of winter. Today the trees are bare; tomorrow there's greenery showing everywhere. I'd spread myself on the back seat of the cab drinking in the beauty of the blossoming shrubbery and, regretting the twelve years I had spent hidden behind a microphone in Radio Éireann's attic on top of the GPO, I'd sing:

Bless 'em all! Bless Séamus Breathnach
Who railed us one day,
'Will ye stop the bloody acting
And get on with the play.'

New York cabbies are great talkers and they talk so fast and range over a wealth of topics even on a short journey. One man broached with me the difficulties he was having in his sex life. Mercifully the journey ended before he got to the intimate details.

Reading the name card on another cabman's dashboard I saw Florence O'Donoghue – a Glenflesk name if there was ever one. He turned out to have been the servant boy at Dineen's, a neighbouring farm, when I was a child. I often saw him with a rifle during the Troubles and, because he took the anti-Treaty side in 1922, he lost out and had to flee to America. We were early at the theatre and we sat in the cab and talked about Glenflesk and Killarney until it was time for me to sign on before half-hour. He was saddened by the number of old people I told him had passed on, and agreeably surprised at the many changes for the better in the district. The ride was free. As he said, 'I couldn't take money from a neighbour's child!' Many of the cabmen go to the theatre. One of them asked me, 'Are you the guy who plays the part of the storekeeper in that *Philadelphia* show?'

The Kerrymen's Patriotic and Benevolent Association of New York got wind of the word that I was in a Broadway show and I was invited to their premises to receive an award. Paddy Murphy went with me. At the door for a joke I indicated that Paddy was my bodyguard. To my surprise this was taken seriously and I was asked if he was one of New York's finest. The term, meaning one of the city's policemen, was lost on me, and winking at Paddy I said, 'Only the finest would do.' Word got around quickly that the tall guy with me was my bodyguard, and I went up in everybody's estimation. We were treated like royalty. When I stood by the podium to hear the citation read, a chair was provided for Paddy in a position where he could cover all entrances and exits. The joke, which Paddy thoroughly enjoyed, had to be played out now, and it wasn't the only absurdity; the one award they had to give was to make me a Kerryman (honorary). And they did just that!

Snowbound in Wilmington and Chicago
❧

The run of *Philadelphia, Here I Come!* came to an end on Broadway and in December we set out on a tour of the States. Our first stop was in Washington where we played in the National Theatre. Our household had a nice apartment there just for one week. I remember the location well because a little distance away on the Y-junction of Pennsylvania Avenue there was a monument by the Kerry-American sculptor, Jerome Connor. It was in memory of the women who nursed the wounded in the civil war. I think they were called the Daughters of the Republic. Down the street from it in the grounds of the Irish Embassy was Connor's statue of Robert Emmet, a replica of which stands in Stephen's Green.

Eoin, Brian and I set out one morning to find a launderette to do our washing. We kept enquiring for one until we were finally directed to a place a distance away in an entirely black neighbourhood. We three were the only white people in the launderette. When I put the clothes in the washing machine I found I hadn't enough coins for the slot. I gave a five dollar bill to a black man and asked him if he would be kind enough to go out and get some change for me. He looked at the note in his hand and said, 'What if I don't come back?' 'You will,' I said, 'your washing is here.' He did come back and we went ahead with the work. As we sat on a bench waiting for the machine to finish, the room filled up. Not all the boys and girls had washing to do – it seemed a kind of trysting place.

I put the damp clothes in the dryer, and after some time an argument started between two people about whose turn it was for the one dryer that was left. Then a strange thing happened. As I was the only white adult there, they assumed I was the owner. I was approached to settle the disagreement. I didn't feel as assured as Aesop's monkey adjudicating between

241

the two cats over the piece of cheese. As they argued their case our dryer gave its last twirl and the swishing clothes came to a halt. I emptied them out and gave one of them the dryer and so peace was restored. I had never before been the odd man out in a crowded room of black people, and because I was new to the States I felt a little uneasy. The children, who saw the world through different eyes, and who had mixed with coloured children at school, were not one bit perturbed.

After our short stay in Washington we were to play for a week in Wilmington, Delaware, and then on to Chicago for two months. Through friends of ours in that city we had already found an apartment, and instead of coming to Wilmington with me, Maura and the children went on to Chicago to await my arrival there on Christmas Day. In Wilmington we played in a theatre in the Dupont complex, and you couldn't ask for nicer weather as we drove there for our last show on Christmas Eve. Back in Dublin all theatres were closed on that day, and in Holy Week the stages were as dark as the words of the Passion on Good Friday. That year Christmas Eve fell on a Saturday and we had two performances, one at five and one at eight. For these back-to-back shows, as they were called, a meal was brought into the theatre, and in the short time before the next curtain-up we didn't have to get out of our costumes or make-up.

Like the first house that afternoon, the second one was a packer. I couldn't help wondering, remembering what Christmas Eve was like in my young days in Ireland, if the people had any homes to go to, or any decorations to put up for the festive season. As the play progressed I found it hard to keep my thoughts from wandering back across the sea to Christmases long ago. There is a scene at the opening of the third act where the family kneel down to say the rosary on young Gar's last night at home before leaving for America. As the Our Fathers, the Hail Marys and the responses swelled and died the thoughts of Gar Public, articulated by Gar Private, always soared westwards across the Atlantic as he visualised what his new life would be like in Philadelphia. But on that night in Wilmington, as the young would-be emigrant's thoughts soared westward from Ireland, my thoughts were soaring in the opposite direction, to my own home in Carrigeen, Glenflesk.

How clear it all became to me, every detail of the kitchen, the picture of the Holy Family, the berry holly, laurel and ivy decorating the walls. The mottoes on the chimney breast, the roaring fire and the Christmas candles in the windows bringing what was to us then a glorious blaze of light. Images of Christmas crowded the mind. Driving to early Mass in the dark in the pony and trap. The sound of hooves on frosty roads, the loud salutations at the chapel gate as neighbours exchanged Christmas greetings, echoed and re-echoed in my head. 'Your decade!' from the housekeeper, Madge, brought young Gar back from his dreams and me back to reality. The reality that was S. B. O'Donnell's stage kitchen in Wilmington, Delaware.

When we came out of the theatre that night the city was blanketed in snow and strangely quiet, as whatever traffic there was seemed to glide soundlessly over the white streets. We had some trouble in getting a taxi. Those at the centre were lazy about venturing to the outskirts in case they couldn't come back. The snow was coming down again and slanting in the rising wind. Eventually we got an empty cab going in our direction. When we got out the last man was lucky. He stepped into the footprints made by the others in the deep snow which was being tossed and swirled in the wind and driven against the walls of the motel. I had to brush it away to find the door handle, and when I opened the door inwards there was a wall of snow almost three feet high between me and the room.

By scooping it outwards with my bare hands, a bit like a rabbit setting about making a burrow, I managed to get in without bringing too much snow with me. I'll never forget the feeling of loneliness that came over me as I shut the door that Christmas Eve and looked around the bare motel room. Granted, the bed was comfortable. There was a dressing table, a wardrobe, a john and a shower; but one picture would have brightened the place. Just one picture with a sprig of berry holly behind it. I got into bed but I couldn't sleep because of the noise the blow-in hot air apparatus was making. I switched it off but then it got so cold I had to switch it on again.

The phone rang. A fellow player, Éamon Morrissey, who

couldn't sleep any more than myself, had rounded up some American and Irish actors from the cast. Would I come down to the lobby? We made ourselves comfortable in a large room and, despite the lateness of the hour, those of us with wives and families called them to send festive greetings. Parcels of good cheer for dear friends in Chicago were raided, and as Christmas Eve merged into Christmas Day, toasts were drunk, songs were sung and on Éamon's insistence I told of Christmases long ago when the world was young and we were all happy by our own fireside.

Next morning at an early hour we were on the road. The snowploughs had cleared our way to Philadelphia airport, where we were to get the plane to Chicago. Flame-throwers were used to clear the snow from the runway. I got a window seat in an aircraft packed with people, parcels and hand luggage, bursting at the seams like the bus from Killarney to Barraduv on Christmas Eve. It was nightfall when I reached the apartment in Chicago and was united with my family. We exchanged presents and had a quiet drink but it was Christmas Day and I hadn't been to Mass. Maura was anxious that I should talk to God before we sat down to our festive dinner. I went down to reception and was directed to a church in Clarke Street, the scene of the infamous St Valentine's Day Massacre in the time of Prohibition.

Brian and Eoin, full of curiosity about the trip, wanted to know if we brought the stage all the way from the east coast. I told them that in Wilmington on Saturday night coming near the end of the show we heard murmuring in the wings. The men of the theatre transport company were waiting and when the curtain came down they descended on the set like locusts and everything – flats, furniture, lighting-board, wardrobe and props – were quickly put in the vehicle reversed into the back of the stage. They were in the lorry in no time and driving through the night, and whatever time it took them to get to Chicago, that set would be in place and lit for us to walk through before we went on tomorrow night. Closing in Wilmington on Saturday and opening on Monday in Chicago, nearly a thousand miles away, was, they agreed, something of a record.

Chicago is the Windy City and the coldest place on God's earth in the winter. The icy breeze blowing across the frozen waters of Lake Michigan would be hard on a brass monkey. The nose, ears and the point of the jaw go numb and turn blue, and the tips of the fingers, even in mittens, tingle with pain. The Wilmington snow soon made its way westwards and we woke one morning to find the snow so deep in the streets that parked cars humped the white blanket like knees-up in a bed. The car antennas stuck out of the snow like the stalks of plants waiting for leaves to grow.

One afternoon I had to make my way to WFMT, a Chicago radio station, to talk on a programme giving publicity to the show. I was well wrapped up for the trip and wearing overshoes which came above my ankles. They weren't high enough and the snow went in over them, adding greatly to my discomfort. While waiting in the anteroom at the station, I took off my shoes and put my socks on the radiator. Unnoticed, I hope, I slipped my feet into my wet shoes when I was called. Once my legs were under the studio desk I discarded the wet shoes and I was interviewed barefoot by the legendary Studs Terkel, author of *Division Street: America*. His book was a collection of his most successful interviews, and one authority said of him, 'Studs Terkel is a wonderfully skilled interviewer, with an instinctive ability to put the question that unlocks defences and coaxes self-revelation!'

About this time Spoken Arts of New York had issued a record by the Radio Éireann Players of two plays by J. M. Synge, *Riders to the Sea* and *In the Shadow of the Glen*. The actors' names for some reason did not appear on the sleeve of the album. As I entered the studio an excerpt from *In the Shadow of the Glen* was on the monitor and going out over the air. You could have knocked me down with a feather when I heard my own voice, and Studs was equally surprised when I told him he was listening to me and my wife Maura on the disc. To put his hand on that particular record was a chance in a million and it gave us something to talk about at the opening of the interview.

Studs himself spoke very little but he had the uncanny knack of drawing speech from his subject, and I talked about radio and theatre in Dublin, the play I was in, storytelling and the place where I grew up in Kerry. When it was over I slipped my feet into my shoes and when I came to the anteroom my socks were dry on the radiator.

But we weren't finished with the snow. After a two-month run in the Schubert Theatre in Chicago the tour was to continue with one-week stands in nine other cities throughout the States. We thought the constant changing would be too much for Maura and the children, and after due consideration they decided to go back to Ireland. They had been almost twelve months away. It was a glorious morning when we set out for O'Hare airport. I wanted to see them off. I would be back in plenty of time for the night show. Our cab driver was Italian, newly arrived but with a fairish grasp of English. We weren't long on the road when the skies darkened and it began to snow. In no time it was coming down thick and fast with fat snowflakes falling on the windscreen. The wipers worked for a while and then failed to function. We had to stop every now and then to clear the soft snow from the glass.

When we got near the airport the snow was so deep that cars were being abandoned on the roadway. A little further on, the thoroughfare was completely blocked and the driver decided to turn around. He reversed into a ditch where the cab got stuck and we were marooned in the snow. This was before the time of telephones in cabs and he went looking for a kiosk to call his company. We were all in our light clothes and we soon began to freeze. The driver didn't come back and I stood in the road to the city flagging down traffic in the hope of being taken back to Chicago. At last when I was nearly frozen to death a car stopped. It was a minister of religion. Little Sinéad was so cold that he opened his greatcoat and put her inside it while he shepherded us into his car.

He said he knew a back road to the airport and he took us there. We were far from the departure area but we found sheltered accommodation with many other stranded people. All Maura's cases were in the cab, and in the cold and excitement of being rescued from it we forgot the hand luggage with her tickets and passport. Now panic really set in. How could we trace the cab driver? We asked for the airport police, and when they came they were flabbergasted to learn that Brian, not yet six, and having an obsession with figures, remembered the registration number of the stranded cab. We gave the police all the particulars, how many pieces of luggage and the names on the destination tags. They went off.

In the blizzard there was no hope of my getting back to the city, and now the full horror of the situation dawned on me. I was going to miss the show that night. I tried in vain to ring the theatre. I calmed myself down by saying that it wasn't a total disaster. We were all alive, and what were understudies there for but to go on in an emergency? Eoin and Brian came to the matinée at the Schubert with me every Saturday. They read their comics in my dressing-room and listened to the show on the tannoy. Now my mind was taken off the concern of the hour listening to Eoin talking to a group of truck drivers sitting nearby. Remembering some dialogue from the play, Eoin asked these disgruntled men, 'Why does a hen cross the road?' I had to smile. The incongruity of it. A child of seven engaging the attention of these hardened veterans of the park-ways. I thought they'd tell him to scram. But no, they wanted to know why. Eoin told them, 'To get to the other side. Ha-ha! Why does a hen lay an egg?' They hadn't a clue. 'Because,' Eoin said, 'it couldn't lay a brick. Yo-ho. Why does a sailor wear a round hat?' They feigned puzzlement, then said, 'Put us out of our misery, kid.' And Eoin capped his own question with 'To cover his head. Ha-ha!' He had run out of dialogue and returned to us.

After what seemed ages the police came back to say that the cabman had succeeded in being hauled out of the ditch, and when the traffic eased he delivered our luggage to the Aer Lingus terminal. Much relieved by this news, although re-gretting that I didn't have the opportunity of paying the cab-man in whose debt I would ever be, we went to the pilots' lounge where there were easy chairs in which we could rest. Later on we were taken by airport car across the runway to the departure area. We checked to find that tickets and passport were safe, but learned at the desk that because of the snow all flights were grounded until tomorrow.

We had a meal in the restaurant and a generous member

of the Aer Lingus staff gave us his apartment a distance away. How great is the goodness of human nature! There was one double bed, and worn out from the day's adventure the entire family got into it. After a while the children complained that there wasn't enough room and they were being crushed. They pushed and pushed until I fell out on the floor where I spent the rest of the night.

Next morning, with the luggage checked in for the flight and Maura and the children sitting in the lounge by the departure gate, we said our tearful goodbyes. I left them bound for Ireland, while I headed back to Chicago. There is a stiff fine levied on any actor missing a show in the theatre, but when I explained my case to the management, they held that my absence was caused by circumstances outside my control and I was forgiven. They were happy enough; my understudy had gone on and the performance had been a success.

I wish I could report that things had gone so smoothly for Maura and the children. According to her first letter, their plane, after many delays, took off from O'Hare airport. Some trouble developed when they were over Canada and they had to make an emergency landing at Montreal. The passengers were taken in buses with a police escort – they had no landing papers – to hotels in the city, and after an early start the following morning they were only a short time in the air when another fault occurred, something to do with the undercarriage. They circled the city several times and came down so low they could see the ice in the St Lawrence River. Because of the long delays due to bad weather at Chicago airport and the emergency landing at Montreal, many of the passengers were distraught and being comforted by the ever-attentive and kindly flight staff.

Finally the fault was rectified and the plane straightened out on its flight line to Ireland. Later Maura had a letter from Aer Lingus congratulating herself and the children for remaining so calm under the trying circumstances at the outset of the journey. Happily for them they were at home in Ireland and we actors were on our way to St Louis on the banks of the Mississippi.

Our hotel there was close by the river and we watched the

big-wheeled paddle boats dock and then sail on. Some of us took the elevator up the inside of the chromium-plated twin arches that have become the trademark of the McDonald's fast food outlets. The view of the city and up and down the river was breathtaking. Modestly hiding away in a corner not far from the braggart arches was an elegant little Catholic church going back to the time of the French.

I haven't mentioned the play reviews we got on the road. They were first class. We won all the way. Bob Goddard of the *St Louis Globe-Democrat* exclaimed, 'Where have you been all my life, Mr Friel? That is the natural question after viewing a memorable stage experience called *Philadelphia, Here I Come!*'

And so the word was in Columbus, Ohio, and over the border in Toronto where we played in the Royal Alexander Theatre. We went on to Cincinnati, Cleveland and St Paul, and our prop money was stolen in Milwaukee. The people in the design department were put to the pins of their collars to dream up imitations of three green Irish pounds, a foxy ten-shilling note and two half-crowns. They did it and the secretary of the Department of Finance in Dublin wouldn't have known the difference from the front row.

Our travels brought us back again to Boston where a critic sporting the name of Kevin Kelly gave us what I can recall as the only bad review of the play. 'It failed to move me,' he said, 'and was little more than blathering bathos.' In Philadelphia, where we had also played on the run in to Broadway, I read a review of the show on the way to the theatre on opening night. I imagine that the critic, on seeing that there was little or no change in the original cast, dolled up his review of our first visit and gave it to the editor, who put it in the paper a day too early. It was an eerie experience seeing our names down for something that hadn't yet taken place. In New Haven, Joyce's *Ulysses*, shot in Ireland, was showing at a city cinema. I went to see it, and it was like a visit home. The auditorium was crowded and my seat was at the very front, from which vantage point my actor friends from Dublin looked larger than life.

We ended our tour of America in Baltimore on 13 May 1967. It had been nearly a year and a half since I had left home. In that time I had seen most of the States except the far west and the deep south. At first I thought I wouldn't like America. I had great confidence in socialism then, my face ever turning to the east, and I felt that the screaming ideology of US capitalism would set my teeth on edge. I wasn't long in New York when I became aware of the wealth of Park Avenue and the poverty of Harlem. As the song says:

> Though gems adorn the great and grand
> There are faces with hunger paling.

In downtown Manhattan I saw poor black women rummaging for food in garbage cans, and people sleeping on the doorsteps in the night-time, something which was not in evidence in Moscow, where I went many years later. In the States the successful white man is cock-of-the-walk, and at that time you'd see no coloured faces in posh restaurants or striding down the concourses of great American airports – unless they were working in those places. On tour out from New York, I felt from the way some of our American crew members spoke to coloured porters in railway stations that in his heart the white man was master, and he still regarded his black brother as a slave. This feeling of superiority manifested itself in unexpected ways. When I got up to give my bus seat to a coloured woman in Columbus, Ohio, all the white people looked at me as if I had two heads.

I was at many parties in Irish-American homes, but I never saw a coloured face. The Irish in England have married Asian and African partners, but I never heard of anything like that in the States. The Irish-American attitude to the coloured seemed to me to be much the same as that of the majority of our settled kith and kin to the travelling people at home. But what a welcome our American cousins have for their white brethren from Ireland. Their hospitality is heartwarming and their generosity knows no bounds. I found friendship to be the hallmark of all Americans. Brendan Behan said of them, 'He who hates you, hates the human race.'

TO BRIGHTON AND LONDON

୧ଙ

Before we had set out on tour from New York each member of the cast had bought a tin trunk similar to those returning Yanks brought home in the old days. These stood four feet high and were two feet broad and two deep. When opened out, one side held drawers and the other a wardrobe space complete with coat-hangers. They were transported with the stage scenery and sat in the wings at each venue, and you took what you wanted from them to your hotel.

Now they were being packed for the last time for our journey back to Ireland. My trunk was shipped by sea and I hurried back by air, anxious to see what the home place looked like after seventeen months away. O'Connell Street seemed bare. Nelson's Pillar had been blown down the year before. I regretted this. During the twelve years I had worked upstairs in the attic of the GPO as a radio actor, I was on the same level as the one-armed one-eyed figure. Every day I promised myself that I would climb to the top. I never did. It wasn't the cost that kept me away. The sign at the entrance read 'only 3d'.

The pillar itself was a graceful Doric column reaching into the sky. I can still see the words sculpted on the four sides of the granite base. Trafalgar was there and I remember February and April. These were cut in lower case and the years in Roman capitals. Seamus Murphy, the sculptor, ever marvelled at the classical proportions of the letters in those words. He held that they were the best example of lettering in these islands. Militant Republicanism is short-sighted. The destruction of the pillar and the equestrian statues of King William and Lord Gough were wanton pieces of vandalism. We should learn to live with our past.

I didn't bring my tin trunk to England. It still sits in the spare room with a large Cunard Line label on it.

We opened our pre-West End tour of *Philadelphia, Here I Come!* in Brighton. Maura and the children came over for a visit and the youngsters enjoyed riding on the toy railway and the many other amenities for young people in the August sunshine. I had a movie camera I bought in New York and I still have pictures of them on the merry-go-round.

Jack Tinker was writing then in the *Brighton Evening Argus* and he spoke of the dewdrop freshness of the play. The English were going to like it. Oxford was our next stop and then into London, but at the last minute Manchester and Golder's Green were added to the schedule because the original date for our play in London clashed with the opening of another show, which meant we wouldn't get our full share of the press.

I had been engaged to take part in a television series called *Never Mind the Quality Feel the Width* with Joe Lynch and John Bluthal playing the leading parts in a joint tailoring business. One was Catholic, the other Jewish, and the comedy in the series arose, as it were, from the collision of these two cultures. I was to play the part of a parish priest, and rehearsals were to begin the week we opened in London when I would be free in the daytime.

Now I couldn't do it because I'd be a couple of hundred miles away. A contract had been signed and there was hell to pay. A proposition was put to me by the Thames Television company. Would I be willing to take a late train out of Manchester each night to London after the show? Without telling my own management of my predicament I decided to chance it. It worked fine for two nights. On the third night I went to the railway station to find that there was a lightning strike. My God! What was I to do? The television show I was rehearsing in London was going out live on Sunday night.

It was difficult enough getting accommodation at that late hour. I found a place, the worst ever in which it was my misfortune to lay my head. The bed was damp and there was a shiny coating of dirt on the bedroom carpet. I had a light overcoat which I wore over my pyjamas between the sheets. I was up at the crack of dawn, got a taxi to the airport and flew to London. I rang the TV people and a courtesy car brought me to rehearsal and back to the airport afterwards for the flight to Manchester.

This is how it was for the rest of the week, and because I was under extreme pressure both the play and the TV rehearsal and broadcast went the best ever. When Oscar Lewenstein and Michael White, the English producers of our show, heard that I was going down to London from Manchester every day, all hell broke loose, because of the risk involved if I couldn't get back for the show. They got after my director Hilton Edwards. Hilton bore down on me like a great three-masted schooner on a small boat. Was it true that I was taking the train from Manchester down to London every day?

'No, Hilton,' I replied. 'I go by plane.'

That seemed to take the wind out of his sails, because he thought for a moment and said, 'You're flying? Well I suppose that's all right.' Strange logic, but it got me off the hook.

After a week at the Hippodrome in Golder's Green we opened at the Lyric Theatre in Shaftesbury Avenue on Wednesday 20 September 1967. At the matinées tea was passed along the seats to the patrons at the interval, and we in our dressing-rooms knew when the time was up by the rattle of the empty cups and saucers being collected by the ushers.

The dressing-room was where I lived when not on stage, and I tried to make it as much like home as possible. There was a couch and an easy chair, a cabinet with drinks in case anybody called round, and I had just one picture. It was a reproduction of Picasso's *The Jester* which I had bought in New York. A white figure with a sad face on a light green background. I regarded it as a sort of talisman. It went with me on tour through the States and it was here in London now.

Outside, the names of the principal actors loomed large on the theatre marquee, and posters of the show were fixed to the wall at pavement level. I was glad that my name was just high enough on the bill that a passing dog with an inclination to raise a leg couldn't reach it. Madge Ryan, who replaced Mavis Villiers and who had a better agent than I, had her name placed above mine, but mine was still safe from the designs of contemptuous London canines. A player whose name escapes me was once asked what he thought of drama critics and he replied, 'You may as well ask a lamp-post what it thinks of dogs.'

But the West End critics were kind to us, though they didn't write about the show with the same gusto as their American brethren. The theme of the play somehow struck a deeper chord with people of the New World. Everyone there of European descent had an ancestor whose last night in his native place was, in many respects, not unlike that of Gareth O'Donnell.

Dominic Roche and Derry Power from the original Dublin production joined the cast in the West End. Dominic, who played the part of the schoolmaster and was no stranger to the London stage, had a story about the Lyric, where we were now. The theatre faces Shaftesbury Avenue, while Windmill Street passes the stage door. An old actor playing there had a short appearance in Act One and didn't come on again until late in Act Three. He had all that time (including two intervals) to kill. Sitting in his dressing-room became boring, and to while away the time he walked each night from his dressing-room, down the long corridor, out the stage door, across the street and into the Lyric Tavern, where he sat on a high stool over a drink and did the Evening Standard crossword.

The play had a long run, and with practice he had his return so well timed that, after glancing at his watch, he got off the stool, walked out of the pub, crossed the street, went in the stage door, down the long corridor, into the wings, and without pausing walked on to the stage on cue. The old actor prided himself on his achievement, but one night he was late. Only imperceptibly. It seems when he emerged from the pub a window-cleaner with a long ladder on his bike was going up Windmill Street.

I am in my element in big cities. In them you can fade into anonymity, and there's no Dublin passer-by to say, 'How's the man?' A chap can be as lost with his thoughts in a crowded street as if he were strolling through a woodland glade. There are city parks in which he can sit and run lines to himself, pubs in which to have a pre-lunch drink and art galleries to visit when the spirit needs lifting.

In the long run of a play the actor has the company of his peers at show time. After the curtain, when the goodbyes are said at the stage door, he is on his own until he meets them again the next night. This is when he misses his family, and mine was back in Dublin where the children had started school again.

Living accommodation proved difficult enough to find in London in 1967. Hotels were out of the question on our salaries. I had to be satisfied with a small flat in Cadogan Gardens, a stone's throw from the King's Road. I had never lived alone, fending for myself, and for a fairly gregarious type of fellow it proved lonely. When the door of the flat shut behind me on Saturday night, I wouldn't see a face I knew again until a half-hour before the show on Monday.

Ever heeding my mother's admonition to 'keep the faith', no matter what strange place I was in, I always managed to make Mass on the Sabbath day. On my first Sunday in Cadogan Gardens I had no idea of where there was a Catholic church. From past experience in foreign cities I had learned that the only people afoot early on Sunday morning were Catholics on their way to Mass. That Sunday at 8.45 a.m. I walked to Sloane Square and noticed a sprinkling of people heading in a certain direction. I wondered if they were of my persuasion. Any doubts I had were soon banished on seeing Garret FitzGerald, who was later to be our Taoiseach, striding along. I tagged on behind and, sure enough, we came to a Catholic church in time for nine o'clock Mass.

The Abbey – A Halting Site

✍

Philadelphia, Here I Come! ran for three months at the Lyric Theatre in the West End. I had been in it off and on from 1964, and continually for almost two years since it had opened on Broadway at the beginning of 1966. It was time for a change. Back in Dublin after a meeting with Tomás MacAnna, artistic director of the Abbey Theatre, I was cast in *Spreading the News*, which was part of a Lady Gregory season at the Peacock. Tomás himself was to direct it.

The Abbey then was a secure place for actors. They were all permanent, some of them working together for as long as twenty years. It was very much like a large family and I felt an intruder for a long time. I likened the house to a caring old bird with her brood sitting comfortably under her protective feathers. But this old bird, though moulting at times, was true to the ideals of the theatre's founders, and mostly sang the native song. It was the song heard in the cities and villages of Ireland. When she sang it well, it was true and glorious and sent a tingle dancing in the blood. She faltered only when she sang to a borrowed tune.

When I joined the Abbey in 1967 many young people were coming in from the school of acting. There was a tendency then to cast juveniles in oldish parts, which meant a heavy application of make-up. I often thought that the young men's heads tended to bend forward under the weight of greasepaint, revealing necks of a natural complexion.

Each actor had an empty cigar box with a hinged lid in which he kept his sticks of Miner's or Leichner's make-up. The sticks were numbered and the most commonly used were No 5, a yellowish shade put on all over the features as a base, and No 9, a red stick applied over the base where the natural colours were prominent in the face. It was much used for florid, outdoor types, of which there were many in the plays of the time. No 15, a paler red, was mixed with No 9 to tone it down for characters with sedentary occupations. A dark stick, No 7, was used if an actor was in the part of an African or Asian, for example the Indian peddler in Bryan MacMahon's *The Bugle in the Blood*.

By rubbing a pared matchstick to No 7, lines could be drawn to indicate wrinkles on the forehead or at the corners of the eyes. Some actors highlighted these dark lines with a streak of white. But the veterans thought this was overdoing it. Cyril Cusack once said that he spent half his life putting in wrinkles and the other half obliterating the natural ones. There was lake, a dark red stick, which was applied above the eyes to set them back, because the old form of stage lighting tended to flatten the face. Lake was also used around the mouth.

Some placed an eye-liner under the eye and put a dot of carmine in the eye-duct with a hint of white underneath. An old actor told me this was to give a little eagerness to the face. The entire make-up job was dusted down with a face powder, and Fuller's earth was used to grey the hair.

A complete set of make-up was costly, and actors entered it in their expenses sheet when making out their income tax returns. One young man fresh from the day job had no make-up. He borrowed it from his fellow players. One asked him when he was going to buy some of his own and he replied, 'I'm waiting to see if I'm going to be kept.'

Cadging make-up was not unknown and there was a tight-fisted thespian who went for ages without buying any. He had an empty cigar box with a hinged lid from which he had cleverly removed the bottom. When it came to the time to prepare for the show, he placed the bottomless container on top of another actor's open box. As they chatted he lifted his lid and helped himself to the other's make-up. When he finished he slapped down the lid and said to his friend, 'Have a good one!'

Tomás MacAnna's production of *Spreading the News* and Molière's *A Doctor in Spite of Himself*, translated by Lady Gregory, was an outstanding success. Music and song were added to both pieces in the manner of Máirín O'Farrell's treatment of *The Playboy of the Western World* in *The Heart's a Wonder*. 'Opera buffa' one dissenting voice called the concoction.

When King Baudouin and Queen Fabiola of the Belgians visited Ireland later on, *Spreading the News* was revived and presented with J. M. Synge's *Riders to the Sea* and *An Pósadh* by Douglas Hyde in a special gala performance for the royal couple. The No 1 Army Band played the Belgian and Irish anthems. During the interval the bar was cleared and the actors in the three plays were invited upstairs to be presented to the King and Queen.

We were arranged in a huge semicircle and Mícheál Ó hAodha, chairman of the Abbey board, brought the royal couple around, introducing each actor to them. When the royal visitors were in front of me, Mícheál was called away and the King and Queen were left looking at me. I guessed that royal etiquette precluded me from speaking to them. They smiled, and it must have been some impishness in my face that made them laugh. We were politely controlling our merriment when Mícheál returned and introduced us. They passed on, the Queen pausing to talk with Bríd Ní Loinsigh, whose performance as Maurya in *Riders to the Sea* was superb.

Next in line to meet us was President Éamon de Valera. He was being neglected tonight because of the presence of royalty. The President's eyesight was failing then. He walked rubbing shoulders with his aide-de-camp and shook hands with the cast. When he was near me he turned to his aide and said in a low voice, 'Who are these?' The aide told him that we were the actors. With a beam on his face he shook my hand with renewed vigour. I spoke to him in Irish, which seemed to please him because his smile broadened considerably.

The event was widely covered in the papers next day and Seamus Kelly, writing in the *Irish Times*, ended his article by saying that, according to the talk in the foyer after the show, the night was stolen by Bríd Ní Loinsigh's Maurya, by Peadar Lamb's Raftery, and humility almost precludes me from admitting that I was mentioned too.

My first play on the stage of the new Abbey was *The Saint and Mary Kate*, adapted by Mary Manning from Frank O'Connor's novel of the same name. I played the part of a daft carpenter called Grog Mahon. I remember Patrick Murray's scenery had a towering contraption supporting a platform on which I did my work. Every night I had to climb up to it in a blackout. It was an unnerving experience. I dreaded missing my footing in the dark. The trick, I found, was to make a mental picture of the object and its direction from the wings while the light was on it. Then let your guardian angel take you by the hand when darkness fell.

The play was set in a Cork city tenement called the Doll's House. Frank Grimes and Bernadette McKenna played the young lovers. For this production, director Frank Dermody brought the new Abbey stage mechanism into effect. You had lifts coming up and going down with the actors at the end of a scene, in the manner of Tommy Dando at the organ in the Savoy Cinema. On a night on which the punters were slow to applaud, when our hands were out of view in the descending lift Frank Grimes and I clapped loudly and the applause was taken up by the entire house. Hard enough having to play to them without having to do their work as well.

I grew to love playing in the Abbey Theatre, although you'd get better acoustics in a ball alley. Actors had to keep their voices above the normal projection level or those sitting under the balcony would never know how the story was going. Much as I liked the work, opening nights down the years proved something of a disappointment. It has long been the practice for managements to paper the house for these occasions. Who were invited? Friends of the theatre, I suppose. Shareholders and board members, many from the press, people likely to give publicity to the event. A sprinkling from radio and television. Somebody seeing a group of RTÉ personnel going into the theatre on opening night remarked, 'A pilgrimage to Knock!' There must have been something in that, because a play that got an outstanding reaction from preview audiences could fall flat on its face on press night. On occasion one even sensed a mild hostility out there in the darkness.

After *The Saint and Mary Kate*, *The Playboy of the Western World* was revived. In my earlier years I had played Christy, 'a young gaffer who'd capsize the stars,' but, in the words of the

Widow Quin, I had 'aged a score' and now I was cast as Christy's father, Old Mahon. Vincent Dowling was the Playboy, Aideen O'Kelly Pegeen Mike, and Maire Ní Dhomhnaill the Widow Quin. Hers was a superbly gamesome widow, and when she came to coax Christy with, 'Come on young fellow till you see my little houseen a perch off on the rising hill,' she didn't say 'house-een' but gave the word the full Gaelicised flavour of 'howish-een' which Synge, the eavesdropper, had heard in Kerry.

Harry Brogan and Mícheál Ó Briain played Jimmy Farrell and Philly Cullen. Tomás MacAnna, a wizard at moving crowds on a large stage, turned in a spectacular production which went to the Edinburgh Festival. Our venue there was the Lyceum Theatre. This was at a time when national anthems were played before the rise of the curtain. 'The Soldier's Song' was first on the turntable. Not everyone recognised it. Half the audience got to their feet. When those standing saw the other half seated they decided they had made a mistake and began to sit down, but by this time those seated thought it was they who had made the mistake and were now getting to their feet and breaking into what one critic called 'uncivilised hilarity'; and so they went up and down like jacks-in-the-box until all were standing and trying to suppress their merriment. Then 'The Soldier's Song' ended and people were settling themselves and reaching for the chocolates, when suddenly the strains of 'God Save the Queen' filled the house, to be greeted, as the audience struggled to stand, with a hilarity as uncivilised as that which had greeted 'The Soldier's Song'.

The incident did the play no harm and the curtain went up to a laughing audience. One paper next day reproached that same audience for their lack of reverence for 'God Save the Queen', but we got a good press. 'Richness', 'Devastating' and 'Splendours' were some of the headings in the Scotsman. 'Synge drew a glorious picture of a browbeaten boy discovering his pride and trying to justify the myth he had created. The devastating climax when hero-worship turns to scorn has been vividly handled by Tomás MacAnna in this production … Vincent Dowling's Playboy was a fine study of bewilderment and bravado. He came out of the night a hunched and pathetic waif and found himself transformed into a hero.'

Other papers praised Geoffrey Golden (Michael James), Mícheál Ó Briain (Philly Cullen), Patrick Laffan (Shaun Keogh) and Máire Ní Dhomhnaill. In the part of Old Mahon I was described by Christopher Small of the *Glasgow Herald* as 'large, hairy, as powerful as a gorilla and much less amiable'. John Calder of the *Daily Mail* said: 'Vincent Dowling as the Playboy and Aideen O'Kelly as Pegeen Mike headed a cast which stormed through a memorable first night like inspired banshees.' And of Harry Brogan's Jimmy Farrell he penned 'the most diabolically comic drunk I have ever seen paralytic on a stage'.

In Act Three of the *Playboy*, at the entry of Harry and Mícheál Ó Briain after getting into 'such staggers' at a morning wake, Harry rattles the latch very noisily. Jerkily the door opens just a little, and one leg, snake-like, investigates the kitchen air before the entire person appears, so full that he is fit to spill. Harry and Mícheál talk about graves and Harry asks Mícheál if he has ever heard tell of 'the skulls they have in the city of Dublin; ranged out like blue jugs in a cabin of Connaught ... white skulls, and black skulls and yellow skulls, and some of them having the full teeth and some having only but one.'

Here Harry holds up, at the end of an outstretched left hand, two fingers. Eyes shut, he rests momentarily. Then, opening one bleary eye and seeing the two fingers raised, he reaches out with his other hand, as fast as is possible under the weight of drink, puts down one finger and wags the other. It is a marvellous piece of grotesquerie in comic hands with sickle-moon thumbs and never fails to make the house erupt.

He told me once how he came across this piece of business. It seems when Harry came to the Abbey first, Lennox Robinson was directing the *Playboy*. When the actor playing Harry's part came to the 'skulls' speech he was shut-eyed, simulating drunkenness, and he raised two digits saying, 'some of them having the full teeth and some having only but one'. 'But,' Lennox called out, 'you have got two fingers up.' Whereupon the actor opened his eyes and put one of them down, to the amusement of the crew. 'Keep it in,' Lennox told him.

Harry, like the actors of his time, was fond of talking about the old days. Acting is a craft and, like Michelangelo's apprentices, novices learn as much from the master's tales as from watching him perform. But the stage wasn't the be-all and end-all for Harry. He was a committed republican from the way he talked, and the Countess Markiewicz was his heroine. John Bull was the enemy and Harry was reluctant to play in London. 'The heart of a rotten empire,' he called it.

When we were in Edinburgh, Phil O'Kelly, our manager, brought the entire cast to a festival news conference held in the freemasons' hall in George's Street. Phil put on what one newspaper man called a *céilí* for the press, by asking the players to do a party piece or talk about the theatre. I told a story which was synopsised in next day's *Glasgow Herald*, and Gabriel Fallon gave a potted history of the Abbey. We would not have an Abbey Theatre were it not for the resurgence of the national spirit at the turn of the century, he claimed, and had it not been for the Abbey Theatre the Easter Rising might not have taken place when it did.

There was vocal agreement from Harry on this, and when he himself got up to speak, with a heavy eye he surveyed his surroundings and said, 'The last time I was in a Freemasons' hall I was raiding it!' He went on to encourage the Scots to engage in a militant nationalism.

THE TAILOR AND ANSTY

✤

P. J. O'Connor of Radio Éireann adapted *The Tailor and Ansty* for the stage. The Tailor, Tim Buckley, was a famous story-teller, and he and his wife Anastasia held court in the long winter evenings in their cottage near Gougane Barra in west Cork. Theirs was an open house for neighbours and visitors alike. Eric Cross, a visitor who came to stay for some years in Gougane, wrote down the Tailor's sayings and stories as well as Ansty's badinage. It was meant as a record for the old couples' many friends, but after some excerpts from it appear-ed in Sean O'Faolain's *The Bell*, the book was published.

The Tailor liked to sing out the title and the name of the publisher, he was so pleased with the project. '*The Tailor and Ansty*,' he would say, 'Eric Cross. Chapman and Hall Limited, 11 Newfetter Lane, London EC4. Eight shillings and six-pence!' Both he and his wife Ansty, God bless them, were as broad-spoken as the Bible, and the book was banned by the Censorship of Publications Board in 1943 as being 'in its gene-ral tendency indecent'. But there was nothing in it that I didn't hear from the men sitting by my father's fire when I was growing up.

Stories like the one about the new Department of Agri-culture bull attracted much local attention. People came in such numbers that the owner of the beast decided to charge 6d a head for the privilege of viewing the animal in all its virile ferocity. One man was hanging back from the entrance to the field, and the owner asked him why he wasn't going in! 'I am a poor man,' the prospective viewer said, 'the father of eigh-teen children.'

'Eighteen children,' shouted the farmer. 'Stand there and I'll bring the bull to see you!'

The animal kingdom interested the Tailor greatly, and he

had a story of a mule which died on the way to Cork with a load of butter. The owner, so as not to be at a total loss, skinned the mule and sold the pelt in Macroom. When he came back the mule had revived and was grazing at the side of the road. His master went into a field, killed a number of sheep, skinned them, and while the hides were still warm, applied the fleeces to the mule's body. 'And that animal,' the Tailor told his neighbours, 'lived for fifteen years after with two shearings a year!'

A cat likes fish, it is said, but will not wet its paws, yet the Tailor knew of a cat called 'the moonlighter' that used to fish with its master. Small animals the Tailor loved, even insects, and he told of the *daradaol*, a slow-moving black chafer sometimes called the devil's coachman, because his tail sticks up like a driver at the back of a vehicle. This bucko told the soldiers where our Lord was hiding, and so the animals lost their power of speech because, as the Tailor said, they'd tell out everything.

Irish was Tim Buckley's first language and he was as fluent in that tongue as the poets of Sliabh Luachra. He brought much of the music and rhythm of Irish to the English he had learned. *Glac bog an saol* agus *glacfaidh an saol bog tú.* Take life easy and life will take you easy. The world is only a blue bag, knock a squeeze out of it while you can, was another saying of his.

The banning of *The Tailor and Ansty* caused a heated controversy in the press and gave rise to a four-day debate in the Senate. In time a new Censorship Board was formed and the book was unbanned, but by then much hurt had been caused to the Tailor and his wife. They, who loved the company of people in their house, were for a time deserted, and worst of all, three priests called on them one day and, forcing the Tailor to his knees on the flag of the hearth, made him burn the book in the fire.

'It was a good book,' the Tailor said, recovering from the humiliation. 'It made a great blaze!' Ansty's only comment was, 'Glory be! Eight and sixpence worth!' That was a lot of money to her.

The Abbey accepted P. J. O'Connor's adaptation of *The*

Tailor and Ansty, and it was put on in the Peacock during the 1968 Dublin Theatre Festival. I was cast as the Tailor and Bríd Ní Loinsigh as Ansty. A young trainee director, Tomás Ó Murchú from Cork, was given the job of preparing us for the stage. My experience as a storyteller and my knowledge of the countryside – I was brought up not ten miles from where Tim Buckley was born – helped me to build the character of the Tailor. Bríd and I thoroughly enjoyed the job of getting under the skin of this outlandish old couple from Garrynapeaka. The stories, the bickering, the reminiscences, the jokes, all added up to a fine night's entertainment.

Strangely enough, the Abbey management felt the Tailor needed a prop, and put on *The Stranger* by Strindberg as a curtain-raiser. But it was plain to all that the Tailor could stand on its own feet. At an early revival, prior to a national tour, *The Stranger* was dropped and the material cut from the *Tailor* script to make room for it was restored.

Bríd and I played in places as far apart as Clonmel and Cahirciveen. In Clonmel we found ourselves part of the activities of coursing week. In us you couldn't have found two less enthusiastic supporters of a sport where ferocious greyhounds are allowed to hack hares to pieces, and we gave the Abbey manager Phil O'Kelly a bandle of our tongues, as Ansty might say, for landing us in such a situation.

We played in an old cinema under the title *Destry Rides Again*. The proprietors had forgotten to take down the sign of the last picture. In Cahirciveen there were no toilets backstage. We had to go down a rickety ladder to a turf shed, and our dressing-rooms consisted of an old caravan parked at the back of the Kingdom Cinema. When I sat downstage to talk to the audience, the audience talked to me.

Arriving in Scarriff, county Clare, we found the hall locked and the caretaker couldn't be found to let us bring in the set and props. After many enquiries it was revealed that he was cutting turf many miles away and had taken the key with him. Here, as in Cahirciveen, there was no house of lords backstage. Cast and crew were expected to use a hedged-in parcel of land at the rear. There were up-to-date facilities for the patrons at the bottom of the hall, but wild horses wouldn't drag an actor through the audience after he is in costume and make-up. I procured a large empty paint tin which took care of the minor necessity.

Leslie Scott, our lighting man, did a brilliant job in getting us properly lit, providing authentic looking 'turf' fires and 'oil' lamps as well as arranging that all house lights would go out as the curtain came across. In *The Tailor and Ansty* I had long solo passages where I told Tim Buckley's many stories or discoursed upon 'Lollipopus', which was what he called Halley's fiery comet speeding through the sky.

On the first night in Scarriff there was one light which didn't go out. It was a bare bulb under the balcony which lit up the entire bottom of the hall and was very distracting because of the arrival of latecomers. I was surprised that Leslie Scott, meticulous man that he was, hadn't it under control. I soldiered on, my concentration wearing thin, until suddenly, nearing the end of Act One, the light went out.

I rushed around to Leslie to ask what had happened. He told me he couldn't find the switch for that light. 'But,' I said, 'you put it out.' 'I know,' he answered. 'It took me some time to find the switch. It was in the caretaker's house next door!'

Interest in the show was so great that it was revived two years later but then, because of the untimely death of Bríd Ní Loinsigh, another actress filled the part of Ansty. Bravely, and with the knowledge of Bríd's outstanding success in the role, Kathleen Barrington took over the part and was acclaimed by the critics for her interpretation. During this run in the Peacock, a play in the Abbey failed to bring the people in. *The Tailor and Ansty* came upstairs and filled the bigger house for two weeks.

I forget how many times *The Tailor* was revived, but on the last occasion my wife Maura played Ansty. P. J. O'Connor always said that he had her in mind for the part when he wrote it. At that time Tomás MacAnna had brought a young man fresh from Trinity into the Abbey, and it was he who directed *The Tailor* this time. His name was Michael Colgan. He built the show out of the new, like the Tailor making a new suit. Maura's Ansty was busy as a bee, all fuss and fooster, bringing new impetus to the part. The Tailor, because of a gammy leg, was anchored in various positions on the set. In Colgan's direction he was orbited by Ansty, stinging him verbally into action with her acerbic tongue. She was an immediate success. With the bantering and mock-warring conflict between husband and wife, the piece played like a racy tune on an old fiddle.

Again a play in the Abbey was a box office failure, and for a second time the Tailor and his spouse climbed the stairs to the mother house and filled it until a new show was ready.

There was a call from the country again and Maura and I set out on a second *Tailor* tour, this time under the managership of my good friend Ronan Wilmot. We went to Derry and Benburb and south to Macroom, little more than a stone's throw from Garrynapeaka where the Tailor once lived. Coming among people who knew him and Ansty inside out was a bit nerve-racking, but we must have been on the right lines because those who came thoroughly enjoyed the evening's entertainment. They faulted me on one word. What Eric Cross wrote as 'keening' the Tailor would have pronounced 'caoining'. I should have known better.

In Macroom on the Saturday night there was only a scattering of people. Ronan Wilmot and John O'Toole, the stage manager, drove out to Gougane near the Tailor's cottage on Sunday. In Cronin's Hotel, after a meal, people who were all dressed up said they were going to Macroom to see their old friend, the Tailor. A good omen; interest was growing, and, sure enough, the house was packed that night and the next. Then we drove on to Bantry for more full houses. The old storyteller was being honoured in his own land.

Maura and I made friends with the Tailor's son, Jackie, and his wife, when we visited the Tailor's one-time famous home. The day we were there, Jackie's cow, what his father used to call the dairy herd, was about to calf. She was a friendly creature, as black as a crow, her barrel large, showing that she was near her time. I minded her out of the cabbages for a while, as I used to mind our own cow when I was a child in Carrigeen. I plucked a wide cabbage leaf and she ate it out of my hand. 'You should have been a farmer,' Jackie said, and he promised that if the cow had a bull calf he would call him after me. So it transpired, and when I met Jackie in Cork afterwards, he swore that the calf, which turned out to be a pet, used to answer to my name.

'Éamon,' Jackie said, 'I sold you in Bantry fair last week for ten pounds.'

SYNGE AND THE DANDY DOLLS

In Hugh Hunt's time as artistic director at the Abbey one of his first productions was *The Well of the Saints*, Synge's famous play about two beggars. Beggars were very much part of the rural scene when I was young. They weren't all travellers who lived under carts or in caravans, but maybe settled families who once had seen better days. Some people, not blessed with a great share of the world's goods themselves, took them into their homes at night, and they slept on straw on the kitchen floor. Many of the lone men were fine storytellers and in the days before newspapers and radio they brought tales of the Fianna and news of the doings in the big world outside.

Mick and Biddy were a well known pair who came by our house once a month. Mick stood outside and Biddy did the begging. She sometimes sat at the other side of the fire from my mother and drank a cup of tea. When she got something for her beg, she'd bring a cup of tea out to Mick and a slice of hot yella buck cake with butter melting at the top. They were as odd as two left shoes. Mick walked ahead of Biddy, looking back now and then, and calling, 'Come on! Come on! Come on!' She took no notice, but plodded away behind him humming to herself a tuneless air.

Despite their oddness they were never the butt of youthful scorn like poor Nellie Mulcahy, a deranged beggarwoman I saw one time in my travels. Nellie loved bus conductors and spent her few precious pennies on short bus journeys so as to be in the company of the man in the uniform cap, and carrying the money bag and ticket puncher. When she was on foot her unkempt hair blew in the wind; she was a pathetic figure in a black shawl and raggedy skirt. The children taunted her as she made her mad way past them on the road to school.

Synge's two beggars are blind. They live in a world of their own, believing themselves to be beautiful people, a fantasy which is fuelled by cruel villagers. Martin Doul boasts of Mary's beauty, of her bright blue eyes and golden hair, and Mary Doul in her imagination pictures Martin as a handsome prince. They are cured of their blindness by a saint at a holy well, and, in the days before the looking-glass, each sees only the other's ugliness. The stark reality brings bitterness and disappointment.

Their fury knows no bounds. They curse, castigate and attack each other with a passion that burns like fire. In time the cure wears off, and when blindness returns we have followed them in their journey from darkness to light and back to darkness again. We have seen their great rage on discovering that their beauty was only a figment of their fancy.

The angry storms having abated, they sit reconciled in the open air. They revert to their previous pursuit of selling peeled rushes to passers-by. (These rush piths were fried in lard, left to dry, and used as primitive candles.) Sounds are everything when sight is no more. The bleat of a sheep, the rippling of a rill or the swish of a bird's wing catches their attention and is talked about. When stillness comes she reaches for his hand; they smile in contentment and are happy again in the world of the imagination.

I was happy when Hugh Hunt cast me in the part of Martin Doul. Physically I was a little too large of frame to fit my description by Mary Doul when she upbraids me in her anger. But I had a feeling for Synge's language. The lilt of it I had learned from my mother when she recited poetry or was carried away in her flights of picturesque prose. I loved the rise and fall of Synge's speech and I gloried in its delivery. His words are not for measured speaking. They must flow, and at times come off the tongue in a torrent.

Mary Doul was played by Máire Ní Dhomhnaill, no stranger to Synge's language. John Kavanagh was the Saint and Patrick Laffan Timmy the Smith. Alan Barlow's set, of large grey boulders against a treacherous sky, captured the dark, bleak mood of the play. Our opening night was 8 September 1969, and of it Desmond Rushe wrote in the *Irish Independent*: 'There are moments which one always hopefully waits for in the theatre, but seldom experiences – those rare and terrifying moments which rivet one to one's seat. Hugh Hunt achieves one of them in his brilliant production of J. M. Synge's *The Well of the Saints* at the Abbey Theatre ... Éamon Kelly plays Martin and Máire Ní Dhomhnaill plays Mary. They are both magnificent. The electrifying moment comes when Martin sees for the first time the woman he has dressed with soft skin, large blue eyes and long golden tresses. His reaction to the reality is a savage eruption of pain. His disillusionment is bitter and total, and he makes the audience share it with him to the full. His playing all through is incisive and superlative, but here he is stunning.'

Seamus Kelly in the *Irish Times* said that Hugh Hunt's direction gave classical treatment to a classical Abbey play.

The Well of the Saints was considered short for a full night's entertainment and it was the practice then to put on a curtain-raiser with it. This time it was *The Dandy Dolls* by George Fitzmaurice, being produced at the Abbey for the first time and also directed by Hugh Hunt. The experts call Fitzmaurice's plays 'folk fantasies' and *The Dandy Dolls* is wild and weird. It is the story of Roger Carmody, who spends his days making grotesque dolls and his nights raiding the presbytery fowl-house. The parish priest comes searching for his stolen goose 'with the cuck on her'. Pat Layde, who played Fr James, asked me many a time what a 'cuck' was. I didn't know, unless it was a tuft of feathers on the goose's head.

The human characters in the play are Roger, his wife Cauth and their child; Fr James, Keerby the priest's clerk and Timmeen Faley. There are also what you would call other-worldly figures like the Grey Man, the Hag of Barna and the Hag's son. The Hag's son seems never to let Roger finish a doll because, as Cauth tells the Grey Man: '... Them dolls are the biggest torment to him in the world. For the Hag's son is against them to the death, and so sure as Roger makes a doll, so sure will the Hag's son, soon or late, come at it, give it a knuckle in the navel, split it in two fair halves, collar the windpipe, and off with him carrying the squeaky-squeak.'

In the end he carries more than the squeaky-squeak, as we hear from Keerby the parish clerk talking to Fr James:

Your goose is safe, your reverence, for it's the wonderful thing entirely I now have seen ... Roger being carried away by the Hag and the Son of the Hag. Riding on two Spanish asses they were, holding him between them by a whisker each, and his whiskers were the length of six feet you'd think, and his nose was the length of six feet you'd think, and his eyes were the size of turnips bulging outside his head. Galloping like the wind they were, through the pass of the Barna mountains, sweeping him along with them, for ever and ever to their woeful den in the heart of the Barna Hills.

Fitzmaurice and Synge were the two sides of the same coin. Synge the outsider who went to the west and to Wicklow and learned the people's language, and Fitzmaurice the insider who wrote in the tongue that was his from the cradle.

Like Synge, Fitzmaurice was a Protestant. He was the son of a parson who married his housekeeper, lost his stipend and turned farmer. George's mother, Winifred O'Connor, was of the old stock, and of course it was from her he heard the language of his plays. Her voice, I would say, echoes through the speeches of his mature women characters. No clucking hens these, but a bevy of songbirds singing it out, arms akimbo, like Maineen in *The Magic Glasses*. The sound of women's voices filled his childhood: his mother talking to the servants, with whom she was all the one, the O'Connor relations coming and going, the women in the neighbouring houses where George, like the young Douglas Hyde in Roscommon, spent much of his time cabin-hunting. Women forever making tapes. As he grew older he moved among and listened to the men, at fair or market, working in his father's fields or talking by the fire at night.

Fitzmaurice's language, like the speech of the people of Duagh in his time, is peppered with Irish words and phrases. 'Boloeeriv' when we first see it in *The Pie-Dish* has an eastern European look about it. Roll it on the tongue and it is nothing more mysterious than the familiar 'Bail Ó Dhia oraibh' we heard from Mícheál O'Hehir when the ball was thrown in at Croke Park.

The word 'shandanagh' has a more homely appearance and turns out to be the old man in the corner, *an sean-duine*. 'Cleakawn' from *claí*, a small or low fence, is another of the many words which speckle Fitzmaurice's dialogue. Words like 'elaygil', *a laoigh ghil*, a dear one, and 'careshuck', *an chiarseach*, the female blackbird. He captured and caged for us a people's speech in lazy flight from Irish to English. What we hear is what was said, but the artist rearranges.

The people who crowded his youthful days were still very vivid in Fitzmaurice's mind when I knew him but briefly forty years ago. Over a glass of stout he would describe a scene at nightfall in Bedford near Listowel, where he was born: youngsters jeering a servant girl from west Kerry because they had heard she spoke Irish. She took refuge in a house into which they followed her and, cowering in the chimney corner, she told her tormentors that she understood Irish but didn't speak it.

But there was warmth, too, and tolerance. He recalled with some pleasure sitting with his father and the family in a front pew in St Mary's Cathedral in Killarney when their neighbour, Dr Mangan from Bedford, was consecrated Bishop of Kerry.

When I met George Fitzmaurice he was in his eighties and walked slowly, his body thrust forward. As he approached you in the street you found yourself looking into the top of his grey felt hat, the brim so broad that it almost hid his stooped figure. When you spoke to him, and you spoke quietly for he was very shy, he raised his head slowly. Gradually the light of recognition spreading from his eyes lit up his face. Then he smiled and there was a softly spoken greeting. He had a big, round, pleasant face and for his age a fine colour in his cheeks. His eyes were blue and, I think, very large; so was his mouth below a long upper lip. He had a curious habit of moving his mouth in a cud-chewing fashion as he listened. An old raincoat came almost to the ground.

If you met him in O'Connell Street in the afternoon, he was on his way to Woolworth's Café in Henry Street. The lunch rush over, he would take a tray to the self-service counter and retire to a quiet corner to have his meal. I took a curious gent of a literary turn to the top of the stairs one time to see him but I wouldn't for the world have allowed anyone to intrude on his privacy.

You could meet him too at night-time, ambling up Grafton Street. He used to go to Mooney's of Harry Street, an honest-to-God pub then, just across the road from McDaid's. He stood by himself, a lonely figure, the support of the counter keeping him erect. It was here one night that I mentioned his plays and I think this put an end to our brief friendship. I had heard the stories ... like the pub he hysed himself out of, never to come back, when a country barman asked him, 'Are you the George Fitzmaurice whose plays do be on at the Abbey?'

I wouldn't have drawn down the subject, but that Mícheál Ó hAodha had asked me to try and persuade him to give Radio Éireann permission to broadcast *The County Dressmaker* and *The Magic Glasses*. He turned me down, but gave his permission subsequently.

I think the last place I saw him was in the Winter Gardens, now gone, at the corner of Cuffe Street and the Green. As ever, he was by himself at the far end of the bar. I had gone in there during the interval, the night Brendan Behan's *An Giall* opened at the Damer. He was curious about the sudden influx of thirsty *gaeilgeóirí*, noticing they weren't regulars. I explained. He regretted he hadn't learned some Irish. It was once a major European language, he told me, judging by the placenames, and spoken in Lisbon, Lisieux and Listowel! He pursed his lips and I thought I detected a twinkle in his eye.

'Fine acting in two revivals at the Abbey' is how the *Irish Times* described *The Dandy Dolls* and *The Well of the Saints* when they were brought back in July 1970 for a short run prior to a London transfer for an international theatre festival. We played at the Old Vic and, the gods be praised, as happened on Broadway and on a former visit to the West End, I had a dressing-room to myself.

Cast and crew were put up in the Irish Club in Eaton Square and a bus brought us to and from the theatre. I rarely sleep after the excitement of a first night, and next morning I was up early and went out for a stroll. The uppermost thought in my head was what kind of reception the press would give the plays. I always fear the worst and for that reason made up my mind not to look at the morning papers. As I walked along, what should I see but the buff shade of the *Financial*

Times stuck in a railing far from a house entrance. I was tempted to have a look but decided against it. When I was returning, the paper was still there. On an impulse I took it and turned to the arts page.

Anthony Curtis wrote: '*The Dandy Dolls* which we saw last night has a fantastical Celtic cricket-on-the-hearth quality … Folk art can be a bit impenetrable if you are not one of the folk and the strange piece, most spiritedly performed, was received with a baffled air by the audience. In England it would have been a Barrie-ish pantomime … in Germany it would have all centred on the moment when they nailed the doll down to the table, highly symbolic no doubt, but being Irish it all ends with a bit of good old-fashioned priest bashing.'

Oh well! The Hag of Barna hits Fr James once with the broom, which he takes from her and drives the Hag and her son from the house as our Lord drove the moneylenders from the temple.

'No such bafflement,' Anthony Curtis said, 'in *The Well of the Saints*.' And he gave a synopsis of the story. 'As always with Synge,' he continued, 'the dice seem to be loaded for pathos, but there is humour well brought out in the main performances of Éamon Kelly and Máire Ní Dhomhnaill, the peatfire in their bellies burnt brightly in the great slagging matches.' He had praise for the cast, for Hugh Hunt's direction and for the settings of Alan Barlow.

The daily and evening papers displayed various degrees of bafflement at *The Dandy Dolls*, but praised the acting of Éamon Keane, Joan O'Hara, Desmond Cave and Pat Layde.

Commenting on the production of *The Well of the Saints*, Michael Billington in the *Times* complained that 'some rather cumbersome grouping – with too many solid peasant figures planted downstage – obscures some of the most powerful theatrical moments such as the blind peasant's first recognition of the faces around him, after his miraculous healing.'

The press was over from Dublin to cover the event. Gus Smith writing in the *Irish Independent* said that 'Missing from the Old Vic on the first night were the Abbey directors. Strange when you consider that this was an auspicious occasion for the company. One also missed the first night reception for the players at the Irish embassy. Surely this is no way to treat members of Ireland's National Theatre on tour. I regret to have to say that the Abbey Company opened at the Old Vic unheralded and unsung. This will not do!'

In fact, two directors, Gabriel Fallon and Roibeárd Ó Faracháin, came at midweek. We saw them in the bus taking us back to the Irish Club. They were deep in discussion and spoke ne'er a word to any of us.

The Irish Club was fairly central, and when free I renewed my acquaintance with the city. I went again to the National Gallery, and fed the pigeons in Trafalgar Square. I went too to the Tate Gallery and bought a reproduction of Jack B. Yeats' *Travellers* – two figures met, and in as lively a conversation as that of any Abbey directors, in a multicoloured landscape in which there were elements of Alan Barlow's setting for *The Well of the Saints*.

I wasn't finished with that play yet. Years later I played the same part in an Irish Theatre Company's touring production. It was directed by Christopher FitzSimon, and Maura O'Sullivan was a splendid Mary Doul. The curtain-raiser this time was *On Baile's Strand* by W. B. Yeats.

To go out where we came in, George Fitzmaurice, who is gradually gaining recognition outside the shores of Ireland, is now neglected at the Abbey. In my many years there I was in but one of his plays, *The Pie-Dish*. I played the part of an honest potter who, wishing to excel at his art, sells his soul to the devil.

DRESSING-ROOM ONE

_&

Dressing-rooms at the Abbey were not allotted according to one's status in a play. There wasn't any one-actor accommodation for those playing leads as in the commercial theatre. In a permanent company like the Abbey had then, permanent actors, once allotted a dressing-room, remained there permanently. It was like a second home to some, and one actor had many of his personal belongings in his desk drawer, including, it was said, the deeds of his house.

In No. 1 dressing-room, situated almost under the stage, there were six actors' places on a long bench in front of six mirrors. The mirrors were lit by twenty-one bulbs, three at the sides of each mirror, and all operated by one switch. In the summertime we nearly melted with the heat. There were lamps on the low ceiling too, but the light bulb inside the door was never put in its socket, because when the door was closed it sheared off the bulb – an indication of how well designed the place was. I dressed in No. 1 over a period of twenty-eight years. The image of the place is etched in my brain.

In the long bench there were six drawers for the actors' make-up and scripts; in front of it stood six stools, an easy chair and a rack on which to hang costumes; and under it was a stretcher bed on which to lie when exhaustion set in. In the daytime, many is the man slept off the effects of a few pints on it. There was a toilet, two wash-hand basins and a shower. There was hot water in constant supply and very tempting for non-residents.

Pale actors in the company dressed together in Nos 4, 5 and 6. The ladies dressed in Nos 2 and 3. In No 1 there were six players, including myself, all of whom came from the regions. Harry Brogan was the only urbanite. Peadar Lamb and Mícheál Ó Briain, when they talked of home, spoke in mellifluous Connemara Irish. At times when those of us fluent

277

enough joined in, our subterranean chamber took on the air of a tiny Gaeltacht.

But there were two other actors present who never spoke directly to each other. Their mutual animosity was manifest. I often opened the door unexpectedly when they were alone to find their voices raised in bitter acrimony. If the walls and mirrors could speak they would reveal the secret of two men passionately in love with one woman. But when cast in a play as long-lost friends, how convincingly they laughed, shook hands and fondly embraced.

Only once did I dress in No. 4. That was when Peter O'Toole played in *Waiting for Godot*, and we were all evicted from No 1 to make room for him. He put a gold star on his door, and his name in Irish – Peadar Ó Tuathail. Other stars who came to our theatre from time to time settled in with the regulars.

Democracy in the dressing-rooms had to do with the no-star system at the Abbey, which was always regarded as a writers' theatre. Actors were never mentioned on the posters. The double crown simply said what was on, by whom, what time and how much to get in. All this was stated clearly so that the contents could be gleaned while passing by on a galloping horse. If you stabled your horse and paid your money into the theatre, you could see the actors and read their names in the programme.

I am convinced that I was the first Abbey actor whose name and physiognomy appeared on a poster. During Tomás MacAnna's second term as artistic director, he asked me to do an evening of storytelling at the Peacock. I became so nervous at the prospect of standing for two hours in front of an audience that had a job been going as barman in a remote tavern in Katmandu I would have taken it.

But one-man shows were becoming popular in the theatre in 1975. Mícheál Mac Liammóir had given the headline in Ireland with his *The Importance of Being Oscar* and *I Must Be Talking to My Friends*. When I got over the shock of being asked, storytelling seemed to me an ideal subject for a one-man show. I had experience of doing longish storytelling spots in concerts, and my part in *The Tailor and Ansty* was in many ways a solo effort.

I got down to throwing some stories together with the theme of emigration, and I called the show In My Father's Time. Tomás MacAnna gave me Michael Colgan to direct it, and, oh lucky me – we got on like two houses on fire. We found that a number of stories told one after the other could sound episodic. There had to be a changing relationship between the pieces, and the links had to be carefully thought out to make seamless the fabric, which we hoped would be colourful and entertaining.

Meabh Browne designed the set, which had as its focal point the fireplace, where storytellers sat since Fionn and Oisín told tales in the king's house in ancient Ireland. Opposite the hearth there was a gable wall, a fly-in roof section overhead, and a freestanding door and window. I was given a say in the selection of the furniture. A súgán armchair, two súgán chairs, a well worn deal table, a dresser full of shining delph, a foldaway settle bed, a wickerwork turf basket with sods piled high, harness hanging from a peg, and a box on which sat a white enamel bucket of water from which I drank with a mug to punctuate a piece, or to tide me over a round of applause. There was one holy picture to preside over the proceedings.

The mantelpiece had an alarm clock, a tea canister, a candle in a sconce, a small oil lamp and letters from America. Socks and an old shirt hung from a line across the fireplace. There were a kettle, a teapot and another pot suspended from the crane, and downstage a butterbox with a hinged lid which became a seat. Inside it was a regular storehouse and the Tailor, who had one, called it his cornucopia.

Michael Colgan directed me so that I used almost everything on the stage at least once. The armchair was for the long, legendary-type story with the red glow of the fire lighting up my face. Pulling a chair out from the table and standing between them was a gateway. Putting a chair on the table, I sitting at the other end became the driver of an engine pulling a train-load of emigrants out of Killarney station. There were journeys to the turf basket to pile the sods on the fire. There was delph from the dresser, tea from the canister and water from the kettle into the teapot to make the cup that cheers.

The table was also a bar or a shop counter to stand behind.

I moved in the set – sat on the chairs, on the butterbox, leaned against the table, sang a song standing by the dresser while putting a reins in the harness bridle – and I tried to do all this with ease and naturalness, without fuss or ado.

Before the performance it would be impossible for me to run the lines, there were so many of them. Instead I topped and tailed the stories, fixed their sequence firmly in my head and thoroughly rehearsed the linking pieces. Opening night came. The heart pounded and I reached out for the hand which guides us mortals in times of stress. The people piled in. They sat on the steps and stood at the back. Tadhg Crowley of the box office said afterwards that for the run we did a hundred and ten per cent business.

The show succeeded beyond all expectations. Because of a misprint in the *Irish Times*, the admission prices at the Peacock were given as 75p and £1000. Seamus Kelly of that paper told his readers that having seen the show it was worth every penny of it. John MacInerney, writing of the evening's entertainment in the *Irish Press*, said, 'Emigration is the focus of many of the tales allowing the storyteller to dovetail accounts of wakes, partings, returns, all night dancing (and how the clergy put the dead hand on all such joy) and matchmaking. Heartbreak and comedy are held in nice balance, and that salty, sly Kerry humour keeps sentimentality alertly at bay.'

So great was the demand that every June for seven years I had a new one-man storytelling show on the stage of the Peacock, all but one directed by Michael Colgan. I toured the country with them. I was in so many places that one man said I must have stopped at every back door in Ireland. One night in the great hall of Magee University in Derry the crewman on the curtain told me at the interval that he was going to watch a football match on the box, but that he would be back before the end. He mistimed his return and when I told my last tale I took a bow but the curtain didn't close. I walked into the wings and pressed a button which brought the tabs across. I pressed another button and the curtain opened. I went out and took another bow. I continued to open and close the curtain and take bow after bow until the audience were rocking with laughter and getting to their feet. I received a standing ovation and gave myself as many curtains as Marcel Marceau.

I was in New York in January 1976 as part of Ireland's contribution to America's bicentennial celebrations. Irish talent was well represented. I stepped into an elevator in a Manhattan hotel and found myself blessed among Siobhán McKenna, Marie Kean, Anna Manahan, Aideen O'Kelly and the singer Mary O'Hara. They were in the Best of Ireland concert in Carnegie hall, as were Peter O'Toole, Donal McCann, Niall Tóibín, Niall Buggy, Donal Donnelly and yours truly, in scenes from *Waiting for Godot, Juno and the Paycock, Riders to the Sea, The Playboy of the Western World, Philadelphia, Here I Come!* and *The Loves of Cass McGuire*. All backed up by Geraldine O'Grady, Eily O'Grady, Frank Patterson, Caitriona Yeats, Jesse Owens, Hal Roach, the Clancy Brothers, the Chieftains and the McNiff dancers. An imposing array – a sight to dazzle the eye.

The show was presented to an Irish American audience in the presence of Jim Farley, the Irishman of the century, and in the lobby there was a photography exhibition showing the works of Fergus Bourke.

Of course the whole caboodle was meant to be held in Madison Square Garden, but the New York promotion committee, once formed, split (in the fashion of many Irish movements), and the energy which should have gone into publicity and organisation went into bickering. The Madison Square Garden plan fell through, and we ended up playing to a fairly packed Carnegie hall, but only for a matinée performance.

Robert C. Roman of the *Irish Echo* declared the show 'an unqualified success … a magnificent production'. He said that everyone associated with the afternoon of the best in the cultural and entertainment arts deserved rich praise. News of it spread across the Atlantic and Alfred Paul Berger said in the *Irish Times*: 'The entertainment itself was pervaded with a kind of gentle, endearing innocence too seldom encountered in this hard-bitten age and area. The entire affair was one large Irish Valentine, unabashedly unsophisticated, and the more winning for that. While Siobhán McKenna and Peter

O'Toole were most in evidence, the performance was well laced with many more or less recognisable names in all divisions
of the arts.'

The Clothes

⋐ॐ

I found that the sense of continuity at the Abbey was a cherished commodity. It hung by a thread of stories told by old actors, parables that went back to the founders of the theatre and to those who practised in it down the years. Many of the tales you could take with a pinch of salt, like the one about a wardrobe seamstress in the old days who was so pious that she wouldn't sew buttons into men's trousers' flies.

The wardrobe was part of the Abbey tradition. When I became a member there was a great stock of costumes used in the theatre's repertoire of native plays. Each director selected garments from this collection for his new production. The store contained costumes designed by the artist Seán Keating for a production of *The Playboy of the Western World* in the 1940s. There were items which must have come from Connemara or the Aran Islands, for their handiwork had all the crude honesty of a country tailor.

From his hand came grey and brown *bréidín* (tweed) coats, collared waistcoats, *báiníns*, trousers and knee breeches for the men. There were red flannel skirts for the women. An assortment of aprons and brown-and-fawn paisley shawls with tassels. These last could have walked off the oil painting by Grace Henry of three shawled Connemara women bunched together on a hill. Among all these items there was a gent's tweed coat, faded and foxy and built in the cutaway fashion of the last century. It came to just above the knees and had large pocket flaps. It was much the worse for wear, with frayed edges and the padding protruding from a tear in the left shoulder. I wore it many times and got so fond of it that I became jealous if I saw it on another actor's back.

It fitted as if it was made for me, and with a neckcloth, knee breeches and long grey homemade stockings, the outfit

283

on me looked the real goat's toe in any turn of the century native play; even more so if topped with a battered, greenish, floppy felt hat and supported by a pair of boots so old and pliable they could have first been worn by Barry Fitzgerald. It was my costume in the character of Old Mahon in *The Playboy of the Western World* and Scots people got an eyeful of it when we took the play to the Edinburgh Festival. The Irish collection, as I'll name those old costumes, was part of the Abbey's continuity.

It was in Hugh Hunt's time as artistic director that a lady from Manchester took over as wardrobe mistress for a while. She must have been flabbergasted at the collection of Aran Islands and Connemara drapery, the likes of which she'd have never seen in the illustrations in her theatre costume textbooks. Anyway she got rid of the whole motley caboodle. What happened to my tweed coat I do not know.

I would have liked if 'the clothes', as Harry Brogan always called the costumes, went to the St Vincent de Paul. And it could be so, for one day I am almost certain I saw my foxy coat on the back of a poor man fingering the keys of a decrepit concertina in Talbot Street. A dark green hat with a scattering of coppers inside lay by his ancient boots. If the coat was mine it was still in show business.

It may be only a fancy, but my feeling is that the old Abbey went out the door with those costumes. The permanent company to all intents and purposes is gone and there are new faces before the footlights.

White-Knuckle Flights

✑

In mid-February of 1976 I was haring across the Atlantic again, on my way to Newfoundland to contribute to the Canadian Association for Irish Studies seminar in the University of St John's. Author Bryan MacMahon, playwright M. J. Molloy, the folklorist Kevin Danaher and many more were on the team from Ireland.

Bryan spoke about Peig Sayers and the vernacular of the storyteller, M. J. Molloy on the making of folk plays and Kevin Danaher on the customs and lore of the countryside. There were readings by the poet Thomas Kinsella, and Eileen O'Casey talked about her husband, Seán.

Bryan and I enjoyed that trip to Newfoundland and rejoiced in the company of the other contributors and the many new friends we made there. We relaxed when our work was over. As we were talking quietly one night in a crowded room, and thinking back to the time when we first met playing in the local drama group twenty-five years before, Bryan said, with an air of pride, 'Ned, we've come a long way.' 'Yes,' I answered, 'only three thousand miles.' He lowered his left eyelid and said, '*amparan*', a Listowel word implying derision. Dineen defines '*amparach*' as a helpless human condition of being bloated with swelling. The familiar expression in strange surroundings made us laugh heartily.

Talking about our own contributions to the seminar, Bryan said that during my show, *In My Father's Time*, his attention was drawn to a group of Eskimos, young men and women who were students at the university, and he wondered how on earth would they respond to the indigenous humour of my stories. At first some were bewildered while others enjoyed the telling, but then some throwaway line or gesture must have reminded them of the idiosyncrasies of an old man in their own village, because they broke into almost uncontrollable laughter. They fell silent and their eyes glistened when death was mentioned, or the pain of parting during the emigration from Ireland in the 1920s.

Many of the Irish fishermen from the Cork and Waterford coasts who sailed, in the last century, to the rich fishing grounds of *Talamh an Éisc* settled in and around St John's. In the streets and in the shops there is a noticeable Irish lilt to the people's speech. At a television station I could have sworn I heard one crewman say to another, 'Are 'ou all right there now, boy?' The taxi drivers' accents sounded Irish, slightly diluted, and Aidan O'Hara, who worked for a long time in Newfoundland, told me that Irish words linger on in everyday speech.

I was in a house one Sunday where worshippers had gathered after Mass. As at home, there was a cup of tea going, and one lady was asked to stay on for a mouthful. 'Oh no,' she said, 'I am in a hurry. There's a *slua* at home waiting for me.' She had a large family depending on her attention. *Slua*, of course, is the Irish word for a crowd.

Irish surnames like Tobin and Brennan gaze down from the fascia boards of shop fronts. The native sense of the ridiculous is akin to our own. A man in a car running eastwards to the sea stopped and asked a Newfoundlander working in a field, 'Is this the road to Ireland?' ''Tis,' the farmer replied, 'but you'd want to be careful. 'Tis flooded beyond the lighthouse!'

There was an arrangement with the university whereby we visitors stayed with Irish families. I was the guest of Dr Michael Mangan and his wife, who is also a doctor. Michael, who hails from Galway, owned racehorses in Ireland at that time, and there was one very famous animal of his called Monksfield, small and compact, which made a great name for himself. When I came home I saw him on TV win hands down at Cheltenham.

Michael had a bar down in the cellar. This speakeasy, as he called it, is a feature of many houses in the States too. There's a counter complete with flap and a little door to get in. Shelves of bottles, many of them of Irish origin, line the back wall. There's a fridge for the beer and the place is decorated with Guinness and whiskey signs brought over from Ireland.

A few tables, easy chairs and a high stool or two. A cosy place for a quiet drink after a hard day. Many is the after dinner-hour I sat outside the bar, Michael inside, as we talked into the night, and the talk was always of home.

As part of an educational scheme St John's University sent me out to speak to dramatic societies throughout the province of Newfoundland. I was to conduct a workshop one evening and put on my own storytelling show the next. My first stop was Labrador. The February weather was vile. Snowflakes flew thick and fast past the window of the plane. By air seems to be the only way of getting about, and the planes fly in the most atrocious weather. In the jolting and buffeting in the storm, passengers hold on desperately to their seats, grasping the armrests in such a tight grip that these journeys are known as 'white-knuckle flights'.

My heart came up into my mouth one time as the plane seemed to stop. Outside the window was white with driving snow, and as there was little difference between the bumping in the sky and that experienced when landing, I thought we were still in the air. I held my breath, waiting for the plane to fall; but the French-English announcement of the bilingual Canadian steward proclaimed that we had landed.

Wahbush is the airport for Labrador. The two places, some miles apart, are known as the twin cities, but in actual fact they are no bigger than a small Munster town, and came into being because of the discovery of large deposits of iron ore. When the snowploughs clear the runways, the channel made looks as if a knife had cut through the icing of a cake with banks of snow at either side. The streets are the same, and so cold, thirty degrees below, that if taxis turn off their engines they can't start them again. It is easy to find a taxi rank. There's a cloud of exhaust smoke over it. Motorists have a heater inside the car and another in the engine.

When the vehicle is parked at home or at work there is a long flex to the heater which is plugged into the electricity. Otherwise the moisture would freeze in the door locks and the oil would solidify in the engine. The streets are always frozen, and a car couldn't negotiate a sharp rise without chains wound round the tyres.

Wahbush and Labrador are three hundred miles inland and eighteen hundred feet over sea level. Because of the altitude, the air is thin and a newcomer falls asleep on his feet. A man brought me out to see the open mining and three times I fell asleep in the car. Trains, miles long, are travelling night and day, bringing iron ore to the coast for export. I was told that the trains were driverless, operated by electricity, but that could have been a Newfoundlander pulling my leg. What took my fancy, though, were the massive tractors with scoops in front for shifting the iron ore. To give an idea of their size, my picture was taken beside one and my head just came up to the axle of the wheel.

The space in which I did my storytelling show in Labrador was a games centre and far too large. It lacked the intimacy of a theatre. A sprinkling of Irish in the audience helped the reaction and forged a bond across the footlights. The workshop the evening before was full of interest for me as John B. Keane's *Sive* was the next play the society was to perform. The Irish, some from home and some from St John's, had plenty of work in the iron ore industry. There were Northern Irish there too, and the city of Wahbush boasted an Orange and a Hibernian hall. Protestants and Catholics tended to drift into separate communities when they settled in the Newfoundland countryside, and the weathercock or cross on the church spires revealed their identities.

In the twin cities only Wahbush had a hotel, where I stayed. My bedroom window overlooked what must have been a playing field in the summer, because the top of a soccer goalpost showed a few inches above the snow. Disposable paper slippers (mine fitted) were provided for one's journeys to the bathroom, and the heat was blown in, which reminded me of a night spent years before in a motel in Wilmington, Delaware. Thank God there was a great log fire in the dining-room.

From Labrador I flew to Gander. As we came in to land, a large bird (in Gander of all places) crashed into the windscreen of the plane and cracked the glass. It could have been serious had the screen been breached. Those flying on to St John's had to take another plane.

I enjoyed doing my own show in Gander, but the workshops, sometimes two a day, became slightly arduous, though the children in the schools were delightful and entered with gusto into my near insane projects. I told a story, which a volunteer among them retold, and then they acted it out on the floor. They improvised with imagination and assumed the characters of the little red hen, the cat and the mouse of the narrative.

The enchanted cake, when it was about to be eaten, ran away, followed by the cat and the mouse and the little red hen. In the chase they were joined by a crumply horned cow and a saddlebacked sow. They passed through a meadow full of mowers, by a barn full of threshers and a riverside full of washerwomen, all of whom joined in the chase. A sly old fox cornered the cake and they all sat around in a circle and had a feast.

They improvised the king's orchard where his son guarded the apples from the great eagle with the feathers of gold, whose eyes were as big as the moon and as bright as the sun. They simulated an aeroplane, complete with pilots ('This is your captain speaking') and hostesses ('Fasten your seat-belts, please') and passengers holding on to their seats in a white-knuckle flight over Newfoundland. They impersonated the storm and the noise of the engines and regretted when I left and took my daftness with me.

My next stop was Cornerbrook where I met the son of novelist Maurice Walsh. He had chains around his tyres as he drove me over icy roads to a secondary school where they were preparing for a performance of Synge's *Riders to the Sea*. In giving them the background to the play, I remembered my holiday in Inis Meáin and my visit to Ceata Bheag's house, where Synge stayed when he came to live in the Aran Islands. Ceata Bheag was busy at her housework when a party of us arrived. She excused herself, went into the room, and came back with a stylish apron and a shoulder shawl. She greeted each person individually in Connacht Irish, which, because of the island's proximity to Clare, had a little of the Munster music. We couldn't have been received more graciously by the Queen of England. She sat on a fireside chair and, like a queen, held court.

I hoped that the actress playing the part of Maurya in *Riders to the Sea* might take her as a model. I told the students about life on the island and about the sea on which the people depended for a living. The ocean was their orchard, their meadow and their garden.

The students read their parts and, in spite of their Canadian-American accents, the magic of the words came through. They laughed at me at first when I tried to teach them the lament – the *caoineadh* – of the women as Bartley's drowned body is brought back on a door from the sea. Finally they got the lilt of it. It sounded great, and the sorrowing mother's closing speech would soften the heart in a stone:

> *It isn't that I haven't prayed for you, Bartley, to the Almighty God. It isn't that I haven't said prayers in the dark night till you wouldn't know what I'd be saying; but it's a great rest I'll have now, and it's time surely.*

When I came back to St John's I wrote a report on my activities – the limbers, the improvisations, the rehearsals, all the phases of the work I had done – and gave it to Mr D. Ferry of the Arts and Culture Centre. He was so pleased with the account that the ghost walked immediately and I got the bread, always a fitting culmination to a bout of hard work. My next stop would be New York. Ted Auletta had arranged with me to take part in a concert presented by Carmel Quinn in Carnegie hall on 6 March.

The morning came for me to leave Newfoundland. It had snowed so heavily the night before that Michael Mangan had to give me his wellingtons to walk from the house to the taxi. I have them still. Many people from the province go down to New York on day trips, and Dr and Mrs Mangan told me that when a man comes to immigration he holds up his passport and says, 'I'm only down for de day.' I did just that and it worked. No delay, I was waved through.

Waiting in my dressing-room in Carnegie hall on the night of the show, I was surprised to hear over the tannoy an artist on stage telling one of my stories. I had many imitators at home but I didn't think the malady had spread across the Atlantic. Imitation, it is said, is a form of flattery. Flattery I could have done without that night, because the story he was telling was on my list for the concert and I had to rack my brains for another and rehearse it in the little time I had left. I went on and couldn't have wished for a better reception.

After the show I met Billy Nolan, a son of Liselton, and a diplomat attached to the Irish Consulate in New York. I shall not forget his kindness to me. For safety's sake I had mailed home most of the fee I had earned in Newfoundland, leaving myself with the plane fare and spending money in New York. By a miscalculation I had left myself short and was unable to afford my next meal. Billy must have sensed my predicament. He stood me a dinner in a Russian restaurant nearby. The waiter, when I told him I was a vegetarian, prepared a gorgeous meal for me, so unlike another American waiter who, when I said I didn't eat meat, wanted to know if I was some kind of nut.

I had to go back to Carnegie hall a few times before I got my fee from Ted Auletta. Some Americans hate parting with money. When I got the dollars I had enough to tide me over to my next engagement, which was with the Irish American Cultural Institute. This was Eoin McKiernan's *Irish Fortnight*, a tour of United States universities in the days around St Patrick's Day.

Eoin had sent me the schedule and a hundred dollars. I'd have no expenses on the road, he assured me. I had my air tickets, which he enclosed, and I would be met at the airport at each venue and put up in an Irish American homestead. The majority of the houses I visited were quite palatial, with swimming pools and as many bathrooms as we had bedrooms at home. The owners were the successful Irish, the grand-children and great-grandchildren of penniless emigrants. They were rich, friendly, hospitable to a fault, and every mother's son and daughter of them as handsome as the famous Kennedy family.

I criss-crossed America, starting in Pittsburgh, where I stayed with Arthur Fedel, a scion of France whose Irish connection was that he had been to Trinity College – on a post-war GI scholarship. In after years he researched the work of writer Francis MacManus for his PhD. Arthur walked with me to the university, where I gave my first show on the night of 10 March. He had a sheaf of fliers advertising the events of the coming fortnight. He handed them out to passers-by, good-humouredly extolling the virtues of what was on offer. To a rather reluctant young lady he said, 'You must be Irish. You have red hair. Take one!' She did.

Eoin McKiernan always had at least fourteen contributors in the air in the daytime, so that there was an event taking place simultaneously in that number of universities that night. Sometimes, arriving at a venue in the early morning, I would meet another contributor setting out. Men half my age were complaining that the gruelling schedule was getting them down.

We had on our list Ruaidhrí de Valera, Desmond Guinness, Diarmuid Ó Muirithe, Michael Hartnett, Aidan O'Hara, Nicholas Furlong, Margaret MacCurtain and many more. I did my show at twelve centres in fourteen days, from Omaha, Nebraska, to Holyoke, Mass., from Albany to San Antonio in Texas, and places in between. Inside two weeks I had experienced the icy cold of Labrador and the heat of old king sol splitting the stones in Texas.

Monsignor Michael McManus was my host in San Antonio. The hundred dollars Eoin McKiernan had given me at the outset was gone and I was on my uppers again. The good monsignor must have seen this in my eyes because, on shaking hands with me as I was going, he left a fifty-dollar bill in my palm.

Dr Rona Fields introduced me to the audience when I spoke at Clark University in Worcester, Mass. Jewish, with red hair and blue eyes, she gloried in that part of her heritage that was Irish. Rochester, Minnesota, brought me to the house of my brother-in-law, Dr Michael O'Sullivan, and his wife Margaret. Familiar faces and talk of home helped me to relax, and after a few beers Michael and I went native and sang 'The Valley of Knockanure'. The lecture room in Rochester stands out in my mind because of the fact that nearly everyone in the audience had a camera or a tape recorder. I was no more than settled in when the lights began to flash and microphones like snakes' heads rose out of the dark and crept towards the platform.

My last engagement was at Fordham University, Lincoln Centre, New York. I stayed with my dear friends Jack and Jeanie Cronin in Yonkers. Next morning I had my last letter from Eoin McKiernan, in English this time. He generally wrote in Irish. He thanked me for my contribution to the Irish American Cultural Institute's Fortnight. 'You have done beautifully,' he rounded off. 'You have demonstrated a great art, and charmed great audiences. You have been a wonderful ambassador for Ireland.'

He enclosed my fee. Jack, Jeanie and I went out for a meal and a few drinks that evening. Tomorrow I would board the Aer Lingus skyship – St Brendan or St Bridget – and hyse home to Ireland.

STORY THEATRE

❦

Lelia Doolan was artistic director at the Abbey after Alan Simpson but her term of office ended abruptly. I thought she was treated harshly. At actors' meetings a number of the male members – the old stagers, some of them in the Abbey for twenty-five years – were less than gentlemanly to her. During her stay Tomás MacAnna came up with an idea for story theatre in Irish at the Peacock, with which she readily agreed. It was to be called *Scéal Scéalaí* – Story Storyteller. Tomás asked me to join him in dramatising some of my stories for the stage, and together we put on paper an evening's entertainment, not unlike the Hail Mary, the first part of which was made by the Angel Gabriel and the Church made the last.

Tomás assembled a cast and we went into rehearsal. As well as the dramatised folktales, we had music, mime, song and dance. The setting was of batik hangings by Bernadette Madden, and the basic costumes were of the same material. In one of my stories about the fairy host – 'The Changeling', it was called – infrared light was used, and on the darkened stage white and light colours showed up dazzlingly bright and gave an otherworldly atmosphere to the scene.

Tomás organised a small orchestra which included Seosamh MacCionnaith, Seán Ó Duibhir, Mary Bergin and Mary's sister Antoinette. Fr Pat Ahern of Siamsa Tíre in Tralee directed the music and song and taught the actors to dance to an Irish tune. Tomás MacAnna was the overall director and, because of his long association with pantomimes in Irish at the Abbey, he had a distinct flair for this type of theatre. His was a rare talent for positioning, grouping and moving actors on stage.

The storyteller, sitting at the side, opened the tale and, as his characters materialised, the actors, as it were, leaped from his imagination and the story became alive. When it was not feasible, visually, to move the story ahead, the storyteller took over momentarily, in much the same way as a narrator in a radio play.

My contributions were mostly in the first half, interspersed with dance and song. We had a giant and a horse, not the pantomime type but the traditional wren boys' animal which roams the streets of Dingle on St Stephen's Day.

It was a happy show and went down well. It was described as 'exquisite', 'spectacular' and 'delicious' by the critics. Desmond Rush wrote in the *Independent*: 'The folklore and folk-music blend superlatively well, which elevates *Scéal Scéalaí* above any other entertainment of its kind I have seen in the Abbey or the Peacock.' Because Tomás MacAnna was unable to accompany us, I as co-author of *Scéal Scéalaí* was made director of our two Gaeltacht tours. We played first in the Taibhdhearc in Galway. I remember when the run was over and the actors were sitting in the lounge of the Ardilaun House Hotel, where we were staying, when news of Bloody Sunday in Derry came on television.

The sight of Fr Edward Daly with his white handkerchief, pleading for a safe passage for the wounded, filled our hearts at once with shock and admiration. When the full tally of those killed by the military became known, anti-British feeling ran high in Galway and throughout the country.

Our next show was in Carraroe in west Galway the following night. We arrived there in the morning and were busy setting up the stage when a group of people arrived and I was told in meticulous Irish that because of the bloodshed in Derry, if the show went ahead that night history would be made in Carraroe. Despite the sweetness of the speech there was no doubting the threat their words carried.

I rang Dublin. The Abbey wanted me to go ahead with the show. They were at a safe distance. I was on the spot and didn't fancy trouble. I discussed the matter with Tadhg Crowley the tour manager and the actors, and we decided to postpone the show for one night as a mark of sympathy with the relatives of the dead in Derry. That night at the time of the show there was Mass in the local church, and the priest invited the actors to intone prayers, from a script which he had given them, for the repose of the souls of the dead, for the comfort of the living and for the forgiveness of those who perpetrated such a heinous crime. He wanted me to pray that God would put Paisley *ar bhóthar a leasa* (on the road of rectitude). I didn't feel like doing so, and made an excuse to get out of it.

Next morning Peadar Lamb and I, with a broadcasting unit hired in Galway, went around the district publicising the fact that the postponed show would be held that night. We turned up the volume to reach houses far in from the public road. People crowded to the doors to listen, and animals in the fields stopped their grazing and wandered in our direction, attracted by the augmented sound of music and speech, something they didn't hear every day.

The show was a success that night in Carraroe and the night after in Spiddal. Our next stop was in Inis Mór in the Aran Islands. The settings, lights, costumes, props and crew went in by boat. Tadhg Crowley, the touring manager, and the actors travelled by Aer Aran. I remember actor Clive Geraghty gave his plane seat to Finnola Eustace who was our stage manager. There was a bumpy landing on the grass runway on the island.

When we got settled up in our lodgings – I slept in the presbytery in a bed reserved for the bishop when he visited his island parish – we got down to setting the scene in the local hall. The ESB didn't go to Aran then and our electric power was from an oil-driven generator. The stress must have been too much for the engine because the power failed half an hour before the show. I had visions of scouring the island for candles and oil lamps which would have been a poor substitute for the lighting effects devised by Tomás MacAnna and Mick Doyle.

Mick worked like the trooper he was on the generator, and by reducing the load to suit the machine's capacity, with only a little time to spare before the afternoon show the lights came on to a mighty cheer.

Schoolchildren made up most of our first audience, and it was heart-warming to see their young faces in the front rows all aglow at the splash of colour, at the music, the dance and the sight of the giant and the pantomime horse. For these children it was their first experience of a travelling show and their reaction was different from their mainland cousins. When the final curtain came down there was no applause. We bowed a second time but there was no putting together of hands. But the children weren't disappointed. From their laughing faces and their animated conversation there was no mistaking their happiness.

Applause wasn't stinted at the night's performance, and when it ended the audience remained in the hall. In a while's time musicians appeared, the seats were pushed back and the local people took to the floor in a set dance. I have never heard dance music played so fast, or with such vigour, and the sound of heel and toe on the boarded floor nearly lifted the roof. We actors joined in the merriment, as our hosts tapped out a welcome to us. Their merry feet seemed to beat out an appreciation of what they had seen on stage.

Next day Fergus Bourke took the cast in costume out on the rocks to take some pictures. The ladies were posing in a group when two young men of Aran came by on tractors one behind the other. They were attracted by the loveliness of the scene, and looked in that direction. To savour the view all the more the man in front stopped his vehicle suddenly, and the man behind, not noticing, ran into him. They were going slowly and not much damage was caused by a shapely leg turning a head.

In Tourmakeady we played in the convent. It was a boarding school, and in the afternoon we gave a performance for the girl students. There was a meal for us in the convent refectory afterwards. That night the local people piled in, and the nuns who hadn't seen the afternoon show came. Backstage opened on to a wide landing with a stairway leading to the college dormitory. The young ladies, taking advantage of the nuns' being at the show, climbed out of bed, and in their dressing gowns sat on the steps like angels draped on a celestial stairway. Bryan Murray, Clive Geraghty and the young actors were the object of their interest.

We stayed in Belmullet when we played in Aughleam, the west Mayo Gaeltacht by Blacksod Bay. When I looked out the window in Belmullet the first morning the streets were crowded; lots of cars parked and moving about. At breakfast I enquired if there was a fair or market being held, and I was told that it was dole day. Out walking later, I saw country people buying vegetables in the shops. I thought this odd while acres of their land lay fallow.

Even though Aughleam was a Gaeltacht, we got the impression from various things that were said in Belmullet that there might not be too great a welcome from the powers-that-be for a show in Irish. We wondered what kind of reception we were going to get.

We arrived in Aghleam next morning to find that the posters advertising the show lay unopened in the presbytery. Better late than never, so we distributed them then and got a broadcasting unit to publicise the evening's entertainment throughout the district and into Belmullet. We didn't meet the parish priest; the curate opened the hall for us. He was a pale-faced, puffy-cheeked man with an inordinate amount of white in his eye. His black hat sat squarely on his head and his countenance ne'er broke into a smile when he greeted us.

There was no seating in the hall, a fact that hadn't been made known to our touring manager when the place was rented. The curate's solution was that those who came could stand. Tadhg Crowley and myself said that on no account would we expect an audience to stay on their feet for two hours. He told us that others who had rented the hall had played to a standing audience, and if it was good enough for them it was good enough for us.

That remark got our dander up, and without putting a tooth in it, we told him that it wasn't good enough for us. Tadhg went into the convent in Belmullet and got two lorry-loads of chairs from the school. God bless the nuns! Now, by placing the loose stools from around the walls of the hall at the front, we had enough seating for the big crowd that came. That night, performance-wise, the show turned out to be one of the best of the tour.

Afterwards the chairs had to be loaded on the transport to take them back to the convent in Belmullet. This, together with striking the set and putting our props and costumes and furniture on the bus, took time, and the curate was furious at the delay. He wanted to lock the hall. 'Mr Keane' he called me as he pulled out the plug of the electric fire where Mícheál Ó Briain was drying his cap in the dressing-room. He ordered us out from backstage.

Tadhg Crowley always made a point of paying the owner of the hall when the show was over. In this case, because of the unfriendliness of the curate, he decided to let him wait. 'There'll be a cheque in the post for you,' he said to him.

Outside the darkened hall there were flashes of lightning, and the roll of approaching thunder. As we piled into the bus all heaven broke loose overhead. I was last on the entry line, and was about to place my hand on the door handle when a flash of lightning ricocheted off it, and little stars danced on the chromium plating. Soon the rain and the hailstones pelted down on the roof of the bus, and almost drowned out the music and song as we sped towards Belmullet.

Next morning our journey was north to Gweedore, where it was a pleasure to play in a fully equipped little theatre.

Our second Gaeltacht tour a year later brought us south of the line from Dublin to Galway. The entire cast and crew travelled by bus, the back portion of which had been converted to take the scenery, lighting, costume and props. On our way to a one-night stand in Reenroe Hotel in Ballinskelligs we stopped by the graveyard in Spunkane, near Waterville, where the well known actress Bríd Ní Loinsigh is buried. Those of us who had worked with her, Peadar Lamb, Mícheál Ó Briain, Joan O'Hara, Máire Ní Ghráinne and myself, went in and dropped a prayer pebble on her grave. The younger people remained on the bus. They said they had never heard of her. Impermanent, indeed, is the actor's craft.

We all stayed in Reenroe Hotel. We dressed where we slept, and walked downstairs ready to go on stage, which was in the hotel dining-room. Not an ideal place. We found that the carpets and window drapes deadened the sound a little. In the bar later a local man said to me that song, dance, music and story were all very fine, but he would have preferred a straight drama. Why didn't we bring Mícheál Mac Liammóir's *Diarmuid agus Gráinne?* I told him that the Abbey had toured the Gaeltacht areas a few years earlier with an Irish version of *The Colleen Bawn*, and that *Scéal Scealaí* was another aspect of the theatre people might like to see.

'Have another pint,' he said, 'and bring a play the next time.'

We visited Cork, Listowel, Ventry and Coolea, where I met many Irish-speaking friends. This Gaeltacht is just over the hill from where I was born. I was in my element here, being the only Munster person in the cast. Kay Kent of the *Irish Times* visited us and stayed with the company till we reached our next stop, which was Ballingeary.

'Going round with the Abbey Company from hall to hall,' she wrote, 'one realises that this village to village touring is every bit as important a part of the National Theatre's work as is playing to its regular audiences in Dublin.'

The Ballingeary hall where we played housed Coláiste na Mumhan (Munster College) where people went to learn Irish in the early days of the Gaelic League. Indeed I had been there thirty years ago on the same errand. A woman in a shop in the village told Kay Kent that I had stayed in her house then. The poster in the window advertising our show had my name underlined in red.

I remembered that summer of long ago and the evenings spent céilí dancing in the hall. Like nearly all the young men who go to an Irish summer course, I fell in love, and we climbed the mountain above Gougane Barra lake together. We strayed the river banks along and talked love in Irish that didn't as yet have the fluency to match the passion of the hour.

While in Ballingeary with the show, the cast stayed in Gougane Barra Hotel hard by the Tailor's cottage and next door to Dinny Cronin's house. Both houses belonged to the Cronin brothers and sat at the edge of the lake shore. In the daytime, rambles by the lake, browsing on the pilgrimage island and strolling in the new forest full of wild life were treats for all of us, but more so for those brought up in the city. Tommy Rogers, a crewman who had never been out of Dublin except for a visit to the Isle of Man, had thought such wonderful scenery didn't exist in Ireland.

Mrs Cronin the hotel proprietress endeared herself to all

with her friendliness and wonderful cooking. The beating of her omelette I haven't tasted at home or abroad. She was a gentle lady and grew in our visitors' estimation when I told them that her brother was a cardinal in America. There was a party for us on the last night. Neighbours came in and one young lady sang the beautiful Munster song, 'An Binsín Luachra' ('The Bench of Rushes'). Young local performers gave a *comhrá beirte* (a comic conversation in Irish) which had won them a prize at the Irish language festival in Dublin. We had music, step-dancing and stories.

We heard of the monster (ollaphiast) which grew so big in the lake in olden times that fish were no longer left to appease its appetite, so it began to eat the monks. The abbot put a curse on it and the giant reptile-like creature, activated by a fierce fire raging in its bowels, worked its way out of the lake and eastwards through Inchageela to Cork harbour. The top lakewater followed in its wake and so the river Lee was formed. A tall tale as old as Methuselah. But the night's entertainment had all the basic ingredients of the show we were doing on the stage every evening.

THE EAGLE FLIES OUT ON THE WREN'S BACK

Later in 1976, and to make a further Irish contribution to the celebrations of the American bicentennial year, the Abbey Theatre was invited to bring a play to the Brooklyn Academy of Music in New York. The tour was also to take in a number of cities in New England. American Actors' Equity stipulates that a visiting company must bring two shows. This would have been a heavy burden on the theatre's resources, so the management of the Abbey hit on the idea of making my storytelling evening the second leg of the tour.

When I was in New York for the Eoin McKiernan Irish Fortnight in March, I put on *In My Father's Time* at the Irish Centre for Harvey Lichtenstein, head of the Brooklyn Academy, to see. He approved, and at the end of November for the third time that year I crossed the Atlantic. Michael Colgan, who directed the show and managed my Irish tour, was with me on the flight, as was the Abbey Company with Cyril Cusack, Siobhan McKenna, Angela Newman and John Kavanagh, to name but a few, who were playing in *The Plough and the Stars*.

The availability of my show and its inexpensive outlay made the tour possible. It was a reversal of the old folktale, I joked with Michael – the eagle was flying out on the wren's back. My set, stage furniture, props and costume had gone on to New York by surface some time before.

The Plough and the Stars was put on in the large auditorium of the Brooklyn Academy and my show in the smaller Lepercq space upstairs. The auditorium of the Lepercq sloped up from the stage edge, and a member of the audience, if he so wished, could walk on to the acting area.

At the interval on the first night this is exactly what Irish people did. They came and sat on the chairs, on the settle, and 'warmed' themselves to the very realistic Leslie Scott fire in my cottage kitchen. They examined and touched everything – artefacts which reminded them of home. Michael Colgan, who came back to the stage to supervise the setting for part two, found them walking away with sods from the turf basket. One woman was putting a *caorán* (fragment of a sod) into her handbag. Michael remonstrated with her. She said that another lady had gone off with a full sod, and why was he making an exception of her? For the rest of the run a crewman had to stand guard, or items irreplaceable in New York would have gone to decorate the sideboards of Irish American homes in Yonkers and Queens. But it was heart-warming that the Irish had turned up in such numbers and I was kept busy afterwards autographing my programme. This was a stylish affair with notes by the folklorist Dr Seán Ó Súilleabháin and writer Con Houlihan.

Michael Colgan and I knew of the tradition whereby anyone with a show opening in New York stayed in that literary and theatrical sanctum, the Hotel Algonquin. I remember visiting it when Brian Friel stayed there during the run of *Philadelphia, Here I Come!* The hotel was a cut above the common and a necktie and jacket were de rigueur in the lobby, the restaurant and the bar. But the porter was known, for a consideration, to fetch a tie and jacket from his cubicle if one came unprepared. Michael and I booked in there before opening night. We were welcome from the outset. I knew the desk clerk, who used to work in the Excelsior Hotel in 82nd Street when I was in New York in 1966. He saw to it that we were seen after.

I was the first to get a cab. I was called from the end of the line and walked past potentates from Texas with ten-gallon hats to the summons of 'Mr Kelly, your cab!' The doorman who hailed me was my first cousin Pat Curtin. He was the son of Tim Curtin from Muingnamunane, near Castleisland, who was married to my Aunt Margaret in Queens.

The Algonquin at that time boasted one of the biggest tomcats I had ever seen. This marmalade monster sat on his bottom in the middle of the lobby and mewed to clients whom he perceived to be cat lovers. I patted him on the head and got a love-bite that nearly took a finger away. The lobby had a newspaper and magazine stand. The owner, a friendly New Yorker, remembered the Irish who had stayed in the hotel. He talked of Jack McGowran and he told me what Brendan Behan said to the lady in the fur coat – a remark positively refreshing if unprintable.

This good man (Pat Curtin must have had him primed) laid aside for me the papers that carried reviews of the show after opening night. I did well, but one reviewer claimed that for a while, until he got used to it, my Kerry brogue had him guessing. The same complaint had been made about the Dublin accent in *The Plough and the Stars*, although Seán Cronin, writing from New York in the *Irish Times*, said the night he was at *In My Father's Time*, the reaction of the audience to my stories suggested that there was no language barrier.

The first paper the magazine man in the lobby gave me was *Newsday*, and Amei Wallach said that '*In My Father's Time*, which is devised and written by Éamon Kelly and nicely directed by Michael Colgan, deals with another side of Ireland from that dealt with in the Abbey Company's first offering, Seán O'Casey's *The Plough and the Stars*. In contrast to the fierce fighting and carousing of Dubliners depicted by O'Casey, Kelly is telling of a more gentle people in rural Ireland and their less belligerent pleasures ... He elicits laughter while evoking the past.'

Mel Gussow of the *New York Times* remembered me from *Philadelphia, Here I Come!* some ten years earlier, and pictured me thus: 'with his hat sitting squarely on his head, his baggy suit looking freshly crumpled, and wearing the bemused look of an aging leprechaun, he begins to populate the stage with fathers and mothers, stonemasons and parish priests, beautiful young women and anxious young men. *In My Father's Time* almost becomes a one-man Irish approximation of *Under Milk Wood*. In the end this is an enveloping evening. We are drawn into Mr Kelly's world – folksy, amiably far-fetched and with a touch of vinegar.'

Patricia O'Haire of the *New York Daily News* headed her piece with 'An Emerald Darlin' of a Storyteller' (you'd have to go to the States to get that one) and ended by saying, 'His theatre training shines through every word he speaks. His timing is beautiful, not a word wasted, not a thought thrown away.'

There were others who saw the show, including Joe Murphy of the *Irish Echo*. No one knocked me and all agreed that my run at the Brooklyn Academy was too short. Nearing the end of the week Michael and I waited anxiously to hear from the Abbey management about our next engagement. We were part of the tour and, before we left Dublin, had received a preliminary list of venues at which we were to appear after New York. Our success at the Brooklyn Academy whetted our appetites for what lay ahead in places like Boston, Philadelphia and Washington.

We checked out of the Algonquin and booked into a cheaper place down the block. It turned out to be a hotel where the homeless on social welfare were housed. On my first day there, who should I see sitting in the lobby but an old actor, James L. O'Neill, who played the part of the schoolmaster in *Philadelphia, Here I Come!* on Broadway. He didn't know me and I realised from the deadness of his eye that he was in his dotage. I told him my name and he mistook me for Emmet Kelly, the great American circus clown. I tried again, mentioning the play we were in together and the Helen Hayes Theatre where we played.

'Sure, I know you,' he said with conviction, 'you were in the cast of *Abbie's Irish Rose*.' I left him to his dreams with his unquestioning eye staring into space.

Michael and I waited for the call. Someone from the Abbey had promised to come and talk to us and we hung around the lobby in case we missed him. While we were having a break in the coffee shop he did come but left again without seeing us. We did the most ridiculous things to pass the time, like trying to figure out how the Algonquin got its name. We called on the ghost of Myles Na Gopaleen to solve that one, and he did.

It seems that the Algonquin was first owned by Quinn, a Clareman, when Manhattan was sparsely populated. One day the Apache and Sioux Indians joined forces and invaded Manhattan. The people, fearing for their lives, flew through the Hudson tunnel into Queens. After some days the Clareman and his staff stole back to the island. They saw no Indians, and what was more important, no arrows. They took shelter where Time Square is now, and the Clareman sent one of his staff to reconnoitre around the hotel. The servant came back in high glee, and said, 'No Indians! I looked inside. All gone, Quinn.'

Dark clouds loomed large on our horizon. The Abbey must have failed to firm up our part of the tour, because we heard no word from the powers-that-be. Our inclusion in the visit had enabled the Abbey to fulfil the American Equity stipulation and get into the States. Now that they were here we felt that we weren't needed any more. This was a severe blow to us, abandoned as we were in New York with one hand as long as the next. Michael Colgan, ever a man of action, proposed that as we had a successful property on our hands, why not try and get some dates and do the show ourselves?

Then a gap came in the clouds and an angel appeared in the form of Paddy Noonan. Paddy owned the Rego Irish Records and Tapes Company and had issued some albums of mine. He was also the leader of a band which toured the States wherever Irish were to be found. We located Paddy in Garden City and he was willing to set up a number of dates for us in Irish neighbourhoods around New York State.

But what were we going to do for stage scenery? Michael hit on the idea of going to Harvey Lichtenstein at the Brooklyn Academy and asking him for our stage setting. It wasn't being brought back to Ireland and would wind up like all Broadway used scenery in a dump in New Jersey.

Lichtenstein turned up trumps. Unfortunately, Paddy Noonan's van wasn't large enough to take the set, except for the freestanding door and window, but we packed in all the furniture and props down to the last egg cup for the dresser. The time was short for publicity. Paddy arranged some outlets. Michael and I spoke on neighbourhood radio – a different station each night. We sat there relaxed in front of the microphone handing out news about Ireland and lauding our show to the moon.

As well as being engaged in publicity, Michael Colgan was the producer, the director, the stage manager and crew of the new venture. He also looked after the front of house and when necessary did his stint on tabs. Paddy Noonan brought in his musicians and we had what we called an 'afterture' of Irish music when the curtain came down.

Our first stand was on Friday 10 December at the Irish Centre in Mineola, New York State. The cottage furniture surrounded by black drapes, with the freestanding door and window and a mock-up fireplace, looked great when the curtain came across. The lighting wasn't the best and, bearing in mind what Bob Hope once said, if the artist is not lit properly his gags go for a burton, I feared the worst. But I used what light there was to my advantage and the show exceeded all expectations.

Saturday saw us in Holy Trinity Church at 20 Cumming's Street in the Bronx. The pastor introduced me, and Michael came to the dressing-room to say that I had better go out quick or the priest would have gone through the entire show. He had already told a story he had memorised from one of my albums, and another he had heard me tell on the radio that morning.

On Sunday we were at Catalpa, Ridgewood in Queens. My two aunts and near relations came back to see me and introduced me to one-time neighbours of my parents, some of whom had been in America since before the First World War. Our last two shows were held under the auspices of the Boston chapter of the Irish American Cultural Institute. We played in a high school theatre at Lexington, Waltham, Mass. Paddy Noonan stored the stage furniture and props in his garage and I used them in a subsequent visit to the States when Brian Collins, Abbey designer, accompanied me.

Back in Dublin I don't ever remember receiving an explanation from the Abbey management about the New York cock-up, but I do recall that there was a request that Michael and I hand over the meagre takings of the shows we did there. Naturally we demurred.

SUSPENDED!

୶

During his term as artistic head at the Abbey, Alan Simpson directed a play by Constantine FitzGibbon called *The Devil at Work*. It was set in heaven and the theme was the creation of the world. Some of us actors played parts outside our range – I was the Archangel Gabriel. I don't think the hair hanging down in ringlets suited my cast of countenance. One ancient wag said I reminded him of a female newsreader he knew on 2RN (Ireland's first radio station, which broadcast from Denmark Street).

Maitias, from Paris, designed the celestial setting, and very beautiful it was too. One critic said, 'it was most elegant, most spectacular and a joy to look at'. At the opening the stage seemed resting on clouds with angels flying about. These heavenly beings were young people suitably costumed on swings. Into the angelic merry-go-round, falling from the skies of an upper heaven, dropped the Archangel Gabriel and the Archangel Michael, played by Geoff Golden. Before the curtain Geoff and I were hoisted high into the flies. Under our finery we wore parachute harnesses. A thin wire, invisible to the audience, was hooked into the back of the harness and we were winched aloft.

It was absolutely essential that we sat correctly into the tackling or agonies lay ahead. It was also very important that there was no twist in the wire, or the actor would spin around and back again. Our heads spun too in the dark upper world of ropes, catwalks and fly bars. The distance to the ground instilled terror, but what was most chilling was a plywood cut-out ground-row directly below; in an accident we were certain to be decapitated.

We were sent aloft ages before the curtain and we seemed to be hours dangling up there. At the dress rehearsal the director came to the front seats and, looking up, proclaimed that our angelic feet were showing. Heavenly hour! We had to be winched higher, which made the adrenalin race like mercury in our glands. Prior to this Geoff had been suspended without pay from the company for some misdemeanour, and on opening night he turned his head and said to me, 'Suspended for a month, and on my first night back I am suspended again!'

The gong sounded, and on the third reverberating stroke the curtain rose and Geoff and I floated down (I forget now if we spread our wings) into a cherubim- and seraphim-filled paradise and alighted on a rostrum upstage. Hands came from behind a masking drape and unhooked us from the wire. God, were we happy to find our feet on firm ground as we walked down and mingled with the other angels. With music, lighting, costumes and a heavenly setting, it was a wonderful sight. A member of the audience told me afterwards that Geoff's descent and mine looked like two figures from the famous painting of the Assumption going the wrong way.

On a bugle call from Gabriel the heavenly host got busy. Architect and engineer angels began work at the drawing board mapping out our wonderful world. The seas were soon filled with fish and the earth populated with animals. The Garden of Eden was created, and the last thing we see at the close of the play is Eve throwing that unfortunate, for us, apple to Adam.

In between there was much activity, and as each animal was planned, a painted cut-out of the creature was run on a wire upstage with a witty comment from the angels on each invention. On beholding a strange shape whizzing across one angel inquired, 'What's this?' and was told, 'That's a yak – useful for crosswords.'

There was also the angels' revolt. Desmond Cave played Lucifer, and Harry Brogan, as Zerubabbe, was one of the dirtiest looking devils you could wish to see. The *Irish Times* described Alan Simpson's production as excellent and the Abbey Company as grand. David Nowlan continued: 'Eric Sweeney's music and Leslie Scott's lighting add to the air of sophistication with which the whole production is endowed, and it is for this sophistication – not all that commonly seen

in theatrical terms in the Abbey – that the evening is ultim-
ately to be commended. Had we been told, even a year ago,
that we would have seen its like in the Abbey, we might not
have believed it. To be believed it must be seen.'

STONE MAD

Apart from Tomás MacAnna and Frank Dermody I worked with many directors at the Abbey. Ray McAnally, who had left the permanent company for a while, came back to direct. I was fortunate to be in his production of *Kolbe*, set in a concentration camp and written by Desmond Forristal. Clive Geraghty played the part of Kolbe, a Polish priest who sacrifices his life so that another inmate of the camp may live. I was a Jewish tailor. Shaven-headed and emaciated looking, Kolbe and I languished in an Auschwitz prison cell. As the Jew and the Catholic priest prepare for death the Jew, with the characteristic humour of his race, suggests that they hear each other's confession.

I ever relished working with Ray McAnally. He got performances out of me which I didn't think I was capable of. He directed *The Loves of Cass Maguire* by Brian Friel and gave me the role of Mr Ingram. I was fortunate to be around at that time and to have the privilege of appearing in so many of Friel's plays. To the other practitioners who excel in the art of play-writing in Ireland give dukedoms, earldoms and knight them, but for Friel reserve the jewelled crown. He is the king.

Like Ray McAnally, Joe Dowling was an Abbey actor who became a director. I remember the two Friel plays in which he cast me. One was *Translations* at the Abbey and the other *Fathers and Sons* at the Gate. It was a joy to work with him. His ability to reassure an actor abated the terror which always seizes me at my first entrance from the wings. Acting is a nerve-racking business. Fellow players have likened opening nights to going over the top in the Great War.

It was Lelia Doolan who introduced me to Patrick Mason. 'This young Englishman,' she said, 'comes to the Abbey as our new voice teacher.' I couldn't help remarking, with as much humour as I could muster, 'When the conquered speak in the tones of the conqueror the conquest is complete.' Patrick laughed heartily, assuring me that no attempt would be made to change the tenor of the native lilt.

Patrick, who at first assisted Hugh Hunt in his production of *The Well of the Saints*, went on to become a director of international repute. He directed Noel Pearson's and the Abbey production of Brian Friel's *Dancing at Lughnasa* in Dublin, London and New York, where the play won Tony Awards for the author, director and players. Patrick is now artistic director at the Abbey.

I remember I was in his production of *The Cherry Orchard* in which I played the part of the old retainer, Firs. The play was in a new translation by Michael Frayn. When he came to a rehearsal one day Patrick asked me to repeat for him what I said about speaking in the tones of the conqueror. I was a bit embarrassed but I did it. Like Patrick, Michael Frayn took no umbrage. The British are bricks when it comes to tolerance, and he agreed with me that small communities should try and hold on to their distinctiveness at all costs.

My last appearance with the Abbey was in a play directed by Patrick Mason. It was *The Only True History of Lizzie Finn* by Sebastian Barry. I had known Sebastian Barry ever since I had been in his *Boss Grady's Boys* at the Peacock Theatre in 1988. That play turned out to be the talk of the town and a great favourite with the critics. 'Barry's writing has a subtlety which puts *Boss Grady's Boys* into a different league from the vast majority of plays that have been written about rural Ireland since Synge,' Tim Harding said in the *Sunday Press*.

Of Jim Norton and me, who played the principal parts, David Nowlan said in the *Irish Times*: '... two of the best performances seen on the Dublin stage this year ... seldom have two characterisations been so nicely balanced in emotion and intelligence. Seldom have words been so well spoken to convey feeling and clarity of thought, silences and actions full of mutual communications.'

Caroline Fitzgerald's superbly sensitive and imaginative production was talked about in the *Sunday Tribune*, and in the *Sunday Independent* Hugh Leonard said the play craved to be seen. Later I was in Sebastian's *Prayers of Sherkin* and saw his magical *The Steward of Christendom* at the Gate with Donal McCann.

Seán McCarthy directed me in Seamus Murphy's *Stone Mad*, a one-man show which had been adapted for the stage by Fergus Linehan and was set in a monumental mason's yard. In the book Seamus tells of his apprenticeship as a stonecutter and describes his work with a gallant gallery of eccentric craftsmen, men with names like the Gargoyle, the Tumbler, the Goban, the Dust, Bulltoes and Danny Melt.

Bronwen Casson designed a very realistic stoneyard (it won her an award) with examples of work in progress – statues, Celtic crosses and headstones – together with all the appurtenances of the trade, including bankers to work on and a small forge. The setting was in the round in the Peacock Theatre and the audience had ringside seats as I worked the stone and told the tales which have made Seamus Murphy's *Stone Mad* the classic that it is.

To give a sense of authenticity to my work with mallet and chisel I went and studied with the stonecutters in Roe O'Neill's quarries in Ballyedmonduff near the foot of the Dublin Mountains. Having worked as a carpenter in my youth gave me a decided facility in the handling and use of tools. In no time, under expert tutelage, I was able to block off the waste on a Celtic cross, and I mastered to a degree the cutting of letters on a monument.

Beforehand each evening I arranged the pieces of stone I had to work on during my almost two hours on stage. One job was the cutting of an inscription on a headstone: 'Walter Poplin. Died March twenty-fifth, nineteen sixty-three. Aged sixty years. RIP.' (Walter Poplin was Big Maggie's husband in the play of that name by John B. Keane, and that's what was written on the note she handed to the stone-cutter Byrne the day of his funeral.) Another task was the sculpting of a design on a Celtic cross.

I left the using of the forge for the opening of part two. Then I heated a chisel in a gas flame in the wings. I came on stage in the blackout with the glowing red chisel concealed from view, and beat it to a cutting edge on the anvil as the lights came up. When finished I plunged the hot iron into water, making a sizzling sound and sending up a cloud of steam. Whatever about the interpretation of the lines, the portraying of a craftsman doing his work with precision and fluidity gave me immense satisfaction. And to my mind nothing like it had been done on the stage before.

Among the messages of goodwill on opening night there was a note from Joe Dowling the artistic director. It read: 'Warmest congratulations on *Stone Mad*, and every good wish for tonight and the run. You had great courage to undertake such a mammoth job, and you have scored a major achievement. It is a personal triumph for you and the theatre is deeply grateful to you. Good luck.'

Seamus Murphy's widow, Mairéad, and her son Colm were in the theatre, which made me a little apprehensive. The only one who noticed this was Con Houlihan. Writing in the *Evening Press* he said I was nervous at the outset but before long I had the audience eating out of my hand. The critics didn't know how to describe the evening. It wasn't a play. I suppose you could call it a 'docudrama', a visit by the audience to a stoneyard where I populated the scene with Seamus Murphy's celebrated 'stonies', told their tales, did their work on stone and paused to blow the chisel dust from the lettering on the limestone tablet.

After a successful run at the Peacock we went on tour. Strong hands shifted the Celtic cross, the holy water font, the slabs of stone and the angel with the broken wing. I was bockety at the knees with fright going on stage the opening night at the Everyman Theatre in Cork city, where Seamus lived and worked, and where he had a legion of friends and admirers.

I needn't have worried. The big-hearted Leesiders took a shine to me, and Maureen Fox writing in the *Cork Examiner* said: '*Stone Mad* is sheer joy.' She liked my playing of the part: '... those who were lucky enough to have known Seamus Murphy time and time again during the evening must have felt as if he himself was speaking.' She also liked Seán McCarthy's sensitive direction and Bronwen Casson's stage design, which set the seal on a wonderful evening.

FIELD DAY AND THE KING'S HEAD

6

I got a chance again to use the sculpting skills I had picked up in Roe O'Neill's quarry when I was cast with Maura in Tom Murphy's *Brigit*, a play for television. Tom, whose praises are sung though I be silent, is one of our foremost writers in the theatre. I was in his *A Crucial Week in the Life of a Grocer's Assistant*, directed by Alan Simpson.

Tom's play *Brigit* is a delicate and very moving piece of writing in which a proud though amateur craftsman, the part I played, accepts a commission a little outside his range. It is to carve a statue of St Brigit for the nuns to replace the one which was knocked over by a clumsy postulant and broken into smithereens. The Reverend Mother tries the religious repositories but can't find a plaster representation of the native saint.

The craftsman takes on the job and carves the figure in bog oak. He works at it day and night. He pours his soul into the creation. He sometimes sings as the big mallet drives the chisel into the wood and when darkness falls his wife and his grandchildren in turn hold the paraffin lamp to throw light on his work. When it is finished the nuns are dubious about the somewhat crude but honest piece of sculpture. However, after consultation with the parish priest, they accept the statue on condition that it be given a coat of paint.

The craftsman, incensed at the idea of painting the beautiful dark bog oak, older, he says, than St Brigit herself, takes the figure from its niche and brings it home. He sits by the hearth gazing into the flames, his hand moving over the work he has so lovingly carved. In a fit of rage he is about to throw it in the fire. His wife prevents him and puts the statue in a place of honour in the kitchen. Her name is Brigit too and, tearfully, she says she sees some of herself in her husband's work.

The play was imaginatively directed by Noel Ó Briain, and I believe it was the last drama to be screened by RTÉ. That was 1988. The following year it won an award at the Celtic Nations Television Festival.

During the troubled times in Northern Ireland, I worked with Stephen Rea in the Field Day Company, when he directed Chekhov's *Three Sisters* in a translation by Brian Friel. I played the part of Ivan Chebutykin, and when the dizzy hour of my first scene came on opening night in the Guildhall in Derry, a British Army helicopter sat in the sky above the stage and all but drowned me out. I had to strive with might and main to make myself heard. When the infernal machine chugged off at the end of the scene I got a hand, more, I think, in appreciation of my fight against the army of occupation than for any gold-medal acting on my part.

One day during rehearsals in the Guildhall there was a bomb alert. All out and down three flights of stairs into the open ground. The adjoining houses and shops emptied into the street and people made for the open space around the hall. I saw John Hume in the crowd. In time word came as to the position of the car bomb. All eyes were directed towards an archway maybe a hundred yards away. Suddenly there was an almighty explosion which left a sickening feeling at the butt of the stomach.

Black smoke billowed from the archway and at its centre there was a red glow tinged with blue and purple. Faces drained of colour and there was a moment of absolute stillness. Some people had to be supported because of the shock. There was a public house at the side of the Guildhall, its windows covered with corrugated iron sheets to save them from flying bomb splinters. We went in there. As the effects of the blast wore off, some had drinks and some had coffee.

There were two English ladies who worked in the show, a mother and daughter. One was in design and the other a costumier. As a delayed reaction to the explosion the daughter fainted, but the mother was unshaken. She had been through the bombing in London during the Second World War.

The proprietor was most kind to us and some of the actors used to drop in there when the show was over and stay after hours. One night late, two RUC constables came into the bar. They didn't take any names but stood at the back in the shadows. When he saw them, Colm Meaney, who played Captain Vassily Solyony in the show, engaged me in a very loud conversation in Irish of dubious ancestry. He was a little in his cups and meant to be provocative. It made for an uneasy atmosphere. After a while the two RUC men left, and at the door one of them turned on his heel and, addressing Meaney, said, 'Oíche mhaith!'

While we were in Derry, BBC Television did a documentary on the work of Field Day. When the camera crew came to my lodgings to interview me I was setting out for the launderette. That would be fine, the director said. They would talk to me in the car. The interview was done as we drove along and while I was putting the clothes in the washing machine. Mine was the last piece of filming and immediately afterwards the crew were to drive to Belfast and back to Britain.

They left, and with my laundry washed and dried I was walking down the street in the Waterside. Putting my hand on the lapel of my jacket I found the miniature microphone which they had forgotten to take. The battery was still in my back pocket, the connecting flex hanging visibly from my trousers belt.

A twinge of panic as I thought of the explaining I would have to do if stopped by the police. The lilt of my southern brogue wouldn't help. I spoke into the microphone, calling the crew and telling them what had happened. I wasn't sure if they could hear me or if they had already left. Noticing a public house nearby I gave them the name of the street and the pub and said I could be found there. Just then a police Land Rover came into view and I held my breath until it had passed me.

I went into the pub, turned up my coat collar to hide the microphone and tucked the flex under my belt. When I ordered a pint – it must have been my accent – the publican eyed me suspiciously. There was nobody in the room off the bar. I went in there, sipped the pint and every now and then talked in a low voice into the broadcasting unit. After what seemed an eternity the BBC people crowded into where I was sitting, and before the publican could see what was happening they had relieved me of their precious sound equipment. A short without a chaser and they were off. Because of their English accents and their delight at our meeting, the publican showed a new interest in me. We became very friendly and talked about the troubles.

I nodded agreement when he condemned the outrages of the republicans, but watching his expression out of the corner of my eye, I knew he was somewhat perplexed by my accent.

During my stay with the Abbey the management was very generous in giving me time off. As well as playing with Field Day and the Irish Theatre Company, I went on trips to America with my storytelling shows and appeared on Irish and British television. The summer of 1977 saw me in the King's Head in London. The King's Head is a dinner-type theatre and is carried on in a large room at the rear of the pub of that name. It is run by Dan Crawford, a Canadian who directs many of the plays himself.

I played there in *Da* by Hugh Leonard. I was in the name part in one of the best roles written for an actor this century. The play was directed by Robert Gillespie, a demanding taskmaster. His hard work paid off and the play was a dazzling success. We cornered all the critics. Speaking of the character of *Da* the *Daily Telegraph* wrote: '... Leonard has the theatrical cunning to make brilliant fun of this crazy individualist, who is uncannily impersonalised by Éamon Kelly.'

As the King's Head is on the fringe of London's theatre world, the actors are not well paid. They work for the lower salary in the hope that the play may transfer. To help me on this reduced salary Dan Crawford offered to provide lodgings for me. I got a shakedown upstairs in the pub, but the room was too near the kitchen and I couldn't stand the cooking smells.

Seeing my discomfort, one of the pub staff gave me his flat a few streets away. It was a one-roomed basement accommodation with no window, just a glass door leading to an open area. I was afraid to open the door at night to let in air in case someone barged in on me from the street.

On my arrival there the caretaker viewed me with suspicion, thinking, I suppose, that the occupant of the flat was subletting. On my second night, at about two o'clock, there was a loud pounding on the door. I opened it and a man and his wife dashed into the room. The gentleman, who turned out to be the Polish landlord, was in a tearing temper. His wife, a big blonde, her face pushed back as if she had it pressed against a window pane, carried a large handbag from which I expected to get a belt any minute.

Accoutred as I was in crumpled pyjamas, I calmed them down as best I could. I explained that I was in a play in the King's Head and that one of the staff, the tenant of this flat, had let me stay for a while. They didn't believe my story: I was an intruder. I had a poster of the play pinned to the back of the door and I showed them my name, the first under the title and high enough to be well out of reach of a dog's pee no matter how low it was placed. The name on my passport, which I always take to London, agreed with the poster.

I gave them a synopsis of my theatrical career, with snippets of my work on Broadway and on tour in the States – I am sure they thought they were making my acquaintance on the way down. They were mollified slightly and withdrew, warning me that subletting was out of the question and to quit when I got other accommodation.

I told Dan Crawford of my experience and he gave me a flat belonging to a woman friend of his who would be out of London for some time. All I had to do in return was to water the nineteen plants and to care for and feed the cat. For days I didn't see the cat, but then on putting my hand in the hot press I felt her soft fur. She mewed defensively and then spat at me, but after I had fed her a few times we became firm friends. It was a first-floor flat and in time she got to know the hour at which I would be coming home from the theatre and sat out on the window-sill to mew me a welcome.

The flat was spacious, two rooms, two beds. It was pleasingly decorated with a large colour drawing of Queen Meadhbh by Jim Fitzpatrick as a centrepiece. I invited Maura and Sinéad over from Dublin. They stayed for a few weeks, and Eoin and Brian, then about eighteen and seventeen, came to London. They explored the city on the Underground, went on a pilgrimage to Wembley Stadium and sat on the Queen's seat.

After the run of *Da* at the King's Head I put on my one-man storytelling show, *In My Father's Time*, at the same theatre. Michael Colgan came over from Dublin to prepare it for the stage, and with the *Irish Post* and the *Cork Weekly Examiner* behind me, a good sprinkling of Irish people swelled the audiences each night. I couldn't have wished for a more intimate space, with a perfect acoustic, in which to do the show.

Mention of familiar placenames or references to scenes of yore and summers long ago would cause a throat-clearing 'ahem' from Irish pockets in the audience. One night a description of an emigration parting at a railway station back home gave rise to a muffled 'Divine Jesus' from the front seat. A quick change to comedy softened the catch in the heart, and laughter again ran through the auditorium.

A one-man entertainment can be a lonely commitment for the actor. He misses the company of the other players, with no one to talk to before the show or during the interval. But the fall of the curtain brought people to the dressing-room, and I met many a son and daughter of neighbours I grew up with in Kerry.

One night I had company on stage when Dan Crawford's black tomcat walked on and sat on his bottom a few feet away from me. He took no interest in the folklore I was dispensing but licked his right front paw and proceeded to wash his face. Delighted giggles kept at a low pitch did not disturb him but I knew that his presence was the end of me. I had lost the interest of the audience, but I gradually regained it by addressing the story to the cat in as soothing and seductive a manner as I was capable of. It worked. A two-hander with a cat, and the audience silently loved it. Sometimes, at some telling remark, he stopped the circular washing motion of his face and, with the paw resting over one ear, turned and looked at me.

The end of the story brought a burst of applause which startled the cat. He looked at the audience, spat once and disappeared into the wings. It was a strange and eerie experience where an animal in all its naturalness took the spotlight off the action and stole the show. While I was on stage thereafter the cat was confined to Dan's living quarters.

Many years later I was back in the King's Head in a production of *Philadelphia, Here I Come!* directed by Dan Crawford. I was in the part of the father, which I had played in Dublin, Broadway and Shaftesbury Avenue twenty-eight years before. This time we moved from the King's Head and it was nice to be told by producer Bill Kenwright that my performance was the deciding factor in bringing the play into the West End.

We were in Wyndham's Theatre, hard by Leicester Square, while another play of Friel's, *Dancing at Lughnasa*, was running in a house down the street. We were doing fine until the IRA caught up with us in the autumn of 1992. Then the bombings began in the centre of London. These tragic events did not affect the theatre attendances at first, but as time went on and the count of the bombings came to fourteen, there were some empty seats in the stalls.

Just a hundred yards from Wyndham's Theatre where we were playing, a bomb shattered the Sussex Arms public house. Five people were injured in the blast and one, David Heifer, lay critically ill in hospital. The following day David died. He came from Luton and was thirty years of age.

What had David to do with the Ireland of the north or south? What had he to do with the invasions or the plantation of Ulster? In what way was he guilty of any crime against the Irish people that he should give his life? He was one of the many in England, including children, who were killed by bombs planted by the young men and women of the IRA. We read in the paper that David carried a donor card and in death he gave to more than one person the gift of life.

The only gesture we could make was to place a bouquet of flowers with the hundreds of other tributes on the fallen rubble of the Sussex Arms, with the message, 'In memory of David. From the cast of *Philadelphia, Here I Come!*'

WHERE HUBERT HUMPHREY AND
PRESIDENT FORD SLEPT

_✄

In the early summer of 1981 I went to America on a story-telling tour organised by Paddy Noonan of New York. I took Brian Collins, the Abbey Theatre designer, with me to set the stage and act as lighting man and tour manager. In New York, while we were preparing to go out on the road, we stayed in an old-fashioned hotel not far from the United Nations building. Because I was commissioned to do a new storytelling show for the Peacock when I came back to Dublin, I got up every morning at six and wrote and rehearsed for two and a half hours. I wouldn't have done it at home, but I have always found the air in America more bracing, urging one on to activity.

We used the stage furniture and props which Paddy Noonan had stored in his garage after the Abbey bicentennial tour in 1975. These included a freestanding door and window, and to give ourselves a homely cottage set Brian and I built a fireplace. This could be folded flat to fit in Paddy's van, and with a full cargo, Brian, I and a driver set out on a tour of places in New England. We visited Boston, Springfield and Worcester.

There was an Irish contact person in each place, and in Worcester it was Jack Finnegan. We slept in his mother's house one night. She was away in California. Next day we were taken to Jack's conference centre, a secluded place deep in the woods. The entrance had no gate, but tied to a post in the middle of a broad opening was a ferocious-looking alsatian on a long chain which enabled him to cover the distance to the piers at each side. Hard by was a helicopter pad in the trees.

Jack rented the centre to political parties and big business combines. A feature of it was a miniature Roman arena-type room with stepped seats looking down on a blazing fire, where men sat draped in large towels after a stint in the jacuzzi. Here Brian and I sat, similarly accoutred, with Irish American men. It was the time of the Northern Ireland hunger strike and the talk was about Bobby Sands. His ordeal affected them greatly. 'If he dies,' one man said, striking his fist in his open palm, 'oh, if he dies!'

We saw the conference and various meeting rooms. We visited the bar and had a meal in the restaurant. That night Brian slept where Hubert Humphrey had laid down to rest, and across the corridor I slept in President Ford's bed. There was a step down to the john in that room and Jack Finnegan told me that the President, who tended to trip himself up, fell into the place to a chorus from his bodyguard – 'He has done it again!'

In the closet Jack showed me the red telephone which, when plugged in at Ford's bedside, was the hotline to Moscow and to the man with his finger on the nuclear button. Finnegan had arranged a radio interview for me at the unearthly hour of 2 a.m., when there would be a hook-up coast to coast. At that time the telephone woke me and, snugly ensconced in the President's bed, I spoke to the nation.

When we went to the midwest and the west coast we had to forget about the set and stage furniture. We got a trunk not too large to be taken on a plane and packed into it essential props like the oil lamp, delph for the dresser and objects for the mantelpiece, or whatever versions of them we would get at each centre.

On arriving at a community theatre or hall, Brian went to the scene dock and prop room and it was surprising what he came up with by way of stage setting. Two old bookcases of different sizes, one on top of the other, made a dresser. He'd maybe fish out a door and a window. With a few boards and sturdy scantlings he made a fireplace with a mantelshelf and gave the lot a coat of fast-drying paint.

There were nearly always black drapes to half-circle the result of his endeavours, and his intelligence and imagination gave me a credible, well lit scene in which to work at every centre.

In Lansing, Michigan, we were at the little theatre in the

university and Brian got very believable furniture for the stage from the folk museum nearby. Here we were both called upon to talk to the drama class. Brian spoke about design and I about my work in the theatre.

From Lansing to Grand Rapids. It was a domestic flight in a plane with a seating capacity of little more than that of the Killarney to Rathmore bus. When the craft came down it seemed about to shake to pieces as it ground to a halt on the runway. In Grand Rapids we stayed with John Tully, a lawyer and possibly the tallest man in America. There was a great gathering of Irish people in his house after the show, some of whom hadn't seen Ireland since they had left maybe twenty years before, and others who had never seen it. When we told them how things stood at home, the conversation turned to the Northern troubles. This was always so when we met Irish Americans. The younger men were very passionate about the North, and crew like fighting cocks.

In Austin, Texas, I was to play in the university theatre, which was in the round. This meant some changes in the presentation. In the house where we stayed, when the owner Kevin O'Connell and his wife went away for the day, we took a table and chairs out to the lawn and re-ran the show with an in-the-round audience in mind.

During this operation we forgot to close the door or to put the mosquito screen in place, with the result that when the lady of the house came back she found the place full of flies. 'Who let the bugs in?' she demanded. We were abject in our apologies while the insect repellent went into action.

Brian, with assistance from the crew, readied and lit the stage and the show worked like a dream. Anyway I had plenty of practice at playing in the round at the Peacock Theatre at home.

Dr Padraig Houlahan, who was with the American Space Programme, met us here, and he and Kevin O'Connell brought us to Maggie Mac's for a drink. Maggie's was a long narrow establishment with a sprinkling of Irish. A small country and western band played at the end. The lady vocalist came to the microphone and said, 'Bobby Sands is very low tonight. He is in a coma now!' There was a silence and she added, 'I'll sing an Irish song.' What she sang was, 'I have heard the mavis singing'.

Next day, Kevin O'Connell drove us to San Antonio, where I met Maureen Halligan. She took me to see Ronnie Ibbs. The theatre where they work, and where I played, is part of a convent university, a fairly big auditorium but we very nearly filled it. Afterwards we had a meal across the street with the nuns and Fr O'Gorman.

New Orleans by air was our next stop. It is a beautiful city and my favourite American place after New York. Strangely enough, the name of the university dean who welcomed us was Éamon Kelly. The evening paper said, 'Stand Up the Real Éamon Kelly'. My name went on parchment as the Mayor, Ernest N. Maoil, conferred on me the title of International Honorary Citizen of New Orleans.

We were back in New York in time to board the boat for Bermuda. This was a cruise on the SS *Doric*, with a full complement of Irish Americans, arranged by Manhattan travel agents. Paddy Noonan with his orchestra and yours truly were on board to entertain them. The Doric was an Italian liner with an Italian crew. The chaplin was Italian also and on the first morning at Mass he wished us all to 'half nice scruise'.

Working at sea was a new experience. I had played in many places, from large theatres on Broadway and in London to village halls in Ireland and Newfoundland. I did a show in the open air in county Cork with arc-lamps hanging from trees around a dancing deck. Cars on the rising ground circled the space with their headlights on the small stage. There was a rookery nearby and I competed with the disturbed occupants. An old lady sitting beside my wife, and unaware of Maura's identity, said as she pointed at me, 'Is that him now? Sainted hour, sure, my old man is as good looking as him!'

On board the *Doric*, the chapel in the morning was the theatre at night. Paddy Noonan and his musicians played there. I did two shows on the way out, two on the way back, and one when we were docked at Hamilton in Bermuda. I had lots of time off during the day to sit in the bar, read by the swimming pool or sunbathe on the upper deck. There were plenty of people to talk to, men who had left Ireland and who wished to talk about it. Sometimes late at night when Paddy Noonan played in the ship's lounge I did a ten-to fifteen-minute stint at the microphone.

I noticed that some of the passengers were grossly over-weight and at mealtimes these were the people who ate as if there were no tomorrows. Their eyes widened and they 'ooh'ed and 'aah'ed at the food before them. We had breakfast, lunch and dinner, and coffees in between, and late at night long tables on the mid-deck groaned under the weight of mouthwatering delicacies. Over the loudspeakers passengers were invited to bring their cameras. They did, and photo-graphed the entire pâtisserie before anyone had time to sink a tooth in it.

We spent some days on the island of Bermuda with its beautiful beaches. I had forgotten my bathing suit and bought one in Hamilton, as well as a sports jacket, all for seventy-one dollars. The sea water had the quality of white wine. One day, lying on the golden sand after a dip, we heard on Brian's radio that the Pope had been shot at in Rome.

A striking feature of the place was the white roofs of the houses. They seemed to be made of concrete. Each house had a huge tank to catch the rainfall as running water was scarce on the island. We fished out and found the house where Tom Moore lived when he was governor there.

We set sail again, north to New York. We docked at the West Pier, where thousands of Irish had first set foot in America. We bade a fond farewell to the many friends we had made on board, and, after a night's rest, Brian and I had three more centres to do in the State of New York: Indwood, Scarsdale in Suffolk county, and one in a city hotel. When the owner of that hostelry saw my stage effects being trundled through the lobby, and when he beheld the dilapidated table, dresser and súgán chairs, he threw a fit and roared, 'Take them away! I didn't order such garbage!'

That show over, we were in the air again, going west to San Francisco, a city in its own way every bit as distinctive as New Orleans. We saw the famous tramcars, which are power-ed from a central electric rail in the street. Don't ask me why people don't get electrocuted by stepping on the rail, but it seems an insulated plunger reaches through a continuous slot to the power which is cunningly concealed below. The trams are very popular and when they are full, passengers crowd the entry platforms and hang from grips over running boards at the side. We rode on one down to the bay, took a boat around Alcatraz, the famous prison island, and under the arches of the Golden Gate Bridge.

The Irish have a fine centre in San Francisco. It is to this meeting place that our country's emigrants flock in the early morning of the first and third Sundays of September to hear the RTÉ broadcast of the hurling and football All-Ireland finals.

It is a well equipped place with a large hall. So large, indeed, that Brian, not trusting the acoustics, asked me to use a microphone. This instrument ties me to one position. I prefer to move in the set, using the chair by the fire, at the table and the dresser. I introduce as much unobtrusive business as I can, and I have been known, in Dublin anyway, to fall to repairing a horse's collar and winkers.

In San Francisco Brian enabled me to move about freely by getting me a radio device with a battery in my hip pocket and a tiny microphone on my lapel.

We played in Sacramento too, where it became so hot on stage that I nearly lost my breath. Here I met an ex-pupil from my teaching days in Listowel Technical School. He told me he was running a small ranch.

The tour over, we returned to New York where I got presents for Maura and Sinéad. At the airport Paddy Noonan paid us. The proceeds when divided up didn't seem all that great; we admitted we'd have earned as much working in the theatre in Dublin. Travel and other expenses were high but we would not have missed the trip, and, as Brian said, not everyone in Ireland could claim to have slept where Hubert Humphrey and President Ford had laid their weary heads.

A Steppe in the Left Direction

⤞

Like the *Skibbereen Eagle*, the Abbey had had its eye on Russia for many a long day. Its actors had played in Edinburgh, London, New York and elsewhere, and it would be another feather in their caps to appear in the famed Arts Theatre of Moscow.

In Vincent Dowling's term as artistic director an invitation came to play in Leningrad (as it was then) and Moscow. The plays the Russians asked for were *The Great Hunger*, a drama by Tom MacIntyre based on Patrick Kavanagh's poem of that name, and *The Field* by John B. Keane.

John B. is the people's playwright. For many years, from Valentia to Belturbet, the rafters of parochial halls have rung to the raciness of his poetic outpourings. From the early 1980s he enjoyed an amazing popularity at the Abbey Theatre. I was in *Sharon's Grave*, which was presented there by the Irish Theatre Company when Christopher FitzSimon was its artistic director. The play was directed by Sheila Richards, who found some of the Kerry dialogue a little strange. I had to plead with her to keep in expressions like 'above in the room' and 'below in the kitchen', because, as she said, the set in which we played had no upstairs.

In 1984 I appeared as Morrisheen Brick in *The Man from Clare*. John B. brings the footballers of Cuas in county Clare across the Shannon to play the Bealabawn team in Kerry. The play was directed by Patrick Laffan and had Ray McAnally in the cast.

Then in 1985 came *Sive*. It was first produced by Listowel Drama Group in 1959 and had a long journey to the Abbey through the halls and ballrooms of rural Ireland. It was directed at the National Theatre by Ben Barnes, with Marie Kean, Catherine Byrne, John Olohan, Meave Germaine and Donal Farmer among those in the cast.

Sive has a chorus of two travelling men, Pats Bocock and his son Carthalawn. I was Pats and Macdara Ó Fáharta played my son. While on stage, they both comment on the night's proceedings in song and in story. Carthalawn plays the *bodhrán* and Pats beats time on the floor with his blackthorn stick. In Act Two, which is the eve of a wedding, there is porter in the house and father and son lower two bottles without taking the containers off their heads.

On opening night, to my exhortation of 'Your best! Your almighty best!' Carthalawn hit the *bodhrán* with such vigour that he drove his knuckles through the skin, but with amazing alacrity and without missing a note he continued to beat out the rhythm on the rim of the drum. There were many revivals of *Sive* – a play with which to make music on a box-office till. My last appearance in it was with an Abbey cast at the Gaiety in 1994.

John B. came to see us once while the play was in rehearsal, but he and director Ben Barnes met and talked over the production beforehand. They became firm friends and 1987 saw Ben directing *The Field*, which had first been produced in Dublin by Phyllis Ryan's Gemini Productions in November 1965 with Ray McAnally as the Bull McCabe. There had also been an earlier presentation at the Abbey with Joe Lynch in the part of the Bull. In Ben Barnes's production the Bull was played by Niall Tóibín, and a vicious bloody Bull he was too. My heart raced with fear as he and his son Tadhg (Brendan Conroy) killed the man who would take their precious field from them.

Big Maggie, with Brenda Fricker in the title role, completed the Keane trilogy directed by Ben Barnes at the Abbey, but it was *The Field* that was to be seen again in a far off land.

Maura and I were to play Mr and Mrs Dandy McCabe. On Saturday 6 February 1988 we packed our bags for Russia. 'Air your woollies for Arbour Hill!' was the call to active young republicans approaching winter in Kerry in the 1940s, and we made sure that only warm clothing was in our luggage. I bought a heavy long black topcoat in the Blarney Woollen Mills in Nassau Street. I had a Russian hat, synthetic fur of course, and with a warm scarf and gloves I was ready to face the severest Russian winter.

On Sunday at 2.30 p.m. we boarded a coach for Limerick and Shannon from the front of the Abbey. The two pubs opposite, the Plough and the Flowing Tide, put up a free drink for thirsty travellers. Danny O'Sullivan, the barman in the Tide, regretted he wasn't going with us. He made me down a vodka to get me in training in case of a Moscow pub crawl.

We stayed overnight in the Two Mile Inn at Limerick and after breakfast we crowded into the coach for Shannon. Our tour manager distributed visas and customs forms, and there was much writing to be done as we drove along. 'Any firearms? Any antiques?' Myself maybe.

The check-in at the airport was a bit hectic. There were the casts of two plays, the crew, the lighting and design people, the touring manager John Costigan and the theatre manager Martin Fahy as well as representatives of the press. A premature announcement to board at Gate 4 sent us all scurrying towards departures, but it turned out that we had plenty of time. Time to go to duty free, pose for photographs and have interviews with press and radio.

'And how do you feel now, Éamon, going to play in the Moscow Arts Theatre?'

'I feel,' I said, 'like an old Kerry parish priest going to say Mass in the Vatican.'

A while in the air and drinks were passed around. I opted for a vodka – neat. It was heart and belly warming. Reds throw it back in one gulp. I sipped it and waited for our first taste of Russian food, only to find that the lunch packs were made up at Shannon. There were the old familiars, Kerry Gold butter, Siúcra Éireann and Galtee cheese.

I sat by the window at the Kildare side as we flew eastwards. It was a beautiful day. The cold land and seas of northern Europe unfolded before me. Gradually the light faded. The days were short and darkness was not far away. Then we were above the clouds and the slanting sun still shone on a floor of cotton wool. As we neared Leningrad we lost height and I could make out roads stretching along the snow covered countryside.

The dark portions I took to be forests. As we descended, the roads seemed to be deserted and we must have gone the breadth of Munster before I saw my first car, the headlights making the snow in front a little whiter. As we neared the city the traffic increased to two or three cars, never more, moving between the clusters of lights that indicated the villages.

We made a perfect descent, like gliding down on a feather tick, and a perfect landing. We were bused from the runway to an austere arrival hall. The passport check was very strict. The official, who seemed to be in army uniform, not only looked at me but peered closer through half-closed eyes and back to the photograph. He motioned me to turn round and take off my hat. Grudgingly, I thought, he let me pass on.

There was a long delay for our luggage to come through. One hour and twenty minutes. John Costigan had warned us about it, having been here before. We had to go through customs again even though our baggage had been checked at Shannon by Soviet personnel. Then there was a big rigmarole about currency and more writing to do.

At last we were in the coach and heading for the city centre. It was not as bright as O'Connell Street. We drew up at the Hotel Europe, a stocky building of three or four storeys with a frowning cornice. Inside, the large lobby with its pillars, plaster decor and gold painted figures reminded me of old-time hotels I had seen in New York.

The riddle of the rooms was sorted out. Sharing was the order of the day. Some resented this, but I was not complaining. My wife and I were in 236, a real relic of oul' decency: not a room, a suite, with a charming sitting-room, beautifully furnished and with a television set, a radio (not working) and a phone. A bedroom opened off, and a bathroom with glazed tiles and brass fittings that must have been put in place before I was born. The door key was huge and the lock so ancient that it took some time to get the knack of opening it.

Dinner was to be at 9.30 p.m. I had a drink first in the currency bar. There were also currency shops where goods could be obtained for sterling or dollars. I had a nip of brandy and needed it at two degrees below. It cost me £1.75. As I paid the barman I said I could have got it for less in the Flowing Tide. 'Spaseeba,' he said and filled a beer for a thirsty tourist. Conor O'Clery of the *Irish Times* dropped in and was suitably chuffed by my remark that the Abbey's visit to Russia was a 'steppe in the left direction'.

The dinner brought me back to a Listowel eating house during race week in the 1940s. All manner of servants helped at table, from fully fledged waiters to women in high boots dressed for the snow. The food was fine and a bottle of Georgian red wine cost four roubles – you'd have change out of a fiver. And so to bed. I bid the porter good-night in Russian. He glanced at his watch and told me the time. Oh well, it was only the first day.

Next morning we were taken on a guided tour of the centre of Leningrad. We visited St Isaac's cathedral, its interior sumptuously decorated with ceiling paintings, mosaics and icons. It was heavily pillared and had massive candelabra converted to electricity; before that the candle grease droppings, we were told, were carted away in wheelbarrows! As well as tourists there were many, many Russians eagerly drinking in every word that poured from the lips of the guide speaking their language, but it was strange to think that this once sacred place was now somewhere to be gawked at and not prayed in any more. Pews, if they were ever there, had been removed to make room for the shuffling thousands who passed through the building every day.

Except for the visit to St Isaac's, this was a short tour and we viewed the outside of well known buildings like the Winter Palace and the Hermitage (which we were to visit the following day). We were shown the Stock Exchange, which is a university now and proper order! At one stop for photographs the company settled into throwing snowballs, much to the amusement of passing Russians.

We rehearsed that evening at the Bolshoi Drama Theatre. The rehearsal room was fitted with a real stage, and had been since 1910! There was even a revolve – but maybe that hadn't been there since 1910. Glasnost, the Soviet Union's department of openness to outsiders, took care of our entertainment.

Next morning we were taken by coach to the Hermitage, only to find long queues outside; but as ever 'Intourist', that magic word, got us to the head of the line. It was a place, indeed a palace, to boast about. The very floors were works of art. Felt overshoes were provided to save the inlaid surfaces. There were massive, ornate ceilings and boulle doors of bulging beauty inside their ogee architraves. It was a tribute to the European art on display that it more than held its own in those luscious surroundings. Inlaid, veneered and carved articles of furniture vied for notice with malachite urns of the most exquisite workmanship.

There were so many items on show here, Olga our guide told us, that if one spent a minute looking at each item it would take seven years of one's life to see them all. But I think one treasures in the mind's video for replay time and time again just one item, and for me that was Van der Helst's picture of *The Family Pig Killing*. There the dead animal hangs by the hind legs down a ladder, its snout just touching the ground. Its waistcoat has been opened from tail to throat and its vitals removed. Already the children are blowing up the pig's bladder to play football, which we kids did in Kerry when Pat Murrell, the townland butcher, dispatched our pig, and for whose bloody death we children shed tears, all to be forgotten as we relished the fresh pork steaks and black pudding the following day.

We went to the Bolshoi Drama Theatre for the first showing in Russia of Tom MacIntyre's *The Great Hunger*. The cast of *The Field* assembled backstage and had coffee while waiting to be seated. Seemingly, there were no seats booked for us, and as the bell went for the start of the play we were ushered around the auditorium to any empty seats that were left. Maura and I were put sitting at the very front and we had no more than impressed our modest behinds on the seats when a gentleman and lady came to say that we were sitting in their places. What else could they have been so excited about! Fortunately, before both sides ran out of body language, an official came and took us to another part of the auditorium.

After many speeches – mercifully short, but long enough as they had to be translated into Russian – the play began. There were earphones. I put these on and there was Natasha, that gifted lady we had already met at rehearsal, interpreting the proceedings in Russian. There is much mime in *The Great Hunger,* and her task was easier than it would be in *The Field.*

Tom Hickey and the cast, under Patrick Mason's splendid direction, weaved and strutted and brought to life wondrously the country people of Kavanagh's poem.

The Russians liked it and that night they gave it a standing ovation. The following evening we went to the opera at the Kirov, Russlan and Ludmila, a wonderful evening of music, song and a little dance, with delightful costumes and stunning scenery. Behind the dress circle was a space the size of a small theatre, a beautifully proportioned, high-ceilinged hall where patrons walked about. Boys and girls, all those good looking young people, linked and strolled, or stood and chatted under the bust of Lenin. Sainted hour, that man was everywhere, like 'that little yellow idol forever gazing down'!

We had the next day off. The stage was being set up for *The Field*. We went sightseeing to the Summer Palace of Catherine the Great. This palace, with the exception of a few rooms, was restored with infinite patience and skill after the devastation of Hitler's bombers. One never realised the full horror of the German invasion of Russia until one heard Olga, our guide, talk about the nightmare that was the siege of Leningrad. Hitler's hatred for Lenin and the Communist system was unleashed with brutal ferocity on the city and on its people. To many of them the angel of death was a welcome visitor after the demons of disease, hunger and mutilation had wreaked their worst. When I see the skeleton on the Derry coat of arms, I think of the siege of that city and I have a vision of a man frying a rat on a fire of broken furniture. Rats were eaten in Leningrad, and to survive did the people stop at that? God bless the mark. I looked into the faces of men older than myself in the streets of Leningrad and dared not think the dark thought.

Later that night we taxied to the Leningrad Hotel, a new western-type establishment with English signs everywhere. In the lettering little liberties were taken. The Russian 'C' is pronounced 'S' and restaurant appeared as 'rectaurant'. Having lived in Leningrad for four days and nearly mastered the intricacies of the Russian alphabet, I sort of resented these English intrusions as I might English signs in the Gaeltacht.

On stage were the Georgian dancers, and we saw the most

energetic folk dancing: high kicking of a spirited nature from the men, but the women were demure and graceful in their movements, and at no time did the men or women touch or dance in very close proximity. I can't understand why people are always praying for the conversion of Russia!

At a late dinner I had two healthy measures of vodka. Oh so smooth! But a deceptive thief; I was nearly on my ear.

Early next morning we went out for a long walk in the city. There were crowds everywhere and the footpaths were as wide as the streets. There were few cars and the architecture could be seen in relation to the human figure. The people were well fed and well dressed for the weather. They had a hankering, I was told, after the western style. Macdara Ó Fátharta exchanged a pair of shoes for a fur hat one night. There was no litter in the streets. Hundreds would stand in a queue and when they moved (queues formed and disappeared at the drop of a hat) the street would be clean. We went to a bakery, got some lovely bread and bought milk. We made tea in our room, with bags from home, and invited Niall Tóibín in for a cuppa. He loved it, the best drop that had passed his lips since he had left Dublin. He got the radio going.

The big day arrived. We travelled by bus to the theatre at 1 p.m., settled into the dressing-rooms, donned our costumes and walked the set. We did a combined technical and dress rehearsal which went very well. It was a commodious place backstage, and there were plenty of spaces with seats where lines could be looked at. There was a full canteen service throughout the day, so there was no need to leave the theatre again.

The show started and we listened on the tannoy. That dear and gifted lady called Natasha spoke over the actors' lines and must have been near enough to the bone for the reaction was very good. Our cue coming up, Maura and I were in the wings. Cue came. We were on! I knew from the moment we hit the light that we were on the ball. The scene worked like a dream. When I burst into song at the end I transposed a line. I hope I didn't throw Natasha. It was a great night.

Afterwards the Irish ambassador came on stage. Journalists, photographers, television and radio people crowded in. It was very exciting. In high spirits we adjourned to the Hotel

335

Europe for dinner. We had quite a night and towards morning there was a potted preview of the reviews.

On Sunday morning I went with Maura to Mass in an old church in a quiet street. It was a pre-Vatican II Latin Mass. The celebrant's back was to us – '*féach anois mé, m'aghaidh le balla*', as the poet says – and he gave a very long sermon. The church was very full, with many people coming and going out of curiosity. Old women concerned for our comfort found seats for us. The courtesy of the people and their warmth were not like anything I had seen in a foreign country before. There were many teenagers there and children – a Russian's love for his child is pleasant to watch. With the crowds it was a bit stuffy so I went outside for a whiff of fresh air. Standing on the steps was a lady of indeterminate age who, without any preliminaries whatsoever, tried to make up to me – all very courteous and graceful, but even with the inclination, and considering my age, it wasn't the time or the place, so I took refuge within the holy walls. John Finnegan of the *Evening Herald* – older than me – told me he had had a similar experience. What these ladies won't do to get to the West!

After Mass there was a procession around the church with the Blessed Sacrament and Our Lady on a litter. Attendant children dressed in white scattered what looked like flowers in the path of the Host. As they passed, old women picked up the flowers and put the petals in their prayer books.

On the second night of *The Field* it really took off, and we got a tremendous reception at the curtain. The goodbyes to the Leningrad crew were very touching, with warm handshakes. The Russians are a shy people and we Irish are reserved, so there were no bear hugs.

On Monday morning we took the coach to the airport. The plane to Moscow was packed and it turned out to be a bumpy flight. The folding table kept falling down on me. There was hand luggage everywhere, and enormous Russian winter coats bulged from the overhead racks. We were in the air for an hour, and when we landed there was another hour's delay for luggage, but while the third hour was still young we were on our way to the city. There was deep snow everywhere. Trees thrust themselves out of the white plain, and in tiny groves and copses gentle birches claimed the attention, very demure and seemly in their winter nudity.

We approached the city. It was so different from Leningrad, which had been architecturally ordered. Moscow sprawled. There were plenty of open spaces. In small parks full of trees, birches again showed their pale limbs. Europe was behind us now, as we saw before us against the clouds the little domes of a cathedral looking as if an invisible angel were holding a hank of onions in the sky.

Our destination was the Russia Hotel, a modern building, part of which rose to twenty-one storeys. It was reputed to have four thousand bedrooms and it was plonked down within an ass's roar of Red Square and the fairytale-like Kremlin. Around the hotel there were many small and very lovely church-like buildings, and it seemed to me that many more must have been demolished to make room for what in this visitor's humble opinion is a monstrosity. A ground to first floor 'fly-up' roadway swept within feet of one of the picturesque churches.

In the hotel there were four entrances and reception areas, and many shops and eating places. When we got to our room, a change from Leningrad, there was so little space because of the two large beds that one of us had to remain in blanket street in the morning until the other had dressed.

That evening Mr Dara MacFhionnbháir, first secretary of the Irish embassy, gave a reception for the Abbey Company and the visiting journalists at the Godanka Restaurant. The food was excellent and my simple vegetarian requirements posed no problems. Groups of musicians entertained us, and actors and press contributed to the general hilarity. It was a great evening and a great welcome to Moscow. *Ambasáid na hÉireann, míle buíochas!*

There was a press conference at the theatre at 3 p.m. next day. Vincent Dowling came over from Dublin for the Moscow opening of *The Great Hunger*. Vladimir Cheranyean from the Ministry of Culture was there and we received a warm welcome. Vincent and Vladimir spoke, and it was mutual admiration nationwise. We heard something about the Russian theatre and especially the famous Stanislavsky Theatre we

were in, but when all was almost said, there was a rift, not between the two nations, but between the Irish. A section of our
press wanted to know from Vincent why these two plays had
been chosen for the Abbey tour of Russia. Why not O'Casey?
Or Synge? But surely Dublin, in the long months leading up
to the Soviet visit, was the place to thrash this out, rather
than seem to devalue what we brought in the eyes of the
Russians. (If I may go into brackets for a moment, I was under
the impression that the two plays we brought were the choice
of the Russian Ministry of Culture, and if people ask for tea
you don't give them coffee.) And one press man – the same
gentleman who started the other questions – wanted to know
why the plays were put on in the order in which they were
presented. So much to be talked about, and time was taken up
arguing as to why the football was put on before the hurling.
We were embarrassed and would have welcomed a hole in the
floor into which we could fall!

Mr Charles Whelan, the Irish ambassador, threw open his
house to us that evening, and a fine place it was. I got a whiff
of home in the shape of some reproductions from the National
Gallery on the walls. My favourite was there, *The Goose Girl* by
W. J. Leech, as well as a representative number of modern Irish
paintings, including Noel Sheridan's *Chair*. This was a happy
occasion. We met people from Aer Rianta who were there on
duty-free business, and a Russian Orthodox priest, a fine figure
of a man, stood radiating charm, as did the figure of Fr Senan
at the Kerrymen's meetings when I first came to Dublin.

The next day turned out to be very interesting. A guided
tour brought us to a lovely park where the wooden palace of
Peter the Great's father once stood, and where he lived while
his stone palace was being built. There were tent-roofed
churches and buildings which housed exhibitions of artefacts
from cathedrals and palaces, an amazing collection of man's
skill in wood and metal. On the way into the park there was a
functioning Orthodox church where a service was in progress.
We mingled with the faithful, were made welcome, and enjoyed the music, hymns, prayerful intonation, incense, gorgeous vestments and flickering candlelight. We added to the il-
lumination by lighting long tapers at the shrines. I was in-

formed afterwards that it was a wake. A line of women in black like Spanish widows were asking for alms and, I supposed, praying for the dead as the old women used to do at the holy wells when I was young.

One day I fell victim to a 'foreign tummy' and nearly conked out. After taking some tablets Vincent O'Neill had brought from Dublin for such an emergency, I found some relief. I spruced up a bit later and went to the Kremlin. The diesel they used in the tourist buses had a vile smell. Black-blue smoke poured from the exhausts, permeated the interior and made a bad tummy worse. We parked outside one of the main gates. There was a long queue at the first palace, which housed yet another museum. There were icons by the score, which were very lovely, but like the Italian triptychs I had seen in American galleries, they were very much out of place away from the altars and churches for which they were first painted. We saw vestments inlaid with pearls and jewels, copes, mitres and croziers of a religion of yesteryear. It was like a theatre wardrobe storing costumes of a show that was not going back on stage again.

Having looked at the royal carriages that bore the tsars, I decided that as far as museums were concerned I had reached saturation point. I took leave of the party and went out in the fresh air. Two cathedrals stood within a stone's throw of each other, one of the Assumption and the other of the Annunciation. Quite near, and closer to the outer wall, was the great bulk of the CCCP government building which housed the Supreme Soviet and the Parliament of the Soviet Nations.

How beautiful the two cathedrals looked, and how varied in size, arrangement and colour those lovely domes can be in that kind of architecture. Like the icons of a while back, to me those two churches seemed a little embarrassed in their new role of museums. They missed, I would say, the incense, the chant and the gentle rhubarb of prayer. But as we had seen the other day, religion is practised in Russia. There are two kinds of churches, those that are functioning and those that are being restored. Nothing of importance is allowed to fall into disrepair. Restoration goes on apace. In fact walking the streets one notices far more reconstruction than construction. Heritage is vital in Russia.

Within the Kremlin a line not always clearly defined separates the public and government sectors, and to overstep this line brings a sharp reprimand from the police. It was my misfortune to do just that, and I have never in my life been spoken to so severely and with such venom.

I escaped to the hotel, and Des Hickey and Seamus Hosey called for me to do an interview for RTÉ radio. What better place than Red Square, and there we went and talked in the shade of Moscow's showcase piece of architecture – St Basil's Cathedral. I don't think there is a more beautifully proportioned pile anywhere in the world. And as in the story of our own *Gobán Saor*, who went to build a palace for the King of England and was threatened with death, the man who fashioned this church, we are told, had his eyes put out so that he wouldn't build a better.

Snowploughs, with a great scoop in front and revolving brushes behind, kept the open space clear of snow. Red Square is a sacred – I don't know if that's the right word – place. You can't smoke there and, like the streets of Moscow and Leningrad, it was immaculately clean. There were no hoardings or advertising of any kind. No neon signs at night, just one massive red star revolving on its turret on the Kremlin wall.

Saturday was the last day for spending our roubles. We had a daily allowance from the Russians, and very grateful we were, but it had to be spent there. The time was short so an early morning shopping spree was organised. We bought what we could lay hands on while the money lasted. In the frosty street an army officer helped Maura over a slippery patch to the safety of the footpath, which was being cleared of snow by elderly women.

The Moscow Arts backstage was as big as another theatre. There were stage lifts and the stage floor tracked left and right into the wings and upstage, so that in our case after the first scene, the 'pub' set glided left and the 'field' set came in from the right. If we needed a third set, the 'field' could move right and another scene could roll in from upstage. All this equipment, together with the flies, made for what must be a director's dream. But what impressed me most was the space. I love space, having worked in the most awful cramped conditions touring around Ireland.

There was a hint of nerves on opening night, but despite this the piece played well. Natasha had made her own of the text, and the reaction right through was just as if we were in Dublin. To sit in a Russian audience, as we did on our nights off, and to be part of their involvement in what goes on on stage was an experience. Soul, as it were, reached out to soul. We were lucky to experience that total involvement from the other side of the footlights. What must it have been like for the actors and the spectators when the great Chekhovian plays were first presented in this hallowed place.

At the curtain the house came down. We all felt we wanted to say: 'We love you! Thanks a million!' and Niall Tóibín, stepping forward, did just that, very gracefully and in Russian, ending with 'Spaseeba! Spaseeba! Bolshoi spaseeba!'

Sunday morning, 21 February, we were all set to go to the circus, but at the last moment tickets became available for the Bolshoi Theatre. We opted for the ballet, myself a little sadly, being an old circus fan, and it also meant that I missed my last chance of riding the Moscow Metro that everyone talks about. We went off then in great glee to the Bolshoi to find that it was 'opera morning': not seeing the world famous ballet on its home ground was a disappointment.

The Bolshoi Theatre's classic exterior, with an equine group dashing forth from above the apex of the tympanum, was but a foretaste of the theatre inside, cathedral-like in its majesty, with a great proscenium opening and a hammer-and-sickle patterned curtain. A loge skirted the entire wall and five balconies were shelved up along the side walls, with a huge box centre back and two other boxes, one on either side of the stage. Everything was decorated and gilded and there was a painted ceiling. In such beautiful and painstakingly re-stored theatres I felt that the drama, ballet and opera had taken the place of religion. The people were streaming in this bright Sunday morning when devout parishioners in Listowel were pounding the flags to Mass.

We nearly overslept the day we went home. Martin Fahy rang just as the porters were calling for our luggage at 4.15 a.m. Luckily the two large bags had been packed since the previous night. We had a hectic half hour to get ready and appear down at the exit. We made it. John Costigan had our passports and tickets and more forms to fill – currency declarations and again the old questions. Any weapons? Any ammunition? Any antiques? No! But there were many sore heads after our last night in Moscow and only a few hours in bed. The porter pressed a Lenin badge into my palm and I pressed some roubles into his. Eventually we were in the coach and had a long drive through the falling snow and Moscow's sleeping suburbs. Snowploughs driving at a furious rate cleared the roads to the airport.

The customs, even with the help of the kindly glasnost girls, turned out to be very slow. And judging by the scrutiny and long delay at the passport counter, it's no cakewalk getting out of Russia. We were shepherded from pen to pen and finally our bags went off, jauntily I felt, along the conveyor belt, as anxious as ourselves to be going home. Then came a surprise, a very welcome breakfast from our hosts, and in no time we were on our Aeroflot plane bound for Leningrad. The trip took an hour, an hour's wait, and then the high skies to Shannon.

We were not allowed off the plane at Leningrad, and we sat out the hour on the runway. Sixty to a hundred college boys and their teachers from St Fintan's High School in Sutton joined us there. It sounded like home already as youthful Irish voices were raised in every section of the plane. We took off at 10.10 a.m. It's a three-hour trip, and Ireland is three hours behind in time. We raced the sun but never beat it. It cast the same shadow in Shannon as it had in Leningrad.

Another shadow fell. And our spirits sagged a little. On picking up the Irish morning papers we found that the summing up of our historic visit to the Soviet Union was greatly at variance with our collective experience.

We were home!

Alone in the Mother House

۶

In October 1990 I took part in a *Sense of Ireland* week in London. I played in the Riverside Studio at Hammersmith. Out walking from the hotel the night before, I lost my way. I called to a man in front and when he heard my voice he quickened his step. Then he stopped and, turning back, he asked me if I was Éamon Kelly. We walked along and went into a pub, and he told me that when he was a youngster in rural Ireland his job was to stand at the kitchen door and, when I came on the radio in *The Rambling House*, to call his mother, who was milking the cows, to hear me.

It was strange, he said, hearing my voice in a London street. At first he thought it was a ghost, which was why he had hastened his step. He told me that his mother and the people of her generation wouldn't miss me on the radio for anything. He turned his head and, gazing past me, he said, 'I was home to her funeral only last week.'

Next morning bright and early I was at the Riverside Studio. Michael Doyle had come over from the Abbey with me, and my set and stage furniture had been shipped across. We set up the scene and in the afternoon while I was resting Michael lit it. That night we opened. There was a great crowd.

I always manage to draw a hearty laugh in the first minute. It relaxes them. When I was telling the story of Fr McGillicuddy and the first motor car seen in our parish, an almighty clap of thunder broke directly overhead. I waited, looking up into the flies until the noise was dying away, and then I said, 'God is getting vexed with me!' The house came down.

Maura and I stayed at the Tara Hotel where we were made very welcome by my friend Eoin Dillon the manager. Bosco Hogan was there. His show *I am Ireland*, about W. B. Yeats was coming into the Riverside Studio after me. We ran into Brian Friel and Patrick Mason. Brian's play *Dancing at Lughnasa* was opening in the National the next week.

After the run, when I came back to Dublin, Noel Pearson, the then artistic director of the Abbey, asked me to see him. The current play in the theatre had opened to the father and mother of a lambasting from the critics. The stalls were practically empty. Would I take over with my one-man show at the Abbey for a few weeks?

It was a tall order and at first nearly knocked the wind out of me. It was all right doing a one-man show in the Peacock, in London or America, but the Abbey – the sacred stomping ground of poets and playwrights! Then I said to myself, what the heck? I had a show fresh in my mind and if it did well in London it should do better in the Abbey.

The name of the one-man show was *English That for Me*, about the time when Irish was being supplanted by the foreign tongue in my native place. It had the heartbreak, the high comedy and the misunderstandings of such a set of circumstances.

Maura encouraged me to go ahead, though my son Brian said I was taking on too much at seventy-six. I did it. Some nights I was put to the pin of my collar to keep going, but strength came after a plea went skywards to relieve me in my hardest hour, and I kept the doors of the Abbey open until Field Day took over with *The Cure at Troy* by Seamus Heaney.

As someone reminded me, I had made a little bit of history that night. I was the first Abbey actor to do a one-man show in the mother house.

It was after Noel Pearson that Garry Hynes came to us as artistic director. Being away from the theatre quite a bit, I didn't figure in too many of her shows, though she did nearly put a halt to my gallop as an actor by miscasting me as Uncle Peter in her ever so controversial production of *The Plough and the Stars*. I refused to do the part when approached, but she got round me. After the first reading of the play I kicked over the traces when I saw that it wasn't working for me. I came home and wrote two letters; one to Martin Fahy the theatre manager, tendering my resignation from the company, and the other to Garry Hynes to the effect that I didn't feel happy in the part. I was going out the door to put the letters in the post when the phone rang. It was Garry, and I'll say this much for her, for a small parcel of humanity she is mighty persuasive. She talked me out of the decision I had made by dint of praise and cajolery.

On opening night, in a cast of shaved heads and some tongues with vague echoes of Belfast, Galway and west Munster, maybe I wasn't entirely out of place. There were Dubliners on stage too, but ne'er a sign of a faded Georgian casement or arched doorway to give the tang of a tenement house. Mollser the consumptive child sat at the corner of a raked stage catching the sun with a mug in her hand:

> 'Mollser, oul' son. What are you drinkin'? Milk?'
> 'Grand, Fluther. Grand thanks. Tis milk.'
> 'You couldn't get a betther thing down you.'

Furniture brought on to the same space gave the effect of an interior. The setting was very different from those of the O'Casey plays we had seen down the years. Old-timers hated the production and the *Irish Times* nearly had a fit. But there were many who loved Garry's very different look at the great man's work, with the stress on poverty and on suffering.

At rehearsals, when I settled down to accepting my role as Uncle Peter, I enjoyed working with Garry. She was often inspired and always inspiring, and the Holy Ghost descended on her many times during the weeks of preparation. She didn't believe in leaving well alone. Frank O'Connor once told me that he could never re-read even his best short story without wanting to change it. That same itch for change motivated Garry. When she had set a scene, if you went to the loo, you came back to find it completely altered. Where before you had entered from the stair landing, you now came up through a trap-door in the floor, as the auxiliaries did in *The Plough and the Stars*. You could never be up to her.

In our last play together, which was *The Colleen Bawn* at the Royal Exchange in Manchester, Myles na Gopaleen descended from the flies to land on the lake shore in Killarney!

Playing Fr Tom, the poitín priest in *The Colleen Bawn*, and watching the plot develop, I couldn't help thinking that in many ways John B. Keane was heir to Boucicault. As in John B.'s plays, Boucicault's characters are colourful and his dialogue comes trippingly off the tongue. *The Colleen Bawn* is set by the lakes of Killarney, and for me who was born near there the language of Boucicault, though not as authentic as that of Keane, is racy of the soil.

That's my story. My journeying is over. I am eighty-four and my next trek will be through the stars to the great beyond, where I hope to meet again those I knew in my wanderings down here: those with whom I shared the craftsman's bench, those who taught me and those I taught in my spell in the classroom, those whose voices rode the radio waves with mine, and finally those with whom I strutted my merry hour upon the stage.

If the humour takes us and there's a playwright handy, Hilton Edwards or the Abbey's Frank Dermody may be tempted to direct a show in some celestial alhambra, where angels with folded wings will sit in the stalls, applaud politely and maybe come round after and say, 'That was great!'

INDEX

578

114

378
16
578
2840

578
37

57
570

114

20 = 102

378

100

500
20 — 100
20
20 20